NON-BINDING LEGAL INFORMATION DISCLAIMER

The author of this Guidebook, Jason Hernandez, is not an attorney, and thus the material and advice reflect his own understanding of federal clemency. The materials in this document do not constitute legal advice, are provided for general purposes only, and are not a substitute for the advice of an attorney. Thus the author accepts no responsibility for any errors or omissions associated within this Guidebook or with any outcomes that result with the use of this Guidebook and expressly disclaims any such responsibility.

IMPORTANT NOTICE: *DO NOT CONTINUE WITHOUT READING FIRST*

This book is created for individuals who are filing for a commutation of sentence and have been convicted of a federal offense.

This book is not created for individuals who are filing for a commutation of sentence in the state. The policies and rules for filing for a commutation of sentence in the state varies from state to state and are different in many ways from the policies and rules governing a commutation of sentence in the federal system.

Nevertheless, this Guidebook can be helpful and used as a resource for individuals filing for a commutation of sentence who have been convicted of a state offense. Indeed, many of the factors, if not all, that a pardon and parole board/governor seek when deciding to grant a clemency petition are typically the same. However, it is strongly advised that state prisoners filing for a commutation of sentence thoroughly review the rules, policies, and any other relevant information pertaining to the state in which they are seeking clemency.

GET CLEMENCY NOW

A Guidebook to Everything A Person in Prison Needs to Know About Clemency and How Families Can Help

www.getclemencynow.org

McKinney, Texas

Copyright © 2020 by Jason Hernandez

All rights reserved.

Published in the United States by Jason Hernandez

ISBN 978-0-578-69604-1

Book, cover, and all other graphics designed by Blake Boring

Edited by Rachel Carter

www.getclemencynow.org

Executive Grant of Clemency

TO ALL TO WHOM THESE PRESENTS SHALL COME, GREETING:

WHEREAS **JASON HERNANDEZ** was convicted in the United States District Court for the Eastern District of Texas on an indictment (Docket No. 4:98CR00014-002) charging violations of Sections 841(a), 846, 856(a), and 860, Title 21, United States Code, for which a sentence of life imprisonment, eight years' supervised release, a fine of five thousand dollars ($5,000.00), and a special assessment of one thousand dollars ($1,000.00) was imposed on October 2, 1998; and

WHEREAS the said **JASON HERNANDEZ** has been confined continuously since his arrest on March 16, 1998, and is presently incarcerated at the Federal Correctional Institution - El Reno in El Reno, Oklahoma; and

WHEREAS the said **JASON HERNANDEZ** filed a petition for commutation of his prison sentence, seeking his release from prison; and

WHEREAS it has been made to appear that the ends of justice do not require the said **JASON HERNANDEZ** to remain confined for the rest of his life, and the safety of the community will not be compromised if he is released prior to the natural expiration of his imposed sentence;

NOW, THEREFORE, BE IT KNOWN that I, **BARACK OBAMA**, President of the United States of America, in consideration of the premises, divers other good and sufficient reasons me thereunto moving, do hereby grant the said application and commute the prison sentence imposed upon the said **JASON HERNANDEZ** to a term of 240 months' imprisonment, leaving intact and in effect the eight-year term of supervised release with all its conditions and all other components of the sentence, including the five thousand dollar ($5,000.00) fine.

IN TESTIMONY WHEREOF I have hereunto signed my name and caused the seal of the Department of Justice to be affixed. I hereby direct the Department of Justice to deliver to the Bureau of Prisons and to the prisoner a certified copy of this document as proof of my action.

Done at the City of Washington this 19th day of December in the year of our Lord Two thousand and thirteen and of the Independence of the United States the two hundred and thirty-eighth.

BARACK OBAMA
President

Photo Credit Malik King

DEDICATION

This book is dedicated to everyone locked down and to all the families who have a loved one trapped in the system.

We see you, we are fighting for you. Now join us, help us, and let's hear your voice in the fight for freedom for those incarcerated.

"Change will not come if we wait

for some other person or some other time.

We are the ones we've been waiting for.

We are the change that we seek."

— Barack Obama, then Presidential Candidate
February 5th, 2008

HOW TO OBTAIN THIS GUIDEBOOK

Due to the extraordinary and uncontrollable circumstances that can come with incarceration, such as having little-to-no-money or no outside support, I have made this Guidebook as readily accessible as possible, regardless if a person incarcerated is in general population, the SHU, Ad Seg, or Administrative Detention.

Below are different ways a person in prison, prison officials, or families of those incarcerated can obtain portions of the Guidebook, or the entire Guidebook, for free or for purchase.

- **Prison Law Library:** The Guidebook is being offered free of charge to all federal prison law libraries. To have the Guidebook mailed to a prison law library, the officer in charge of the library at the prison will need to send an email directly to me at getclemencynow@gmail.com with the subject title: *"Request For Free Clemency Guidebook for [name of prison and security level, e.g. 'USP Beaumont']."* They will need to include the appropriate address it must be sent to in order for the prison's law library to receive it. The Guidebook must be shipped to prison staff/officials and not a person incarcerated at the prison in order to receive a free copy for that prison.

- **Available Online:** A PDF of the entire Guidebook will be viewable at www.getclemencynow.org. It can also be downloaded and printed for free by anyone with Internet access. This allows a prison law library, your Unit Team or a loved one on the outside to print out a copy for free.

- **Purchased and Shipped Directly To You From Amazon:** The Guidebook can also be purchased from Amazon. Prisons do allow direct shipping from Amazon so anyone can purchase this Guidebook and have it mailed to a person in prison.

- **Purchased Directly From Me:** Anyone on the outside can send an email to getclemencynow@gmail.com requesting to purchase the Guidebook from me and have it sent to them directly. However, because I am not a book distributor, prisons will not allow me to directly send books to people incarcerated in the prison. You must have it mailed by Amazon or download the Guidebook off the website and mail it to the person incarcerated.

TABLE OF CONTENTS

Contributors 8

Foreword by Mark Osler 11

Introduction: Why I Created This Guidebook 12

Part One: The Federal Commutation Process 16
    The First Steps to Clemency 16
    Step One: Understanding the Federal Commutation Process................ 17
    Step Two: Gathering Information for Your Application......................... 22
    Step Three: Filling Out the Application 24
    Question #1 25
    Question #2 25
    Question #3 26
    Question #4 26
    Question #5 27
    Question #6 28
    Question #7 30
    Things You Should Keep in Mind When Answering Question 7 31
    How Should I Organize and Format My Answer for Question 7?.......... 32
  Step One.. 32
  Step Two 34
    Creating Your Memorandum and Things to Consider When Doing So 35
        Factors Demonstrating Sentence Is Too Harsh, Unfair, and/or Unjust 35
        Your Life Prior to Incarceration.. 35
        Your Life During Incarceration 36
        Your Release Plan... 38
        Concluding the Petition 39
    Attachments: Adding Letters of Support and Other Documents to Your Petition for Commutation 39
        Letters of Support: Who Should I Ask to Write a Letter for Me?...... 40
        Should I Write a Letter Directly to the President? YES! 43
        Other Documents to Consider Including 44
        Putting Your Petition Together 44
        How Do I Send in My Application? 45
    Final Thoughts.. 47

CONTRIBUTORS

Part One Contributing Writer

Courtney M. Oliva is the Executive Director of the Center on the Administration of Criminal Law at NYU School of Law. Before joining NYU, Oliva served for several years as an Assistant United States Attorney in the District of New Jersey and as a Special Assistant Attorney General with the New York State Office of the Attorney General. Prior to becoming a prosecutor, Oliva spent several years in private practice representing individual and corporate clients in government, regulatory, and internal investigations and securities litigation. She received her BA from Brown University and her law degree from the University of Chicago Law School.

Part One Contributor

Mark Osler is a law professor at the University of St. Thomas (MN) whose work advocates for sentencing and clemency policies rooted in principles of human dignity, ideals of the Christian Faith, and is considered a leading expert on clemency. A former federal prosecutor, he played a role in striking down the mandatory 100-to-1 ratio between crack and powder cocaine in the federal sentencing guidelines by winning the case of Spears v. United States in the U.S. Supreme Court, with the Court ruling that judges could categorically reject that ratio. In 2011, he founded the first law school clinic specializing in federal commutations, and he trained hundreds of pro bono lawyers who were filing petitions during President Obama's Clemency Initiative.

Part Two & Three Contributing Writer

Jessica Sandoval, MPA, is the National Campaign Strategist for the Unlock the Box Campaign to End Solitary Confinement at the ACLU's National Prison Project. She is the campaign lead and is responsible for the development and implementation of campaign strategies, provides technical assistance to campaign states, oversees the Jurisdiction-based Campaign fund, and manages the national campaign steering committee. She has 25 years' experience reforming the youth and adult justice systems, she uses her organizing and advocacy expertise to develop and administer strategies and tools to support state campaigns aligned with the mission of the "stop solitary" movement.

TABLE OF CONTENTS

Part Two: How to Advocate for Clemency **48**
    Fighting for Your Freedom From a Prison Cell 50
    Contact List: Who Should I Contact? What Do I Send Them? 53
    You Know Who Your Targets Are: Now What Do You Send Them? 56
        Introduction Letter 56
        Profiles 57
        Additional Documents You Can Create and Mail Out 59
        Staying Organized 61
        Gaining Support From the Outside 62
    What Next? 64

Part Three: Advocating From the Outside for Someone on the Inside **66**
    Questions to Ask Yourself Before Making a Commitment to Advocate 68
    Things to Consider When Seeking Assistance or
    When Someone Offers Assistance 70
    What to Do First? 71
    Social Media and Using It to Bring Awareness and Freedom 71
    Creating a Petition for Support 77
    Ways to Gain Support and Who to Reach Out to 78
    Advanced Advocacy Tactics 81
    Lobbying 81
    Panel Discussion 84
    Organizing a Vigil or Rally 84
    Items You Will Need to Create to Make the Most Out of Every Engagement 86

Part Four: The Last But Most Important Steps You Must Take In Order To Obtain Your Freedom **90**
    Personal Steps 91

In Conclusion **97**

Acknowledgments **98**

Recommended Reading **99**

Appendix **100**

Notes **211**

TESTIMONIES

"I found Jason at a time when I was completely hopeless as to how to help my fiancé who was serving life without parole. And he showed me how to not only put together a powerful clemency petition but also how to fight for my husband's freedom."

ANRICA CALDWELL,
Fifth Grade Special Education Teacher, Fiancé and Advocate For David Barren who's life without parole sentence was commuted to thirty years.

"When my clemency petition was denied in 2016 I thought I would die in prison. After reaching out to Jason, who told me what was good and bad about my petition and what I should change and add to it, I refiled and was granted clemency."

CORY BLOUNT,
Sentence of life without parole was commuted to thirty years by President Obama.

"Today Obama granted my clemency. I just wanted to let you know that my life sentence is over. I did 22 years 6 months and 16 days. But God blessed me. Thanks for your advice on how to fill out the clemency application."

MR. JAWAREIL,
Sentence of life without parole was commuted to thirty years by President Obama

"My brother was sentenced to die in prison for a nonviolent drug offense. But thanks to Jason showing us how to put a clemency petition together he is now a free man!"

BARRY ROACH,
Brother and advocate of Kevin Washington, who's sentence of life without parole was commuted by President Obama and is now free

"Jason helped our family by guiding us as to what we would need to do to advocate for David's freedom and take matters into our own hands in a way I could have never imagined. David is still not free but without Jason's help no one would know anything about David's case."

LIDIA PEREZ,
Advocate and Fiancé of David Diaz who is serving a sentence of 37 years to life in a California prison

FOREWARD *By Mark Osler*

Americans believe in freedom. It's in the songs we sing, the pledge of allegiance, and the political slogans both parties rely on. Yet there are only a few among us who fight for actual liberty. That group includes soldiers, public defenders, free speech activists, and those who take risks on behalf of others. It also includes Jason Hernandez. This book—painstakingly written from experience, study, and discussion—lays out the key tools that can lead to freedom through the Constitutional device of clemency.

Clemency is the wild thing of the Constitution: it is unrestrained by checks and balances, resting instead within the soul and conscience of the president. The Constitution's pardon power allows the president to grant two primary forms of clemency: a pardon (which removes some of the effects of conviction) or commutation (which shortens a sentence). There have been and will be presidents who are brave enough to use the pardon power to free those who are incarcerated for irrationally long sentences. Sadly, the number of people serving those sentences in our country is much too large.

The good news is that American citizens and our leaders are coming to see that fact. The recognition by both Republicans and Democrats that we incarcerate too many people for too long has finally become a majority view, and the movement is now towards a more reasonable and humane system of criminal justice. That means that no matter who is serving as president, clemency will hopefully become a primary tool for reducing incarceration and right-sizing sentences that are far too long.

Jason Hernandez did something remarkable: he wrote himself to freedom. He prepared his own commutation petition and then bolstered it with a follow-up letter to President Barack Obama (who, in fact, read the letter). Jason was one of the first people to have his sentence commuted by Obama. He knows how clemency works because he has both earned his own freedom and helped others do the same. In this book, he gives specific and worthwhile directions on how those in prison can follow his path. While clemency is never guaranteed and is still too rarely granted to even the most deserving petitioners, this book can help readers avoid the most dangerous traps and greatly increase their chances of success.

In 2011, I started the first law school clinic in the country focused on federal commutations. Since then, my students and I have prepared dozens of clemency petitions and corresponded with hundreds of people in prison. In 2015, New York University professor Rachel Barkow and I set up a pop-up law office to prepare clemency petitions during the Obama administration's clemency initiative, and worked with hundreds more. I have also gone into federal prisons to talk about clemency—how it works and what it means. Through all of this, I have seen the depth of the tragedy in our criminal justice system and the waste of human potential. Still, I couldn't write the book that Jason has. I have never had to work two hours to afford one stamp and an envelope, or draft a document on a broken typewriter, or wait in line to make a phone call, or suffer any of the other unnecessary indignities that those in prison must push past. Jason does know all of that, and it is woven within the rhythm and wisdom of this book.

For those who read this book and succeed, I ask for a commitment: When you are in freedom, take inspiration from Jason and the many formerly incarcerated individuals who have came out and helped others succeed. Join us in trying to change the clemency system as a whole so it can work to free more people who have proven themselves deserving. Stand with us to revive this forgotten part of the Constitution. It's a good fight, and we need you.

Mark Osler is the Robert and Marion Short Professor of Law at the University of St. Thomas (MN) and is co-founder of the Clemency Resource Center at New York University.

INTRODUCTION *Why I Created This Guidebook*

If you are reading this book it means one of two things: Somehow you have ended up in prison for years, decades, if not the rest of your life. Or you have a loved one or someone you know behind bars, and they will continue to be there for a very long time unless something short of a miracle happens.

In either scenario, you probably don't know what can be done to attain freedom, if anything at all. And, if so, how it can be done, where to start, who to talk to, what to say when you find out who to talk to, and what to continue to do when you face rejection after rejection.

Well, the good thing is that I have been on both sides: in prison advocating for my freedom and others, and on the outside advocating for the freedom of those in prison. And I have been successful on both sides of the wall.

In 1998, I was sentenced to life without parole, plus 20, 20, 20, 20, 40, 40, 40, 40, and 80 years for conspiracy to distribute controlled substances. When I went to prison, I learned about the law and taught myself how to research and create habeas corpus motions and petitions. I became what is known as a "jailhouse attorney." In twelve years of being in prison, I filed every motion you could possibly think of—and some more than once. Direct appeals, writ of certioraris, 2255's, 2241's 3582(c)(2)'s, Rule 60(b)'s: You name it, I filed it. But you can only file so many motions, and after 12 years of being in prison there were no more motions that could be filed. Simply put, with no release date, I was left for dead.

The one thing I noticed after filing so many appeals and motions for myself and others was that they never allowed me to tell my/our story. They never let me illustrate that I wasn't a bad person growing up, just a person who made a bad decision and that I had amazing parents who still loved and cared for me and would help me if released; these motions never allowed me to talk about how I had not had an incident report throughout my entire incarceration, never failed a drug test, never joined a gang. They never let me mention the education I had attained and the programs I completed, how I had changed my way of thinking, how I now felt remorse and contrition for what I had did and understood it was wrong. The motions never let me talk about my accomplishments while incarcerated or the things I was doing for other people in the prison, like mentoring youth and volunteering on the Inmate Suicide Watch Program. And most importantly, these appeals/motions never allowed me to talk about what I would do if I were freed—my goals and the dreams I had of not only bettering my own life but also the lives of others.

I knew that if there were some remedy that allowed me to set forth all of these facts then it would happen—I would gain my freedom.

After spending nearly every aching hour in the law library all day, year after year, learning everything about the law that I could, I found that there was, indeed, one remedy that did allow for me to state all the above and more. But, more importantly, this remedy also gave the authority to one person and only one person to release me from prison. A remedy I knew absolutely nothing of, never considered, or that no prisoner ever mentioned—clemency. An executive power that allows the President of the United States (and governors and clemency boards for state offenses) to reduce the sentence of any federal prisoner.

Granddaughter advocating for the release of her grandmother Eva Palma, serving life without parole.

But there was a reason the prisoners never talked about it, or why I never heard about clemency: the chances of receiving clemency were extremely rare. If you were a drug offender and/or minority, the percentages of you receiving clemency were substantially reduced. Someone serving life without parole being granted clemency had only happened once before in history.[1]

Nevertheless, I believed I had a chance. So, I went to the law library to do some research on clemency and how to prepare a petition. There was nothing. Not even an application. Even the old school jailhouse attorneys knew nothing about clemency, which was strange because they knew everything about the law. In addition, I asked the officer who ran the law library if he could order a book on how to do clemency or one that explained it further, and after he searched for a few days nothing came up.

I would eventually obtain a copy of a Petition For Commutation and on the second to last page there was a page titled, "Reasons for Clemency," where I was supposed to explain why the President of the United States should release me. I knew if I only filled out that one page there would be no way my clemency would be granted. But at the bottom of that page in small words was stated, *"If you need more space you may complete your answer on a separate sheet of paper and attach it to the petition."*

I knew right there and then I was going to be able to put a petition together so compelling and convincing that if the president were to read it there would be no doubt he would release me. And thus, I began to construct a Petition For Commutation like my life depended on it—because in fact it did.

But there was still the important factor of getting the petition in the president's hand. To make him aware I existed and that there were many more just like me trapped behind bars with no way out. *"How does one do that?"* I thought. It's probably hard, if not impossible, for someone free to reach the president, but for a prisoner to accomplish such an extraordinary feat? Chances of getting struck by lightning in a prison cell were probably better.

It just so happened that for the past three years I had been reading books on how to start a business, how to market, and how to network. These books illustrated how to create press releases, flyers, and pamphlets—and I learned the power of imagery and how one can make people who don't know you take notice of your business and support it.

But the most significant part was learning about the Internet, Google and social media outlets such as Facebook, Twitter, and other various websites. It dawned on me that this was my chance. That was the way we were going to bring myself and others out from behind bars and into the free world.

So along with creating an out-of-the-ordinary clemency petition, I launched a clemency campaign from prison on behalf of myself and others called Crack Open The Door. Through my brother Stevie, I was able to further this advocacy on the outside using social media.

At first, admittedly, no one listened to my brother or me. No one answered the letters or documents I sent, and not only did they not respond to my brother's emails or phone calls, many would go on to block him from contacting them. Those who did respond informed us that though our cause was a valid one: *"Clemency was something not used on prisoners like [me]."*[2]

The Beginning: What you see here is the first photo and symbol for Crack Open The Door. In this photo are nine individuals serving life without parole for crack cocaine: 8 Black, 1 Latino. I felt this would show the disparity created by the crack cocaine penalties in a way statistics couldn't. I sent this picture to everyone and anyone who I thought would listen and help and my brother Stevie did the same on the outside. Of the nine individuals in this picture six would receive clemency from President Obama; two would receive a reduction of sentence based on a Guideline change made retroactive. Unfortunately, Russell Ellis, age 60 and incarcerated nearly 25 years, is still serving a sentence of life without parole.

CAN-DO's 4th White House Vigil
Sept 16, 2016

Photo Credit Malik King

But through persistence, faith, and the refusal to give up, we fought, day after day, month after month, year after year, to make connections. Even then we only made a couple, but were of the greatest magnitude one could hope for. We made contact with the author of The New Jim Crow, Michelle Alexander, as well as the ACLU's Vanita Gupta, Zeke Edwards, and Jennifer Turner. And we connected with advocates such as Nkechi Taifa of Open Society and Anthony Underwood who was fighting for his father, William Underwood, to receive clemency.[3]

Then, on December 19th, 2013 (26 months after I filed my petition and sent my letter), something extraordinary happened. Something that no one thought possible: The President of The United States, Barack Obama, responded to my plea of clemency by reducing my life sentence to twenty years, along with seven other individuals. We were called "The Obama 8."

It was a day I had dreamed of since my arrest and conviction in 1998. A day that would change the rest of my life and that of my family forever. However, that day also brought sorrow and sadness for I knew many other great individuals who were just as deserving of clemency. Many who I said I would help set free, many who didn't believe it was possible.

I would be released on August 11, 2015 after serving nearly 18 years in prison. By then, fortunately, President Obama had started his clemency initiative, which had set out to review and commute the sentences of thousands of people in the federal prison system. But there were missteps in the process that would limit the number of those that would actually be able to seek relief.

As a result, families who had a loved one incarcerated with no representation and were uncertain about how to navigate the clemency process began to contact me for help. I was able to help some of these individuals, but knowing I couldn't help everyone, I began to teach prisoners, family members, teachers, and law students how to do clemency petitions.[4] But along with the petitions I knew we would have to advocate in order for the voices of their families and loved ones to be heard.

Luckily, there were advocates like Nkechi Taifa, Amy Povah of CANDO, and others who were already mobilized and advocating for clemency. I was able to join with them on social media campaigns, mini-docs, op-eds, lobbying in Congress, speaking at colleges, appearing on TV, and at rallies and vigils in front of the White House and the department of justice. You name it, we did it.

Ultimately, President Obama would go on to commute the sentence of 1,725 prisoners: 500 of them were serving life without parole sentences. It was an amount that far preceded any president before him, but far from what should have been. This was a shortcoming many blamed on the Obama Administration—and while there was fault on their part, I mostly contribute that to criminal justice reform advocates and civil rights organizations not devoting the resources, time and preparation to clemency, or understanding how it should be implemented on a mass scale, and how to adequately represent the ten's of thousands of prisoners who warranted a reduction of sentence. I, myself, am also to blame. For though I helped nearly half a dozen individuals receive clemency from President Obama, I should have been prepared and in the position to help dozens more, if not hundreds.

That is the reason behind this Clemency Guidebook: To give you, the people in prison, and your families, the tools, knowledge, and know-how to create your own clemency petition. And also how to advocate from prison—or with a loved one on the outside—and have your voices actually be heard. So that you don't have to sit back and hope and pray that one day an attorney, organization, advocate, or celebrity takes interest in gaining your freedom: you can now do it yourself!

Because one thing I know is that regardless of who the president or governor in office is, regardless if they are liberal or conservative, regardless if it is their first year or last year in office, regardless if you've been in prison one year or twenty, regardless of your crime, regardless of how many rejections you've received, it is the prisoners and their families, and only them, who are going to fight day in and day out. Weekends and holidays, year after year: they don't care about any of the other stuff that says it can't be done or that you don't deserve a second chance.

Indeed, clemency is seldom granted, but I believe it's because there are not enough people applying for it, and there are not enough organizations pushing and advocating for it. I believe if the president (or governors) were explained why clemency is required and justifiable for one person or on a mass scale, then it would happen more often.

I envision a day when there will be mass clemencies to release the many thousands of prisoners who are serving excessive and unjust sentences, just as the "War on Drugs" resulted in mass incarceration and the stripping of rights of millions and millions of people.

I also believe this movement must be led by us: the incarcerated, formerly incarcerated, and families of the incarcerated.

As the Godmother of Criminal Justice Reform Michelle Alexander prophesied and so movingly stated over a decade ago:

> **"** *If Martin Luther King, Jr. is right that the arc of history is long, but it bends towards justice, a new movement will arise: and if civil rights organizations fail to keep up with the times, they will be pushed to the side as another generation of advocates comes to the fore. Hopefully the new generation will be led by those who know best the brutality of the new caste system—a group with greater vision, courage, and determination than the old guard can muster, trapped as they may be in an outdated paradigm."*
>
> The New Jim Crow: Mass Incarceration In The Age Of Colorblindness[5]

Michelle Alexander was referring to me, to you, to us.

Clemency vigil outside The White House

Photo Credit Malik King

PART ONE
The Federal Commutation Process

THE FIRST STEPS TO CLEMENCY

This Guidebook will help you and your family and friends understand the federal commutation process. The Guidebook will cover these topics:

1. **THE COMMUTATION PROCESS**
   What government agency handles applications? How does the application process work?

2. **GATHERING INFORMATION FOR YOUR APPLICATION**
   What kind of documents should you try to gather before you fill out your application?

3. **FILLING OUT THE APPLICATION**
   What are the dos and don'ts of writing your application? What do you need to keep in mind? How can you make your answers organized and clear?

Note: This guidebook was created under the reality that you could be in a prison that is consistently locked down, in the SHU, or under administrative segregation. With that in mind, several documents are included that should provide you enough information and material to explain the clemency process. The process of how to fill out a petition is listed in great detail, giving you what you need to perfect a clemency petition straight from a prison cell.

Step One *Understanding the Federal Commutation Process*

The first thing you need to understand is how the federal commutation process works. The information below will help you understand the difference between a pardon and a commutation and will give you an introduction into the Office of the Pardon Attorney (OPA), which handles commutation applications. Finally, this section will explain the way applications usually get handled once you submit one to OPA.

What is a federal pardon vs. commutation and what's the difference between the two?

A federal pardon is the action of the President of the United States that completely sets aside the conviction for a federal crime. The authority to take such action is granted to the president by Article II, Section 2, Clause 1. Under the Constitution, only federal criminal convictions may be pardoned by the president.

A federal commutation is not the same thing as a federal pardon. A "commutation" is a decision by the President to shorten the punishment for your crime. This is usually done by shortening the sentence of someone who is in prison. Sometimes, this means that you can immediately leave prison since you've already served the duration of the shortened sentence. Other times, it means that you have a shorter amount of time left to serve.

In addition, the president's power extends only to federal court convictions, to convictions adjudicated in the Superior Court of the District of Columbia, and to military court-martial proceedings. However, the president cannot pardon or commute a state criminal offense. Instead, you should contact the governor or other appropriate authorities of the state where the conviction occurred to determine whether any relief is available to you under the state law.

> NOTE: The process set forth in this Guidebook for filling out and filing a petition for clemency apply to applications that will be sent to The United States Department of Justice Office of The Pardon Attorney. This Guidebook can be referred to when preparing a clemency petition in a state case, but it is strongly recommended that you research the state clemency rules before filing a clemency petition. Each state's rules and process vary from one another and differ from the federal level. However, I would say the elements that a governor or Pardon and Parole Board look for when considering clemency are going to be similar to what the OPA and President look for.

What agency handles commutation requests?

The Office of the Pardon Attorney (OPA) handles all requests for federal sentence commutations. The OPA is part of the Department of Justice (DOJ). The DOJ sets the rules that apply to commutation petitions. The OPA's website has information about the commutation process, including instructions on how to fill out the application and what factors the OPA looks at when it reviews your application.[6]

The following are in the Appendix:

- *Petition for Commutation of Sentence. Appendix A*
- *DOJ Commutation Instructions and Governing Rules. Appendix B*
- *DOJ Standards for Consideration of Clemency Petitioners. Appendix C*
- *DOJ Frequently Asked Questions of Clemency. Appendix D*
- *BOP Clemency Program Statement 1330.15. Appendix E*

You should be able to get a copy of Appendix A and B from the law library.[7] If this is not available in the law library or you don't have access to the law library, you can ask your case manager for the documents. See Appendix E, BOP Clemency Program Statement 1330.15 ("*An inmate may request from the inmate's case manager the appropriate forms (and instructions) for filing a petition for commutation of sentence*").

How does the federal commutation process work?

The current process has lots of different levels of review by different attorneys. Generally speaking, commutation requests are reviewed in this order:

1. The OPA receives and reviews applications. Sometimes, the OPA has to ask other federal agencies for information in order to review your application. The OPA makes recommendations to the Deputy Attorney General (DAG) at the DOJ;

2. The DAG's staff reviews applications that get recommended;

3. The DAG reviews applications that get recommended and then makes a recommendation to the White House;

I KNOW NOTHING ABOUT THE LAW, CAN I REALLY PUT ONE OF THESE PETITIONS TOGETHER? YES YOU CAN!

In 2016 an elementary school teacher contacted me by the name of Anrica Caldwell. She had a friend in prison named David Barren who was serving life without parole and wanted to know if I could create a petition for him because there was no one else who would help. I told Anrica I couldn't do his petition, but I could teach her how to put one together and highlight the steps she could take to put a spotlight on David's case. I knew with Anrica's education, but importantly her passion, she could not only put a clemency petition together but could do it way better than any lawyer could. I just had to make her believe that it was possible and give her guidance and a little overview. She filed a petition for clemency on behalf of David, and on January 19th, 2017, President Obama reduced David's life sentence to thirty years. A huge victory. Nonetheless, Anrica still fights for David's sentence to be reduced even more.

4. Attorneys from the White House Counsel's Office reviews applications that get recommended;
5. The White House Counsel then makes recommendations to the president;
6. The president then makes a decision on whether to deny or grant your petition for commutation.[8]

The president, however, is not constitutionally required to follow the rules of the Department of Justice or the OPA and has wide discretion to exercise his/her clemency powers whenever he/she believes it is warranted.[9]

How long will it take for these steps to happen?

According to their website, OPA is not able to say how long it takes to process an application and make a decision. However, you should be prepared for this to take a while.

> **HOW LONG CAN IT REALLY TAKE TO GET A RESPONSE?**
> After I sent my Petition for Commutation, it took me 26 months to get a response from the President. From my personal experience I have seen it take up to three years to receive a grant or denial. However, under President Obama's Clemency Initiative denials and grants were being issued within a few months sometimes. You never know. All you can do is be patient.

Will the prosecutor from my case review my application?

Yes. It is the OPA's policy to ask the head federal prosecutor (the U.S. Attorney or the Assistant Attorney General) from the office that handled your case to look at your application. The federal prosecutor's opinions are very important to the recommendation that the OPA eventually makes. Generally speaking, the prosecutor can oppose your application, support your application, or not express any opinion about it. They are supposed to let the OPA know what position they take within 30 days.

Can the BOP weigh in on my application?

Yes. If OPA asks for the BOP's opinion on your application, the Director of the BOP is allowed to make a recommendation about whether you deserve a commutation. ("BOP" Bureau of Prisons). If the OPA asks for the BOP's opinion, the director will ask the warden of your prison for their written opinion about your application and more than likely the warden will request a recommendation or report from your Unit Team.

> **NOTE:** You are not notified if the prosecutor, the judge or the BOP are asked to respond to your petition for commutation. Nor are you given any documents or information as to what their position is on your petition. I've never heard of this information being provided to a petitioner and from my knowledge there is no policy statement or rule saying you can have access to it.

Do I need to serve a certain amount of my sentence before I can apply for a commutation?

No. You do not have to serve a certain amount of your sentence before you can apply for a commutation. However, the OPA will look at how long you have already served when you apply. Basically, if you have not served very long, then the chances of your application being granted are not very high.

Can I use a commutation request to get out of prison because of a medical condition or because I am very sick?

Yes. There is no policy stating clemency cannot be granted based on a medical condition. However, because there is a "Compassionate Release" statute 18 U.S.C. 3582(c)(1)(A) that allows a prisoner to seek a sentencing reduction for a severe medical condition/illness, a clemency petition seeking relief solely on this basis will not be looked upon too favorably by the OPA. If you have already submitted a compassionate release request to your warden, the OPA more than likely will not consider your commutation application until your compassionate release request gets decided on. However, if your medical condition is not severe enough to file for Compassionate Release, you can definitely include any medical or health issues (good or bad) you have in your petition when you start to describe who you are as a person today—which we will discuss later.

What if I have a petition pending but want to supplement it?

You are allowed to supplement your clemency petition, months or years after it is filed. Indeed, due to the amount of time it typically takes to get a response it is recommended to offer documents showing you have completed additional educational programs, stayed incident free, gained the support of a highly respected person(s) or anything else of significant importance. I would recommend, however, being strategic when doing so:[10]

- → Supplement only when there is information of extreme importance or when you have several new developments that need to be addressed or raised;
- → Don't supplement your petition every time something comes up. Let things accumulate;
- → Be very conservative with how many times you do supplement: once or twice should be sufficient (I supplemented my petition only once).

Recent Clemency Victory!

In 2018 I started a clemency project with Texas A&M Law Clinic. The project consisted of me speaking with the students about clemency and then assisting the students in preparing petitions for commutation for certain individuals in the federal system that I was advocating for.

Thereafter, I reached out to longtime friend Amy Povah, the founder of CANDO Clemency and a clemency recipient of President Clinton, and inform her of the project and asked did she have a particular person she would like to see a petition being prepared for. Amy strongly recommended Crystal Munoz whom Amy had been a longtime advocate for.

A petition along with an addendum was prepared and filed in November of 2018 with the Pardon Attorney's office.

On February 18, 2020 President Trump granted Crystal Munoz clemency: Crystal was released within 24 hours.

Much thanks and appreciation to the many hands that contributed to Crystal receiving clemency: one of those key people being the lovely Alice Marie Johnson.

Navajo woman receives clemency from President Donald Trump

Crystal Munoz and daughters Sarai and Nova
(Photo courtesy of the Munoz family)

Most and foremost, all the gratitude in the world to Amber Baylor, Associate Professor of Law and Director of the Criminal Defense Clinic at Texas A&M University: who trusted me, a person who was formerly incarcerated and a felon, to share with her students the meaning, purpose and power of clemency: a lady is now free from prison as a result of it.

And to the students who put this petition together and who I told, "You don't have to wait until you get a law degree to make change. You can do it now, from this classroom." Those students are: Mark Thorne-Thomsen, Jason Tiplitz, Megan Cloud, Enrica Martey, and Ryne Thacker.

Step Two — Gathering Information For Your Application

The next step in your process is gathering information that you need to complete the commutation application. This section will describe the legal documents that will be helpful to you when you fill out your commutation application. It will also describe the prison documents that will be helpful to you.

 **TIP:** Before you dive in and start filling out the application, take a moment to get organized. Try not to rush. If you want to make your application strong and accurate, you should make sure you try and gather the documents below before you begin writing or sending anything to the OPA. In the Appendix is a Check List of things you will want to do before you start to fill out your application. *See Appendix F, Clemency Checklist*

Do I need to get all the legal documents from my case?

You don't need to get every single document from your case. But you should definitely want to have or review your **Presentence Investigative Report** (PSR/PSI) before you file anything. This is the document that the Probation Officer created before your sentence. The PSR should have been given to you, your defense attorney, the prosecutor, and the judge. It has a lot of information that you will need to fill out the commutation application. It is also a document that the OPA, the DOJ, and the president will have access to and will more than likely rely upon in making a decision whether to grant or deny your clemency. The PSR also has all your criminal history, which you will have to fully disclose in the petition. Failure to fully do so may give the appearance that you are trying to be deceitful.

How do I get my PSR?

You are not allowed to possess your PSR in prison. So, you should start by writing or emailing your defense attorney and asking them to send your family or loved ones a copy of the PSR. If they receive the PSR you will have to get certain information through phone calls or mail since you are not allowed to have it in the prison. Another way to review your PSR is to inform your case manager or counselor that you want to look at it, and then set up a time when you can read it in-person. You should then write down all the information you will need to fill out the application.

Are there other legal documents I should try to get?

Other legal documents might contain helpful information. The list below is a *general list* to help you think about what might be helpful to you as you put together your commutation application. But remember: *every single case is different*. Not all the documents listed below will be necessary for your application.[11]

1. **Judgment of Conviction:** This is a document that has to be filed with your sentence. It contains the length of your sentence and supervised release. If you were ordered to pay a fine, or to pay restitution, it will also have this information.

2. **Complaint, Indictment, or Information:** These are the documents that list what you where charged with. These documents might also contain facts about your crime(s). It might also list your co-defendants.

   a. Having names of co-defendants might be useful in finding out what kind of sentences they got. Depending on the facts of your case, you may be able to point out that co-defendants who were more responsible than you somehow got much lower sentences.

3. **Sentencing Transcript:** Usually there is a written transcript of what was said at your sentencing. This might include any helpful facts that your attorney raised, as well as arguments made by the prosecutor. It would also include anything the judge said before they sentenced you.

   a. If the judge made comments suggesting that your sentence should not be so harsh, the transcript will help you point this out in your application.

4. **Court opinions from any appeals you filed:** If you appealed your case, you should try to get court opinions from your appeals. This includes appeals and habeas petitions (Title 28 USC Section 2255) made to your sentencing judge, to the Court of Appeals, and the Supreme Court. If you cannot get the actual opinions from your appeals, try to find the case citations so that you can include them in your application.

What prison records should I get?

All federal prisons keep records about you. These records should include your initial evaluations from when you first entered prison, along with regularly scheduled evaluations, and evaluations done when you are transferred between prisons. They also might have regular progress reports, employment and school records, and any discipline reports you received while in prison. You should try to get these records, because the OPA will definitely look at your prison record and behavior when they read your application. Here is a general list of prison records you will want to get and read over:

1. **Inmate Skills Development Plan Progress Reports:** These reports are updated regularly once you are in prison. The reports will have information about what you have done in prison, including:

   a. Education classes you have taken
   b. Jobs you have been given
   c. Discipline reports you have received
   d. Your academic progress and goals
   e. Your job progress and goals
   f. Your mental and emotional health and goals
   g. Your family relationships and goals

2. **Internal Prison Files:** Federal prisons have special units designed to collect information about prisoners, such as possible gang membership. You do not have the right to see this information. However, you can ask if they have you confirmed as a gang member or associated with a gang.

   a. When you begin the process of preparing your clemency petition, ask the Special Investigative Services (SIS) at your prison if they have you connected to a gang. When I asked, I was informed they did have me as a confirmed gang member even though I wasn't. I then took the steps to have this gang classification removed.

   b. The OPA does not mention anything about gang affiliations being a basis for denying a person's clemency, but this is probably something that the OPA will look at in determining if you are a safety risk if released.

Once you gather the PSR and other records stated above you are ready to start the process of filling out your application.

Step Three *Filling Out the Application*

This section will discuss the federal commutation application. *Appendix A, Petition for Commutation of Sentence*. It will give you general information about the seven questions that are listed in the application. This section will also give you general advice about other helpful documents that you can include with your application, such as letters of support and education and job training certifications.

TIP: Once you have read through the entire application and instructions, don't rush to write down your answers. Write them out on a separate sheet of paper, so that you can copy them down in the application. This helps keep the application neat, and it also means you get to keep a copy of your answers.

The "Relief Sought" Question:

If you are only asking to have your sentence shortened, then you should check the box "Reduction of Prison Sentence Only." If you were ordered to pay a fine or restitution and also want to have that amount reduced, then you will want to check the box "Reduction of Prison Sentence and Remission."

QUESTION 1

Question 1 asks you for a variety of personal information. You should know most of this information, such as:

1. Your first, middle, and last name
2. Your BOP Reg Number
3. Your Social Security Number
4. Your birthplace and birthday
5. Your citizenship status
6. Your current place of incarceration
7. Whether you have ever applied for a federal commutation before and the dates of any decisions on your earlier applications

If you don't know the answer to all these questions, you should be able to find them by looking at your BOP Progress Reports and your PSR.

QUESTION 2

Question 2 asks you to identify *"Offense(s) For Which Commutation is Sought."* This includes:

1. Whether you pled guilty or went to trial and were found guilty
2. Where you were convicted
3. What crimes you were convicted of
4. The date you were sentenced and the length of your sentence
   a. Any fines or restitution you were ordered to pay
   b. The length of supervised release or special parole
   c. The length of probation
5. How old you were at the time you committed the crime

You should be able to get answers to these questions from your Judgment of Conviction or your BOP Progress Reports. Both of these documents will tell you what crimes you were sentenced for, the date you were sentenced and information about your sentence length, supervised release, and any fines or restitution.

QUESTION 3

Question 3 wants to know everything pertaining to the amount of time you were in prison and the sentence that was imposed by the district court. This includes:

1. When you began serving your sentence[12]
2. When you are getting released
3. Whether you qualify for parole
4. If you paid any fine or restitution that you were ordered to pay

You should be able to find answers to #1-2 in your BOP Progress Reports. These records will have the date you were transferred to BOP custody and their estimate of your release date.

QUESTION 4

Question 4 wants to know if you have any active appeals relating to your crime. If you or your attorney filed appeals challenging your conviction or your sentence, you should determine the following:

1. Appealed your case to the U.S. Court of Appeals and is it still active
2. Appealed your case to the U.S. Supreme Court and is it still active
3. Filed a habeas corpus motion (also called a 2255) and is it still active

Remember, if you have any active appeals or are able to file a timely appeal then your commutation application will more than likely be rejected. If you have any available remedies for relief such as a Title 18 USC Section 2255 motion or a Title 18 USC Section 3582(C)(2) motion and file for a Petition for commutation your petition will more than likely be denied by the Pardon Attorney's Office. However, the President has the authority to grant clemency to any prisoner, at anytime, regardless if a prisoner has an appeal pending or availability of another vehicle to challenge their conviction/sentence.

Jason with Josie Ledesma (left) and Geneva Cooley (right) who were both sentenced to life without parole for a nonviolent drug offense. Josie would spend nearly 25 years in prison before her sentence was commuted by President Obama: Jason assisted with her clemency petition and advocacy. Geneva would spend 17 years in prison before a court reduced her sentence: Jason assisted with the initial steps that would lead to her freedom.
PHOTO TAKEN 2019.

Questions 5, 6, and 7:

The last three questions in the application are the most important ones. Government attorneys will care a lot about how you answer them and what you say and don't say. You should take your time and think carefully about how you will answer them.

QUESTION 5

"Provide a complete and detailed account of the offense for which you seek commutation, including the full extent of your involvement. If you need more space, you may complete your answer on a separate sheet of paper and attach it to the petition."

This question wants to know about your federal crime(s) and your role and involvement. You should make sure you are honest and open about what you did. Everyone's answer will be different, but here are certain dos and don'ts to keep in mind:

- → **Give a factual account of what you were convicted of:** Question 5 is a little tricky. It does not mention "accepting responsibility" or "taking responsibility," but that is what the government attorneys want to see. If you do not state what you did the government could see this as a sign of not accepting responsibility. Basically your answer should reflect the elements of the offense of conviction.

- → **Never blame anyone or anything else:** Do not blame any of your co-defendants, any victims, or anyone else. Do not blame "the system" or "society." Do not say or suggest that what you did was minor or not that bad. If you do any of these things, this could be weighed against you.

- → **Keep it simple:** If other people were involved in your crime, do not spend time talking about them or what they did. Focus on yourself and your actions. Court decisions usually give a short but thorough explanation of what happened in your case: look at those for examples. The key thing is to admit each element of the crime. You don't have to go into a full account of your offense.

- → **Do not argue:** Do not try to argue about the facts of your crime. Remember, government attorneys will be reading your PSR to determine the facts of your crime. You should not try to argue that the PSR or the prosecutor or judge was wrong about the facts or that the relevant conduct used to base your sentence is inaccurate. Nor do you have to put down everything alleged in the PSR or at trial. Again, stick to the elements of the offense. The OPA will compare what you write down to the judgment in the case. That means you will want to be accurate as to what you were convicted of.

What about addressing violence?

The OPA is looking at your application to see if you have changed, and whether you will be a danger to the community if your sentence is commuted and you get released early. So if your crime involved violence, you should not ignore it in your answer. Here are some tips for writing about conduct that involved violence:

- → **Don't sugar coat.** Don't ignore it or pretend it didn't happen. Don't make any excuses for what you did. But, as well, you don't have to give specific details as to what actually happened. It's the elements of the offense that are important.

- → **Keep it simple.** You don't need to go into a lot of detail about what you did. Keep your descriptions short and plain.

- → **Don't argue.** You might be tempted to say "this isn't really violent," or "nobody actually got hurt." Don't do that! If government attorneys think you are not taking full responsibility or trying to downplay what happened it more than likely will be weighed against you. If you think anything is a mitigating factor I would recommend not asserting it under Question 5 and waiting to do so when answering Question 7.

 TIP: If you have a hard time answering Question #5, remember that it's the judgment that matters –you need to admit to the crime of conviction, but you don't have to elaborate or go into every detail. There will be examples to look at in the Appendix so don't stress too much on it.

QUESTION 6

"Aside from the offense for which commutation is sought, have you ever been arrested or taken into custody by any law enforcement authority, or convicted in any court, either as a juvenile or an adult, for any other incident?"

"For each such incident provide: the date, the nature of charge, the law enforcement authority involved, and the final disposition of the incident. You must list every violation, including traffic violations that resulted in arrest or in a criminal charge, such as driving under the influence."

This question wants you to list all of your past arrests and past convictions. This includes federal, state, or local arrests and convictions, from when you were a juvenile and adult. This question is important, because government attorneys will be looking at your criminal record carefully. If you hide something or forget something in your answer, there is a chance the government will think you are being dishonest and deceitful. This is why it is so important to get your PSR, because it will list all your arrests and convictions (most of the time).

Here are some tips to keep in mind when writing your answer to Question 6:

→ **Use the PSR:** Question 6 has to include every arrest and conviction from your PSR. Government attorneys will look at your PSR to see what your criminal record looks like. If you leave something out of your petition that is listed in your PSR, this will make it look like you are hiding something and could hurt your application.

→ **List everything:** If you know about an arrest and/or conviction that is not in the PSR, then you should list it, even if you do not have all the information relating to it. You can take a chance and hope the government doesn't find out about it but I wouldn't recommend that. If you leave something out it could make the OPA view you as someone who is deceitful and untruthful, which could also lead them to viewing actual claims you allege in your petition as untrue.

→ **Keep it simple:** Question 6 only wants a list of your arrests and convictions. You should not try to explain the facts of every arrest or conviction you have.

→ **Do not argue:** It does not matter if you think your arrest or conviction was misstated in the PSR. It does not matter if you think your arrest or conviction was false, unfair, unconstitutional, or corrupt. You must still include it in your answer.[13]

NOTE: Even though I put a lot of emphasis on disclosing every arrest and conviction you have, there may be some you have forgotten about due to lapse of time or because you were arrested so often you can't remember them all. If this is the case, don't let this prevent you from filing your petition. Just put down those you know of. However, I would say that if you were arrested and/or charged with something significant (e.g. DWI, assault, drug charge, attempted murder) and you don't list it and the OPA were to find out about it through their own investigation of you, they would probably come to the conclusion that you couldn't have forgotten about something so severe and are trying to intentionally hide it. In any event, the most important advice I can give you in answering Question 6 is to LOOK AT YOUR PSR!

Norris Henderson

FROM INCARCERATION TO NOW FIGHTING FOR THOSE INCARCERATED

Norris Henderson is the Founder and Executive Director of both VOTE and Voters Organized to Educate. In 2018 Norris served as the statewide campaign director for the Unanimous Jury Coalition, a ballot campaign that ended non-unanimous juries in Louisiana. During his 27 years in prison, under a wrongful conviction, Norris was a jailhouse lawyer, who co-founded the Angola Special Civics Project, and a hospice program and also drafted a successful parole reform law for Lifers.

Questions 5, 6, and 7:

The last three questions in the application are the most important ones. Government attorneys will care a lot about how you answer them and what you say and don't say. You should take your time and think carefully about how you will answer them.

QUESTION 7

"State your reasons for seeking commutation of sentence. If you need more space, you may complete your answer on a separate sheet of paper and attach it to the petition."

Up until this question, the OPA has been focused on your crime and your criminal record. Now is your chance to tell the OPA who you are as a person, why you deserve commutation, and what you plan to do with your second chance.

Your main objectives in answering Question 7?

Question 7 does not have any limits on what you can say. However, when you answer Question 7, you want to do four things.

1. You want to set forth any reasons you have that demonstrate your sentence is inequitable, no longer just or necessary.

2. You want to show the OPA that you have changed since you committed your crime and went to prison.

3. You want to show them who you are as a human being, that you are someone's father/mother, daughter/son.

4. You want to show them that you have a reentry plan in place and goals, and that you are not a danger to commit another crime if you were to receive a commutation and released early

Do I need to talk about my crime(s) when I answer Question 7?

Being that Question 5 of the petition asks you to set forth a detailed account of your crime and involvement, typically you wouldn't discuss your crime in Question 7 again. However, being Question Five is only asking for a factual account of your offense, you may find it necessary to discuss how you became involved in the criminal conduct you were convicted of. For example, if your crime is a drug offense, you might want to set forth why you began selling or how you got involved (e.g., addiction). Or if your offense is the result of being in an abusive relationship, you might want to give some background on how you met that person and set forth when the abuse began and how it escalated over time (e.g., battered wife syndrome).

Talking about your offense and what led up to it is a slippery slope. You might not want to bring it up at all and there may be no need to. But if you do, be sure you don't come off as trying to portray yourself as a victim or as trying to gain pity or make excuses for what happened. The focus should be on giving the reader an understanding of your personal life.

Example: When I spoke of my offense in my petition, I noted and conceded I was the leader/organizer and the crime I committed was very serious. I did note as well that my drug offense did not involve the typical characteristics that a crime like mine usually would or that others would perceive it to have (e.g. shootings, guns, violence, involvement of kids, gangs). However, I was clear to point out that I did not believe because my crime did not involve those elements it was okay doing what I did. It was told in a factual manner not argumentatively. See Appendix G, Jason's Memorandum in Support of Petition for Commutation.

Things you should keep in mind when answering Question 7:

1. **Always be honest.** The OPA who reads your personal statement will already know a lot about you and your criminal case. They will also know about your time in prison. Lying or hiding information will not help your application.

2. **Think about the "big picture."** Sometimes people write only about their crime and then their time in prison. Think bigger: your life from childhood to your current age, and your plan/goals if granted clemency. This might seem broad, but remember, the people who read your application do not know you. They only know what's on the record from your trial, PSR, and prison reports. Your personal statement is your chance to explain who you are and the things that happened in your life.

    a. For instance, who are you as a person? As a father or mother? As a sister or brother? A husband or wife? As a student? What role does religion play in your life? Are you a mentor to other prisoners?

    b. The Standard Application Form will not ask these questions. Only you can tell the decision makers these answers.

3. **Take responsibility.** Do not blame other people or outside forces for why you are in prison. If the OPA thinks you are not taking responsibility for your actions, they will probably weigh this against you.

4. **Show remorse.** This goes along with taking responsibility. The OPA will want to see that you understand what you have done is wrong and that you are sorry. If you cannot be remorseful, then your application will probably not be looked upon favorably.

5. **Do not come off as argumentative.** When setting forth the basis for your claims, you want to be matter of fact and not argumentative or rely on theories. You can support your claim by citing reports, studies, research, and court decisions.

6. **It's not an appeal brief.** Claims relating to the prosecution of your case should not be alleged: e.g., ineffective assistance of counsel, unlawful search and seizure, improper jury instructions, defective indictment, conviction/sentence is based solely on hearsay from cooperating witnesses, etc.,. These claims and those that are similar should have been addressed on appeal or habeas corpus.

RELITIGATING COURT FINDINGS AND CAN IT REALLY RESULT IN YOUR CLEMENCY PETITION BEING DENIED?

To illustrate the importance of not re-litigating court findings and the impact it can have on your petition if you do, consider the extraordinary case of Corey Blount. Corey was sentenced to life without parole in 1998 for distributing crack cocaine. He filed a clemency petition under President Obama's Clemency Initiative and was denied in 2016. I had been in contact with Corey and his daughter since my release and when I heard he was denied, I was shocked. I felt if anyone should receive clemency it was Corey. Something had to be wrong, so I asked to see his petition. When I read it, I determined, based on my belief, he was denied because he had relitigated drug quantity. I sent him my petition for clemency, he re-did his, I reviewed it and with a couple of additions we re-submitted it: but this time with no argument or suggestion the drug quantity was in error. And amazingly, Corey's life sentence was commuted to thirty years. A blessing without a doubt, but we still feel Corey should have received twenty years and he is still seeking clemency today.

How should I organize and format my answer for Question 7?

Below I will set forth the format I typically use and one that has been used by other individuals involved with clemency work when answering Question 7. However, there is no wrong or right format to use to answer Question 7. Indeed, I rarely use the same format twice, and the order in which claims and factors are presented change from petition to petition. Regardless, below is a guide on how to structure and format your response to Question 7.

Step One:

Question 7 of the Petition for Commutation provides space for you to state the reasons you are seeking commutation. On this page you want to state the main reason(s) on which you are seeking clemency. There is nothing that states you must have more than one reason for the president to grant you clemency. However, one reason may not be sufficient or strong enough, and it may take a number of factors to convince the OPA and the president that your case is unique and that clemency is warranted.

> **NOTE:** President Obama's clemency initiative stated prisoners who met a certain criterion would be considered for a commutation of sentence. That criteria was: (1) would be given a lesser amount of time if sentenced today; (2) nonviolent, low level offender with no ties to large scale organizations, gangs, cartels; (3) been in prison ten years; (4) no significant criminal history; (5) demonstrated good conduct while in prison; and (6) no history of violence prior to or during incarceration. It should be noted that this criterion was applied in a flexible manner and hundreds of people received clemency who did not meet every criteria.

Following are examples of factors, by themselves or in conjunction with others, that have been relied upon to grant clemency and the basis for doing so:

- **Committed the offense at a young age:** Science has proven that the brain does not fully develop until around the age of 25. Courts have, over the years, relied on this fact to give a lesser punishment to defendants under the age of 21 and especially for those under 18.

- **First time offender:** Research has proven that a first-time offender or an offender with minimal criminal history is less likely to reoffend.

- **Punishment is not considered reasonable and/or cruel:** With crime and punishment being reevaluated all across the United States there are many penalties for offenses at the state and federal level that have been deemed excessive and unnecessary. You should be able to do a nationwide evaluation on your crime and punishment through the law library and see if there are any changes in perception of punishment as it relates to your offense. Look for court decisions, articles by professors or organizations, or changes in the law in different jurisdictions.

- **Change in law that is not retroactive:** This includes a U.S. Supreme Court ruling that impacts your sentence but was not made retroactive by the court. Or if the punishment under a Sentencing Guideline or statute that you were sentenced under has been reduced but not made retroactive could also provide a basis for clemency.

- **Judge was mandated to impose a sentence they disagreed with:** There are times where the sentencing judge expresses that they would impose a lesser sentence if they had the authority but because of mandatory minimum sentences they are unable to. In cases where a judge did not make a specific statement or mention of wanting to impose a lesser sentence you can always write them a letter and ask to support your clemency.

- **Battered Woman Syndrome (BWS):** BWS is a medically recognized condition in which women suffering from mental and emotional abuse remain in the relationship despite a repeated pattern of violence perpetrated by a spouse or boyfriend.[14]

- **Significant amount of time incarcerated:** Significant amount of time incarcerated varies from offense to offense. From what I have seen, being in prison half of the time you were given is considered significant or if the amount of prison time you received is a life sentence or equivalent (thirty years or more), twenty years of incarceration (depending on the offense) is considered significant.

- **Extraordinary post-conviction act or conduct:** This typically would involve more than just completing regular and required courses and something more significant like no incident reports (or minor/minimal), obtaining a degree (or degrees), being an educational instructor, or creating programs for prisoners to better themselves. Also passing all drug tests, no connection to gangs, or saving the life of a prisoner, guard, or staff member.

- **Elderly or Illness:** Seeking early release through illness or disease is typically limited to extreme cases where one has limited mobility, brain function, or death is imminent. At that point, it's recommended to pursue release through 18 USC Section 3582(c)(1)(A)—the act that allows federal prisoners to apply for early release if they can present certain "extraordinary and compelling" reasons. The BOP typically defines the age of being elderly at sixty-five-years-old. If your age or health isn't quite at the level of what is stated above but it is close, then I would also mention it as being a factor to be considered.[15]

- **Family Circumstances:** If a serious illness or death of a family member occurred while you were incarcerated and you're the only person able to care for your children or immediate family member, then this is also something worth mentioning.

- **Actual Innocence:** An actual innocence claim is typically reserved for the courts and habeas corpus proceedings, but there are times where statute of limitations and other procedural hurdles don't allow a court to review a claim and clemency can be the only remedy. It is the extremely rare case where clemency is granted to someone alleging actual innocence. In fact, there is no evidence a commutation has ever been granted to a federal prisoner on this ground. However, there is no policy saying it can't be used, and governors have reduced the sentences of death row inmates when the reliability of the conviction was in question.[16]

In setting forth your issues for Question 7 of the petition you want to be very concise and fact specific. Because of the limited amount of space provided on page 5 of the application, I recommend not going into too much actual or supportive detail on this page. *Appendix H, Eva Palma's Answer to Question Seven of Petition for Commutation; Appendix I, Evelyn Pappa's Answer to Question Seven of Petition For Commutation*

For those factors that need further information to support them, or if you want to assert other factors or information, you can do so with additional pages (which we will discuss next). The basis and reasons you are relying upon do not all have to be stated on page 5 of the application.

TIP: I typically will advise the OPA that I am adding additional information by stating the following at the bottom of page 5 of the clemency petition: *"For additional facts, information and documents in support of Petition for Commutation please see attached memorandum."*

NOTE: In answering Question 7 you can either do so in first person or third person (regardless if you are doing the writing yourself or if someone is doing it for you). Every clemency petition I have prepared or assisted in preparing was done in third person. There is no right or wrong way when it comes to this. It's all based on your preference and what you are comfortable with.

Step Two:

Question 7 also states: *"If you need more space you may complete your answer on a separate sheet of paper and attach it to the petition."* These additional sheets, if necessary, are normally referred to as a memorandum, or addendum (hereinafter "memorandum").[17] They are used to clarify, modify, or support your basis for clemency.

There is no set format on how to create a memorandum or requirement that one needs to be added to support a petition for clemency. However, to assist you I will include actual petitions and memorandums you can reference.

You should typically want your memorandum to be sectioned in four different parts:

    a. Factors Demonstrating the Sentence is too Harsh, Unfair, or Unjust

    b. Your Life Prior to Incarceration

    c. Your Life During Incarceration

    d. Your Release Plan

The order above is a good one to follow but there's no set format: the order is entirely up to what you feel is best. There is no recommended length of how long or short the information should be in support of each section. The rule I would follow is, "Less is best."

Creating Your Memorandum and Things to Consider When Doing So:

- **FACTORS DEMONSTRATING SENTENCE IS TOO HARSH, UNFAIR, AND/OR UNJUST**

When setting forth information in support of the factors you are relying upon to show that your sentence is too harsh, unfair and/or unjust, you are going to want to rely on statements or decisions by individuals who are highly respected (e.g., professors, judges, civil rights organizations, Congress members, the president, or his staff).

A factor can also be supported by studies, research and science that have been done by credible sources (e.g., professors, government agencies, civil rights organizations).

Your presentation of the facts should not be argumentative. You are only trying to restate and summarize information, findings, and research, and how they relate to your conviction/sentence or you.

- **YOUR LIFE PRIOR TO INCARCERATION**

In setting forth your life prior to incarceration, the objective is to get the OPA familiar with you, your background, your family, and anything that might relate to your character as a person. Whether a certain factor can be weighed against you rather than in support of your character is a consideration you will have to make in order to determine what to assert and what not to assert.

Some of the factors about your life you should consider:

1. **Your family life growing up:** Where were you born? Siblings? What was your family like? Who raised you and took care of you? What kind of challenges did you face? Were you raised by a single parent or neither parent? Did you live in poverty? Did you take care of other people in your family? If important family members or loved ones were gone from your life because of illness, death, or incarceration, you should explain this. Or did you grow up in a relatively safe environment and were you raised in a good home? Were you part of a church?

2. **Your education growing up:** How far did you go in school? Did you graduate? Why or why not? Did you go to trade school, to college? Did you have any special interests or skills? Did you face any challenges in school or were you top of the class?

3. **Your work history before prison:** Did you have any jobs before prison? What was your position and day-to-day duties? Is there something extraordinary about how you attained your position? Did you serve in the military? Were you unemployed? Laid off?

4. **Your survival story:** Were you the victim of trauma or violence or crime? Is it something that impacted you back then or does it continue to impact you today? What have you learned about your trauma?
    a. Sometimes people who commit crimes were also victims of crime or have suffered traumatic experiences that they have not been able to deal with such as child abuse, sex trafficking, gender based violence, domestic or sexual violence, or addiction of any kind, including a history of addiction in your family.

5. **No survival story or severe hardships:** If you experienced a childhood or life with very little to no significant hardship(s) you should state so. There is no way to tell whether a story of sorrow or privilege works in favor or against your clemency. So tell the truth or tell only what you think supports your clemency—but never lie.
    a. Sometimes we make mistakes or commit a crime simply because of stupidity regardless of everything being pretty good in our life. Or sometimes a person comes from a privileged background and has never had to face consequences for wrong-doing and this results in a person spiraling out of control. If this is your situation, consider stating so.

TIP: There is no way to determine how the OPA will look at certain factors of your life in comparison to your offense. Hardship or a life of privilege could be weighed against you, in support of you, or have absolutely no bearing at all. As with everything else recommended in this Guidebook, you must make the determination of what to say and not to say and/or how to frame it if you do decide to state it. Bottom line is that there is nothing requiring you to state anything personal about your life or that of your families. To give you a personal example I decided not to include the fact my brother JJ was murdered in prison because I felt it would be weighed against me and my family as a whole. However, I am sure they became aware of his passing at some point of the process.

- **YOUR LIFE DURING INCARCERATION**

In determining whether to grant a petition for clemency, the OPA is going to want to know everything about what you have done and haven't done while incarcerated. The OPA will review your progress reports from prison and may even ask for the prison to supplement it with an updated report and ask for a recommendation from the Warden.

In addition to reiterating the significant parts of the progress report, you will state other important information the report leaves out (with documentation to support) that pertain to your character and rehabilitation while you've been in prison.

Ways to demonstrate one has achieved extraordinary rehabilitation:

1. **Your behavior in prison:** When you first entered prison, you might have gone through an adjustment period and in doing so had discipline issues. Or, you might have never had an incident report during your entire incarceration.
   a. Your prison record is important, because the OPA will be looking at how you have changed since you started your sentence. This is an opportunity to highlight your good behavior in circumstances that can be very challenging. Being able to state you have no connection to prison gangs, have passed all drug test given, or have no incident reports will go a long way.
   b. If you took courses on anger management, drug and/or alcohol addiction, or other self-help topics, you can point to this as examples of you trying to improve yourself and your situation. Again, I would recommend not listing or attaching certificates of every program you took.[18]
   c. Some people turn to religion as a source of comfort and guidance. If you have become a religious leader in your prison, or you mentor other prisoners or participate in regular religious services, this is also an important fact that you can write about, because it will show your personal growth.
   d. Payments on court issued fines and restitution can be viewed as a person's acceptance of responsibility of a crime they have committed. If you have not paid the entire amount or paid only a small percentage of the total amount, I would still state it, especially if you have consistently been on a payment plan and consistent with payments.

NOTE: You should also explain what brought about the realization to change and dedicate your life to becoming a better person. Was it an event you witnessed? A book you read? A religious experience or conversation; something that happened to you or a family member? At what point did it occur? This could be a very important and powerful narrative for the reader that humanizes who you are.

NOTE: Depending on the type of incident report(s) you have received and the frequency of them, you can expect they will not be looked upon favorably. You may want to consider stating mitigating factors (if they exist) that put the incident in perspective. However, again, you take the risk of possibly coming off as a person who is never at fault for any wrong-doing. Thus, it may be best not to say anything at all. Circumstances to consider if you decide to speak about incident reports:

- *The date it occurred:* When a person goes to prison it takes time to learn the rules set by the prison and the prisoners. During that process you make mistakes, you get in trouble.

- *Entered prison at a young age:* The younger you are the more stupid mistakes you make, whether you're free or when you're in prison. If your incident reports occurred when you entered prison at a young age and you have not obtained any since, it is a sign you have grown up and matured.

- *Incarcerated at a violent prison:* The chances of you getting in trouble at a United States Penitentiary are pretty high whether you are looking for trouble or not. I am not suggesting this gives you a free pass on any incident report(s) you receive, but I would say based on an entire overview of your clemency petition in conjunction with the type of incident and facts surrounding it the OPA can make an assessment if your conduct was more the result of the violent nature of the prison rather than the violent nature of yourself.

- *Incarcerated at a violent prison but you've received no or minor incident reports.* Typically, when a person is in a setting that is violent and a lot of gang activity and negative behavior is rampant, it typically leads one to act the same, especially when that person enjoys committing such acts. However, if you are in this type of environment and you have stayed on the straight and narrow, I think it speaks to the testament of someone ultimately being a good person who just made a bad mistake (or mistakes) at one point in their life.

- *No excuse or explanation at all:* There isn't always an excuse or justified reason for doing something we weren't supposed to do other than being a bone-head. Again, you may want to stay completely away from trying to explain an incident report for it could be weighed against you. You decide.

2. **Your education or job history in prison:** You may have taken courses to get your GED or a college degree; been part of programs or groups inside the prison that have helped you rehabilitate; been admitted to honor dorms or had your custody dropped as a result of clear conduct; taken courses to get job-certified; or you may have taken courses on religion or led the choir or your own church gatherings. If your prison does not have a lot of education or job-training opportunities, or you have been in the SHU for a great majority of your time, you can also point this out when you discuss what you have taken.

   a. Your efforts to get an education and job skills are important factors, because they show that you have set goals and have gotten skills that will improve your chances of successfully reentering society if you leave prison. Depending on what you have taken, you can talk about how your specific courses and trainings have prepared you to find a job and financially support yourself if you are released.

   b. This is especially important to mention if you are assisting as an instructor for programs and courses or have created programs/courses for prisoners (educational/self-help/religious).

   c. If you have not taken a lot of classes as a result of being in a maximum-security penitentiary, which offer very little programs and are constantly on lock-down, then you should explain so. As well, a person can be signed up for a class/program for years and not be allowed to participate because they are serving a life sentence or de facto life.

TIP: When I was in USP Beaumont, my sentence didn't prevent me too much from taking courses because nearly everyone there had a significant sentence. However, the prison didn't offer many courses and by my second year in that prison I had completed everything offered. Therefore, what I began to do was take correspondence courses. When I went to El Reno FCI, I continued taking correspondence courses because it was difficult to get enrolled in classes because of my life sentence. I can't say for sure, but I think the fact I continued my education on my own and paid for it on my own went a long way in showing my commitment to change and my rehabilitation. I would recommend you do the same if you can afford it. See Appendix J, Correspondence and Educational Courses

3. **Your family life today:** Who is your family today? Are you married or have a girlfriend/boyfriend? Do you have kids? Are your parents alive? How has prison challenged your family?
    a. Family ties are important, because you will need support if you get released from prison early. If you have been fortunate to be able to regularly speak with and see your family during prison visitations, you should highlight how hard you have worked and what you have done in order to maintain these bonds.
    b. During long periods of incarceration, unfortunate circumstances can sometimes occur in your family's life, such as a severe illness, death, or some other tragic occurrence. If it is a situation where your release in some way can contribute to bettering the situation then state that clearly.
    c. Prior to incarceration you may have been financially secure. If you are still providing for your family from your savings or some other type of legal income, you may want to state that. Or if you are making money inside the prison from UNICOR or another job and are sending money to your family monthly or for holidays and/or special events, then state that as well.

- **YOUR RELEASE PLAN**

In setting forth your Release Plan, you want to provide information that will illustrate what your life will look like immediately upon release, including the first year of your release and anything long-term you wish to accomplish.

Everyone's release plan will look differently, but the idea is to demonstrate that you have a plan. It doesn't necessarily have to be grandiose or involve wanting to save the world, and you definitely don't want to sound like you are making stuff up to show how great of a person you are because it will more than likely have the opposite effect. After spending time in prison, it's perfectly fine to just want to get out and be with your family or start a family of your own and enjoy life and not necessarily volunteer in community projects (indeed, the OPA might not be fond of the idea of you being involved in the community based on your offense). And if that is what you want to do—simply take care of your family and enjoy life—then state it in your petition.

The OPA and the president's main concern is that if you get a commutation, you will commit a new crime. You need to show them that you have thought about life after prison, you have a plan, and not only will you not commit another crime, but you will get out and most likely succeed.

→ *Support system:* You may have offers from family and loved ones to stay with them if you are released from prison and assistance with other things you will need when released, like a car, job, transportation, and support. List who these individuals are and how they will help.

→ *Counseling:* If you are going to counseling in the prison (e.g. AA/NA) and will continue to do so when released, try and determine what providers are in your city and reach out to them and let them know your situation. Make a notation of this and their response in your memorandum.

→ *Education:* Some prisons offer a lot of courses that put you in a good position to further your education upon release or provide you with the skillset and hours to eventually get certified. If you plan to further your education/attain certification, then state this and how it will impact you.

→ *Job:* If you had a job before prison, or if you took vocational programs while in prison, then talk about what your job skills are and how they can help you transition back into your community. Maybe you know of someone already who is willing to hire you? State who they are and the name of the business.

→ *Housing:* It is also helpful if you can write about where you will live, who owns the house, and give any pertinent information about them and their character (if you can, include a letter of support from a highly esteemed person of the community speaking of that person(s) integrity that you will be living with). If you don't have a place to stay, reach out to organizations in the city where you will be released and see if they will offer a letter saying they will house you or find out if they have a system that helps people coming out of prison secure housing.

→ *Life lessons:* What have you learned about yourself since you went to prison? How have you changed and improved? How have you learned from your mistakes? What have you done to make the best of your situation?

NOTE: All of the points above are not equally important. However, having a plan for (a) work, and (b) housing are especially key. As well, I think everyone has the tendency to want to express that they want to go out and make a change. You have to think about the OPA's view of you and if they would see it more as a benefit or detriment having you working with youth, women, etc. Again, I think the OPA will put more emphasis on where you will be living and working when released rather than how you will be giving back to the community.

- CONCLUDING THE PETITION.

In this last part you want the request for commutation and prayer to be directly to the President of The United States. It should be sincere and concise. You can state a length of time you believe your sentence should be reduced to, but it is not necessary. I would caution that if you do set a specific amount of time then pick a reasonable amount. If you are seeking an amount of prison time that is considerably low, it could be viewed negatively against you and your acceptance of responsibility.

TIP: As you will notice at the conclusion of my petition, I requested that my life sentence be reduced to anywhere between 17-24 years. This requested amount of prison time was based on the amount of imprisonment I faced if the crack cocaine I was sentenced for was converted to powder cocaine. As you will also notice, I recommended that my supervised released be extended with an ankle monitor for the first year. *Appendix G Jason's Memorandum in Support of Petition for Commutation.* That was my strategy to demonstrating: "I know I did wrong and I should be punished severely." As I state with everything else in the Guidebook, you have to decide what you think works best for your chances of receiving clemency. For at the end of the day, you have to live with what you decided to state or didn't state.

Do you have any examples of memorandums?

Yes. The Guidebook has actual memorandums that have been filed and/or that were granted. You should read each thoroughly and take from each petition ideas on how to format a memorandum and what to include in your petition. My petition is included but remember it was done nearly ten years ago and there are certain things I would not have included if I could do it over. Therefore, those aspects of it have been blacked out. *Appendix K, Eva Palma's Memorandum in Support of Her Petition for Commutation; Appendix L, Evelyn Pappa's Memorandum in Support of Petition for Commutation; Appendix G, Jason's Memorandum in Support of Petition for Commutation.*

Attachments: Adding Letters of Support and Other Documents to Your Petition for Commutation

You are allowed to include other documents that you believe will help your application. Generally, people who have received commutations have included:

1. **Letters of support:** These are letters that talk about who you are and why you deserve a commutation. They can come from family, prison officials, community leaders, Congress members, etc.[19]

2. **Employment and education certificates:** These are usually certificates you received from programs in prison and job courses that show that you passed a course.

Letters of Support: Who should I ask to write a letter for me?

You should ask people who know you well and have known you throughout different parts of your life, even after you were sent to prison. Include the people who have seen you do good things and be a good person, who will be able to talk about who you are and give a better picture of your best qualities. Other people will be able to talk about how you have changed and matured. These are important things to write about, because government attorneys will be concerned about your risk of committing another crime if you are released, and they will also want to see that you understand and take responsibility for your actions.

Here are some broad categories that can help you think about who to ask:

1. **Family:** Your parents, siblings, wife/husband, and children are people who know and love you. For instance, if you have children who were young when you went away and have grown into teenagers or young adults, they can talk about what your absence has meant to them. You definitely want a support letter from whoever you will be living with. I would recommend avoiding distant relatives. They dilute the more powerful letters you will include: Remember–quality is more important than quantity: *Appendix M, Letter to President by Eva Palma's Daughter; Appendix N, Letter to President by David Barren's Son; Appendix O, Letter to President by David Barren's Mother*

2. **Religious leaders:** If you are religious or have grown close to a religious leader, you should consider asking them to write you a letter (can be a religious leader you knew before prison or meet in prison). Or, if your parents belong to a church, their religious leader can write a letter talking about your family and how they will be a positive source of support for you if you are released. *Appendix P, Letter to President by Church Official for David Barren*

3. **Community leaders:** Are you returning to the community you lived in before you were sent to prison, or perhaps you are going to live somewhere new where your family has moved to? Either way, community leaders can talk about the support you will receive (e.g., city council members, city or state employees). They can vouch for your family, and they can talk about the community network of support you will receive if you leave prison. *Appendix Q, Letter to President by Community Member for David Barren: Appendix R, Letter to Governor By Homeboys Ind. for David Diaz*

4. **Former teachers, professors, instructors, counselors:** Probably nobody knows you better than those who taught or mentored you in school or college. And these individuals have no reason to lie and more than likely wouldn't anyway, thereby making their comments about you even more impactful.

5. **Prison officials:** You may have developed a good relationship with your counselor or case manager, or even the supervising officer or warden at your prison. Their words will carry a lot of weight, because they have personal experience seeing you in prison and will be able to talk about how you will be a productive member of society if you are released.
   a. Keep in mind that some prisons do not let their employees write letters for prisoners. You should check with your prison to see if officials can write letters for you.[20]

6. **Your attorney:** You might consider asking the attorney who represented you in your criminal case to write you a letter of support. They may be able to verify an important factor you are alleging (e.g., you were wanted to plead guilty and accept responsibility but the government would not allow you to unless you cooperated, or you suffered abuse at some point in your life but it was not allowed into evidence or presented for some reason).

7. **Your sentencing judge:** It is extremely rare that a judge will write a letter in support of your clemency, but it does happen. In determining whether your judge would do so, you should consider any comments made to you at sentencing. If they did make a comment in regards to the excessiveness of your sentence but don't actually write a letter in support of your clemency, the transcript is still just as valuable.

8. **The prosecutor on your case:** A letter from a prosecutor will be even more rare than getting one from a judge. If you learn that the prosecutor no longer supports harsh sentences, you might consider asking them to write you a letter. If the person who prosecuted is no longer a U.S. Attorney, you should still try to locate them and request a support letter.[21]

To Write The Judge/Prosecutor Or Not?
We know the OPA is going to ask the judge and the prosecutor in your case whether they support/oppose your commutation. However, it is not known in this communication whether the OPA will include your petition/memorandum, which illustrates all you have done since being in prison, support letters, letter showing remorse and accepting responsibility to the president, etc. You can be pretty sure the prosecutor/judge will have no idea what has been happening with you or your family since you've been in prison. And it puts one at a severe disadvantage to have the judge/prosecutor make a decision on whether you deserve clemency based solely on what they remember of you at sentencing. So in addition to a letter, you may want to consider attaching the most impactful documents of your clemency petition or even sending your entire clemency petition for them to review. Again, sending your entire clemency petition (depending what is stated inside) could potentially be weighed against you by the judge or prosecutor and dissuade them from making a favorable recommendation as to your clemency. You need to decide if it's best to send a letter and additional material or nothing at all.
Appendix S, Letter to Sentencing Judge by Jason

THE IMPORTANCE OF TURNING OVER EVERY STONE, BECAUSE YOU JUST NEVER KNOW.
When I was incarcerated, I sent a letter to the investigating officer in my case and then I had my brother reach out to him asking if he would write a letter supporting my clemency. *Appendix T, Letter to Investigating Narcotics Officer by Jason.* Amazingly, he agreed. My juvenile probation officer also wrote a support letter asking President Obama to release me as well. However, I will admit I did have a strong feeling they both would be willing to do so or would not oppose my clemency.

What should a letter of support have in it?

A letter of support should do two things. First, it should support you and your application for a commutation. Second, it should talk about who you are as a person. These letters should be all about who you are, who you have become, and how you've grown. This includes talking about things that may have been hard in your life (like abuse, poverty, drug or substance addiction, etc.).

Since your relationship with your letter-writers will all be different, their letters will naturally also be different. In addition to stating who they are, they should also describe themselves (e.g., army sergeant, school principal, preacher). Here are some broad themes you might want them to cover:

1. **How do they know you? How long have they known you?** For instance, friends and loved ones who have known you for a long time can talk about how they have seen you grow and mature. Employers, teachers, community leaders, etc., will want to state how they know you and met you and the impression you left on them, as well as give an example of a situation that shows your honestly, integrity, and/or love for others.

2. **Have they been personally affected by your incarceration?** For instance, your family members will be able to talk about the sacrifices they have made and the challenges they have faced. If you have children, they can talk about what it's been like having a parent who is incarcerated. They can also talk about important life events that you have missed, such as the birth of a child or grandchild, graduations, or family deaths, to help personalize the hardship of your incarceration.
    a. Every family is different. If your family faces challenges in being able to regularly visit you, these letters should describe what that has been like. If your family has made a lot of sacrifices to be able to see you, this should also be discussed. But if your family has been able to see you consistently, then be sure to state it.
    b. Your family should also be accepting of the fact that you did something wrong and you deserve to be punished for it. Statements like *"well the crime wasn't really that bad,"* or *"rapist get less time"* should never be used.

3. **Why do they think you deserve a commutation?** They should explain why they support your application and why you deserve to be released early. They should be encouraged to share specific stories and examples about you that show your good character, your commitment to your family and friends, the role that religion plays (if you are religious), and why they believe you have matured and will be a productive member of society.
    a. Depending on your relationship, the letter writer can talk about your relationship, how you have had a positive impact on them, the fact that you have made the best out of a hard situation in prison, and how you have continued to improve yourself.

4. **Why do they think you will be successful when released from prison?** Remember, the OPA is concerned with the chance that you will be released and commit another crime. Letters of support can address this by talking about what they would do for you if you were released from prison, or how they will provide you with the social, emotional, and/or financial support you will need as you begin the reentry process.

5. **Identification components properly stated:** All support letters should include the following and be sent to you and attached to the clemency petition you put together:
    1. Be addressed to the president
    2. State that the letter is in support of commutation followed by the prisoner's name and federal prison number.
    3. The sender's name, any distinguished titles, and contact information (phone # and/or email) clearly printed.

Where can I find more information about writing letters of support?

There are websites that talk about how to write letters of support and what facts you should try to include. Here are a number of resources that you can provide for the people who will be writing your support letters.

1. throughbarbedwire.wordpress.com
2. www.change.org/p/charlie-baker-support-my-son-arnie-king-by-signing-his-petition-to-commute-the-life-without-parole-sentence-so-that-he-can-become-eligible-for-parole-release
3. commutationnow.blogspot.com/p/tips-for-writing-letters.html
4. www.cannabischeri.com/prison-outreach/writing-effective-clemency-support-letters-for-marijuana-prisoners/

Can you attach too many letters?
I believe you can. And this is probably the biggest mistake people filing for clemency make. I personally recommend only letters from immediate family and if it is a rather large family then I don't recommend a letter from everyone. When it comes to letters from highly esteemed people in the community or from prison staff, you obviously cannot have enough. If someone is offering you a place to stay and/or work upon release, you will definitely want to secure those. Outside of that, I would keep a limit on letters from people who are supporting claims about your character before prison and during. Again, quality over quantity.

Should I write a letter directly to the President? YES!

Your memorandum is going to state that you have changed, you are remorseful, you accept responsibility, and you have goals, and the overall presentation of the information included in your petition should support those factors. However, you should consider supporting these statements with a personal letter to the president stating that you acknowledge what you did was wrong and you are sorry for it (unless you are claiming actual innocence).

What should my letter say?

In preparing a letter to the president, you want to follow the same advice that has already been set forth in creating your Memorandum:

- → **Keep it short:** Explain why you are reaching out to the president and the basis for your commutation. The letter should be kept at about a page in length.

- → **Take responsibility and show remorse:** Explain that you are sorry for your actions and make sure he/she knows that you understand the harm your actions caused. As has been explained in previous sections addressing remorse and acceptance of responsibility.

- → **Show who you are now:** Talk about how you've matured and how your time in prison has helped you change. State that you understand what a privilege it will be to have a second chance to repair your bonds with your community and your family, and to have another shot at freedom.

- → **Give your word:** Make a personal declaration, a promise to the president that if you were granted clemency you would honor their decision by going out and being a law-abiding citizen and that you would never take your freedom for granted.

- → **How to send letter:** Your letter should be attached with your clemency petition along with your other attachments. You can send the letter directly as well but mailroom policy changes sometimes. So be sure to attach it to your petition.

My Letter To The President
Of all the far-fetched things I did during my advocacy in prison, and to this date, sending a letter to President Obama was probably the most out-of-the-ordinary thing I did—or anyone requesting clemency had done before. But I felt that if he knew of me, and the many others like me, that he would show us mercy. Therefore, I sent him a letter directly on September 23, 2011. I wouldn't find out until nearly 7 years later that he actually received my letter and read it. See: *To Obama: With Love, Joy, Anger, and Hope,* by Jeanne Marie Laskas, page 112.

For Examples of Letters to the President see *Appendix U, Letter to the President by Jason; Appendix V, Letter to the President by Evelyn Pappa.*

Other Documents to Consider Including

→ *Certificates and Awards:* Your Inmate Skills Development Plan Progress Report should document all the certificates, programs, classes, and awards you received while in prison. In addition, your case manager will attach this document with your petition. Therefore, I would recommend not including a copy of all of the certificates you receive and only include those that are not documented in your Inmate Skills Development Report and are of significance (e.g., associates degree, college course, student of the month).

→ *Extraordinary Activities:* Are you teaching a course in prison that you created? Writing articles for a prison newspaper or have had writings published on the outside? On the Inmate Suicide Watch Program? Receive an award from the prison? Include these in your application or anything of this nature.

→ *Change.org Petition:* A petition with signatures from people in your community or from other parts of the country can show public sentiment and approval of your sentence being reduced. In listing a Change.org petition as an attachment, don't attach all signatures. Simply attach the Change.org petition and the page that states how many signatures you have received. *More information on whether to create a petition and how to do so is included on page 77..*

→ *Family picture:* To add more to the human element of your clemency petition, you might want to consider adding a family photo from a visit. If you don't have one currently, ask your family to send you one. You want the best clarity as possible and a full-page photo. Do not include an actual 4x6 photo as it might get lost. You will want to photocopy it on the exact size paper you are using for the petition and add it as the last attachment. *(For suggestions on dos and don'ts of family photos, see page 59.)*

This is our Mother: Elisa Castillo. She has **life Without Parole** For A nonviolent drug offense: She is 64 and has been in prison 11 years. If our mother does not recevie clemency....**she will die in prison.**

Putting Your Petition Together

Your completed clemency petition should be organized, easy to read, and easy to take apart. Here are some things to keep in mind when you actually put everything together and the order it should be in:

1. *Cover Page:* Should clearly state what is enclosed: *"Jason Hernandez Petition To Commute His Sentence of Life Without Parole."* Include who it is from, the address, the date submitted, and a small picture of you on the cover (if possible).[22]

2. *Table of Contents:* What information will be provided and the page it will be provided on.

3. *Petition For Commutation:* The actual petition.

4. *Memorandum In Support of Petition:* The document listing all the facts and reasons supporting your clemency. This document should also have a cover page.

5. *Attachments:* Each section of Attachments should have a cover page as well (e.g., *"Attachment A: Jason Hernandez's Letter To The President"* or *"Attachment B: Family Support Letters On Behalf of Jason Hernandez"*). Stay away from labeling attachments with tabs (everything you send will be copied and tabs could get in the way).

6. *Family picture:* A family picture at the end, I believe, helps add that final element, showing that the granting or denial of your petition impacts not only you but your loved ones. It humanizes you and allows the OPA to basically look into the eyes of your loved ones and understand you are a human being and not a number.

7. *Do not staple:* I know this will be hard to do, but the OPA does not want you to staple, glue, bind, or tape any part of your application. I would recommend using one of those huge paperclips or using a hole puncher and inserting it in a folder that has three fasteners. Your application will be copied many times so that different attorneys can review it, so you want to make it easy for them to take the pages and documents apart. Will the OPA return your petition/memorandum if it's stapled? I've never seen it happen. But whether you decide to staple it or not, be sure to number all the pages of the Memorandum and the attachments so if somehow the documents get mishandled they will know the order it goes in.

8. *Make copies:* Try your best to keep a copy of what you send to the OPA, because everything that you send becomes part of your clemency file, and the OPA cannot send things back to you. As well, other people, advocates, and organizations may want to look at your petition and other document and you will want to send them an exact copy of what the OPA has on file.

How do I send in my application?

The BOP has rules about how to file commutation applications. PS 1330.15 says that you should give your completed application to your case manager, and that your case manager will forward it to the warden, who will then send it to the OPA.

PS 1330.15 also says that your case manager is supposed to document when you handed in your application, and that they have 30 days to make sure it gets to the OPA. I would recommend checking with your case manager periodically to determine the date it is actually sent to the OPA.

You can mail it yourself to the OPA, but it typically will not be processed until the BOP attaches all required documents. So I think it is best to submit it through the prison you are at. When, and if, you add additional material at a later date, I would recommend sending that yourself: there is no guidance from the DOJ or the OPA on the proper procedure for a prisoner to add additional information once your Clemency Petition has been accepted and filed.

Can the BOP refuse to send in my application?

No. PS 1330.15 says that staff may not refuse to process your application, even if it seems like you are not eligible.

What else will the BOP send to the OPA?

Whenever the BOP sends in your commutation application, they have to give the OPA certain documents, which include:

1. Your petition
2. Your PSR
3. Your JOC (judgement of conviction)
4. Your most recent Inmate Progress Report

As you can see, many of these documents are the same legal documents you should be trying to get to help you fill out your application.

You Submitted the Commutation Application: Now What?

The OPA has a section on its website where your Unit Team, friends, loved ones, and/or attorney can look up information about your petition: *www.justice.gov/pardon/search-pending-clemency-case-files*. You can look up information about your application by your BOP Register Number or your name. If you want information about your pending petition, you should check with your case manager, who can access the OPA's website and look up the status of your application. Keep in mind that it can take weeks or even months for the OPA to process your application and include it in the lookup feature.

The OPA's lookup feature only allows people to see whether an application is pending. It will not give you any information about *where* in the process an application is. If your case at one point showed up in the lookup feature but now does not, this means that you either received a commutation, had your commutation request denied, or had your case administratively closed.

Khalil A. Cumberbatch

FROM INCARCERATION TO NOW FIGHTING FOR THOSE INCARCERATED

Khalil A. Cumberbatch, formerly incarcerated and Governor Cuomo Pardon Recipient, serves as Chief Strategist at New Yorkers United For Justice. Previously, Khalil served as Associate Vice President of Policy at the Fortune Society and was also JustLeadershipUSA's Manager of Training—a national organization dedicated to cutting the United States Prison population in half by 2030.

FINAL NOTE

All the information that you have just been presented with cannot guarantee that you will receive a commutation of sentence. However, I believe I have given you a blueprint for how to create the most powerful commutation petition that you possibly can, either with the help of someone or completely by yourself.

PART TWO
How To Advocate For Clemency[23]

"*Those closest to the problem are closest to the solution but furthest from resources and power.***"**

– Glenn E. Martin, Founder of JustLeadershipUSA

Note: This guidebook was created under the reality that you could be in a prison that is consistently locked down, in the SHU, or under administrative segregation. With that in mind, several documents are included that should provide you enough information and material to explain the clemency process. The process of how to fill out a petition is listed in great detail, giving you what you need to perfect a clemency petition and advocate straight from a prison cell.

Advocating for clemency can sound pretty intimidating for a parent, spouse, sibling, or for someone who is in prison. Especially if you have never done any type of advocacy before. And even if you are familiar with advocacy, how do you translate that into advocating for clemency? How do you do so from prison?

One might also ask what purpose a clemency campaign serves when the sole decider (whether it be a president, governor, or parole board) will probably never see anything that is initiated or carried out…. (or will they??).

If you are having doubts as to whether you can really have an impact on your release or that of someone incarcerated, consider this:

In front of The White House

- → I advocated from prison with no knowledge whatsoever of what advocacy was (honestly, I didn't even know the word existed until I got out of prison and was told I was an advocate).

- → I utilized the Internet, having no idea what it was (with the help of my brother, who also didn't know much about the Internet). I learned how it worked and what social media is (Facebook, websites, Google) strictly through reading about it in books and magazines.

- → I didn't then (and still don't) have a law degree.

- → I never created an actual 501©(3) nonprofit, but I was still able to assist people incarcerated and their families on how to advocate for clemency (and several received it).

- → Lastly, President Obama (I would later find out) knew about me way before the Pardon Attorney ever did via the letter I sent him and, we believe, also through our social media.

I'm sure the first thing you picture when you hear the word "advocacy" are people doing rallies, knocking on doors, standing on a pulpit with a microphone, ads on the radio/TV, etc. But let me tell you, it doesn't have to be all about that to be effective. Besides, if you are in prison, you can't participate in those activities anyway.

Think of advocating for clemency as more of raising awareness and educating people about an injustice or inequity imposed on you or a group of people who are incarcerated. You can start doing this all from your prison cell, as I did, or from your bedroom at home, as I did as well.

With knowing how things are in prison and on the outside, this part of the Guidebook will illustrate:

1. How to advocate for clemency from prison for yourself or a category of individuals incarcerated, without any outside help

2. How to advocate for a loved one incarcerated or a category of individuals incarcerated

3. How someone incarcerated and someone on the outside can work together to advocate for clemency for themselves or a category of individuals incarcerated

FIGHTING FOR YOUR FREEDOM FROM A PRISON CELL

What should I do first?

The most important step and decision you have to make is, who are you fighting for? Are you advocating only for your release or the release of other people in your same situation? Are you fighting for those who were convicted of the same offense, received the same sentence, or are actually innocent like you—or whatever your basis for saying you deserve clemency is? I'm not going to say there is a positive or negative in going at it alone or for a group of people. Each situation is different and a decision you will have to make on your own.

If you choose to proceed in the manner that I did and advocate for a body of prisoners, then you need to set a criterion you are advocating for and stick to it as much as you can. There is no set number of factors you must have, but make sure that whatever you choose is as clear and short as possible. As you will later see, these factors will be in letters you send out and might have to fit on a t-shirt, poster, or even a business card.

What is your objective?

Once you determine whether you are advocating solely for yourself or a segment of incarcerated individuals in similar positions, then you need to determine what your mission is. What are you fighting for? What are you seeking? What is the ultimate goal?

Obviously, it is a commutation of sentence. However, you can advocate for more than one form of relief, but you must be specific as to what you are requesting and realistic in that what you are requesting is reasonable and attainable.

→ **What is the goal? Be specific:** If you have life without parole, are you asking for a commutation of sentence to life with parole? Or a thirty-year sentence reduced to twenty-years? Maybe extraordinary circumstances have arisen that you strongly believe justify your immediate release? Whatever it is, be sure to state exactly the length of time you are advocating for and state why it is appropriate.

In addition, you can advocate for a change in the law that resulted in your sentence. If you are seeking to change a sentencing statute or policy that required an unwarranted/excessive sentence in your case, what policy or statute is it? What is the process for changing it? And what exactly should it be changed to in order to prevent what happened to you from happening to others?

→ **Be realistic: Is it reasonable and attainable?** Let's be honest, you might think you have already been in prison too long or that you should have never been to prison in the first place. Well, you need to throw your personal feelings out the window and advocate for a sentence (or change in the law) that many of the decision makers and people of influence would consider appropriate and reasonable based on your offense or your situation (e.g., pardon attorney, congressmen, sentencing organizations, academics). Certain literature, other advocacy organizations, and prior grants of clemency should give you an idea of what is reasonable to ask.[24]

> **NOTE:** I personally advocated for two different forms of relief: (1) that nonviolent crack cocaine offenders sentenced to life without parole should have their sentences commuted to 20-24 years; and (2) that the guidelines which mandated a lwop sentence should be amended to reflect a punishment range of 30 years to life without parole.

Do you have to become a real organization? NO! But you must act like one.

I'm sure when you think about "organizations" you immediately think of those like the NAACP, the ACLU and others that you may have see on TV or read about. You're probably thinking to yourself: *"It's just me and my brother/wife or me by myself, there's no way I could become an organization, right?"* or *"I wouldn't know where to start,"* *"Attorney fees etc., etc.–do I have the money for an organization?"* *"How do I even register it?"* *"Do I need a board?"* *"A CEO, COO, President?"* I personally didn't do any of those things when I started and still haven't. In any event, you are currently in prison so you can't do any of it anyway. And for those who may be on the outside assisting with the campaign, I'd tell them to stay away from all of this stuff as well. You don't need to be a 501©(3) to be effective.

> **NOTE:** Later, I will also explain the mentality and commitment you must have for a Clemency Campaign, but let's stick to things you must do now.

Nevertheless, whether you have someone helping you out or you're by yourself, you should try to see yourself as an established organization and act as if you are one from the start. As far as a CEO, COO, president, secretary, etc., are concerned, guess what? You are all of them. Does that mean your Organization is less real? No! Everything you do has to be done with the utmost importance, as if you are the ACLU or the NAACP. You are going to have to address everything you do in this manner if you want to attain your freedom and that of others. This is serious sh## here. If you are not thinking about how to attain your freedom from the moment you wake up to when you are in your bed at night—and living out those visions throughout the day—you might as well step back because you could actually be hurting other people's chances in prison from getting clemency. And I don't know how to tell you that in a clearer way.

Branding Your Advocacy

Determining the name of your campaign/organization is extremely important. It is your flag, your coat of arms, it is how your campaign and organization will be identified from here forward.

Also keep in mind that you are not starting a company or business so the normal standard of creating a name that is cool, like Starbucks, Apple or Amazon, should not be the goal. Nevertheless, you should treat your name just as importantly. As well, once you come up with a name you very rarely, if at all, want to change it. I'm not saying there is never a reason to do so, but just try to be certain that when you do pick a name, you have thought about it very thoroughly.

> **NOTE:** When I started my campaign, I wanted something catchy and symbolic for who I was fighting for and what we were seeking, so I went with Crack Open the Door. Which I will admit now might not be the best choice. When you read it by itself, it doesn't have any relationship to prison, drug laws, life sentences, clemency, or even an indication that it relates to the criminal justice system. So, though I knew what it stood for, no one else did unless they were familiar with the campaign.

Here are the names of some well-known organizations advocating for clemency that demonstrate what they are about in their name:

- → Michigan's Women's Justice and Clemency Project
- → CAN-DO: Clemency for All Non-Violent Drug Offenders.
- → Buried Alive Project
- → Mercy Me 924(c)[25]

If you choose to advocate solely for yourself, you should strongly consider something with your name in it. It will make it easier for people to distinguish and locate you if you end up getting someone to create a social media presence for you on the outside.

Below are the names of some actual clemency campaigns for individual people:

→ Clemency for Elisa Castillo

→ Free David Diaz

→ Libertad For Eva Palma

→ Clemency For Evelyn[26]

I think you get the objective, right? Short and have your first or full name in it.

Creating a Mission Statement

Your mission statement is the foundation for why you are advocating. In a sentence or two, it sums up the essence of your organization/cause. It will guide your decision-making processes and should make people want to learn more about your organization and what you are advocating for.

A good mission statement explains three things:

→ **Why** your organization exists

→ **Whom** it serves

→ **How** it serves them

Most importantly, a mission statement hits all three points in a succinct, clear, and memorable way. Unfortunately, many mission statements are vague and ambiguous, while others are too wordy.

Examples of mission statements that pertain to clemency that are clear and effective are:

→ Michigan Women's Justice and Clemency Project: *"The Clemency Project advocates for the freedom and human and civil rights of battered women prisoners through clemency petitions, legal & advocacy efforts."*

→ Buried Alive Project: *"Working to dismantle life w/o parole sentences handed down under federal drug laws through transformative litigation, legislation and humanization."*[27]

If your campaign is solely for you, your mission statement is going to be more concise and usually shorter. For Josie Ledesma, for example, our mission statement was, *"Seeking clemency for Josephine Ledesma who has been in federal prison over 24 years on a sentence of life without parole for a nonviolent drug offense."*

Now What?

Okay, so your clemency petition is filed, or you are about to file it, you have a name and mission for your cause, and you feel confident to start reaching out to people in the free world. But for the moment, it's just you and you have no outside help. Now what? Trust me when I tell you not to get discouraged. If someone comes along to help, then great. But believe me when I tell you that no one is better equipped to get this going than you are. Nobody knows your case better than you. And if that statement is not true, then you need to make it true. You have to start setting the foundation and developing materials that demonstrate an injustice in your case; you have to become an expert on the topic or topics which you are relying on to demonstrate you should be released. Whether that means locating statistics that show your sentence or conviction is unfair, or writing reports that set forth in clear and convincing detail that what is happening in your case or that of others is a manifest injustice. Or any other type of advocacy you can do straight from your cell, just like I did.

All you need to do this is a typewriter, copy machine, glue stick, envelopes, and stamps. If you have access to a law library on a daily basis, then that is even more helpful. If that library has LexisNexis or any other computer law system, you are about to be on your way.

But before I start explaining how to go about your advocacy, there is something else you need to start working on: **contacts**.

> **NOTE:** Becoming an expert on the laws and authorities on which you are seeking clemency is imperative to gaining your freedom. In addition to establishing the basis for your freedom there may come a time where, from prison, you are communicating with top criminal justice reform advocates (as I was) through direct mail, emails, or phone calls. When that time comes, you must be knowledgeable and an expert on the issues you are relying on. Don't expect that those people who you are hoping to reach will be experts on the issue. You might have to educate them yourself.

Contact List: Who Should I Contact? What Do I send them?

Who cares about you being released or the cause you are fighting for other than your immediate family members and friends? You might be surprised. Your mission? To find those who are aligned with your cause and make them aware you exist. And also, to find those who don't know or don't care about you or your cause and make them aware of it and why they should care.

> **REMINDER:** Later I will discuss how someone who is part of your campaign and dedicated to its mission can locate individuals, organizations, politicians, entertainers, etc., but for right now we are approaching this as if it's just you.

I am sure while incarcerated you have done a lot of research and may have found court decisions that cited stats, reports, research, etc. As well, I would imagine you read legal and prison brochures like FAMMGram, Razor Wire, and articles in the newspaper or magazines that coincide to your cause or criminal justice reform in general. You should have notes of all these references, but if not, then go back through those cases, pamphlets, newspapers, and magazines and write down all the names of people you feel might be passionate about your cause. Write down everything about them: who they work for, their title, the city they might live in, the name of the document or article they wrote or how you became aware of them. Same thing goes for organizations, until you have a solid list of people who might care or be able to help your cause.

FROM MY EXPERIENCE
At my prison, I was able to get the addressees of these individuals and organization from either the law library clerk, the officer who ran the library, or my case manager/counselor. If that didn't work, I would ask a friend to get it from a family member on the outside. Regardless of who you ask, make sure to not only list the person's name or organization, but also any other useful information that can help them locate the right address. You want to ensure that when they search for that person or organization online they will more than likely find them and get the right address.

People You Should Contact:

Organizations and Criminal Justice Reform Advocates: There is a very good chance that there is a state/national organization, grass-roots campaign, or a group of families who are seeking the release of someone incarcerated similar to you. Their approach might not be clemency but rather a change in the law or parole. Nevertheless, your goals are both the same: to get people out of prison.[28] In most cases, organizations and campaigns collaborate to some extent.

A lot of the time, organizations are fighting to change a law but are not actually seeking clemency for those imprisoned by the law they seek to overturn or amend. You may be the one to encourage them to kickstart a clemency campaign that advocates for the release of the person or persons you are advocating for. *Appendix W, Letter to Michelle Alexander by Crack Open The Door*

Colleges (Professors, Students, Clubs): Colleges across the United States have taken a huge interest in criminal justice reform by holding panel discussions, conferences, clinics, and sometimes even working on actual clemency petitions. You name it, some type of criminal justice reform at a college is being performed or on the verge of happening near your hometown/state or in the area you are incarcerated in.

Find out what law schools are in your state or place of incarceration and determine if they have programs that help people who are incarcerated and/or a clemency clinic. If you locate a college and they are not doing anything related to clemency, make them aware of what other colleges are doing and see if they would be interested in working with you or assisting your cause.

Media and News Outlets: There is no bigger validation to the public that a cause is just than when the news or media does a story on it. Whether that be a newspaper, magazine, local/national news, radio, etc.

When reaching out to reporters or people in media, don't make the mistake of thinking it is their job to research your issues and to devise a way to make your advocacy work newsworthy: that is your job. You need to sell them on why they should cover the story and also make their job as easy as possible. Basically, put everything in their lap. For example:

- → Have summaries of personal stories for the reporter to consider of people who are incarcerated and of their family members on the outside with contact information (e.g., profiles which I will talk about in a few).

- → Make them aware of any national trends and stories that have come out and how your advocacy relates to it with names of article(s), outlets, and reporters.

- → Give list of facts and statistics pertaining to incarceration on a national and state level.

- → Give facts, statistics, history, and any pertinent information relating to the basis for which you're seeking clemency and on the issue of clemency itself.

- → Set forth in your fact/figure sheet any quotes given by elected officials or civil rights groups relating to the issues you are raising.

> **NOTE: The following words are used interchangeably; cause, campaign, organization.**

→ If a reporter you are reaching out to has done a story relating to your advocacy or on criminal justice reform, mention the story and how your story/issue relates to it.

→ Reporters are pressed for time and what might be a story for them today might not be a story for them tomorrow. So if they respond back to you with a certain time/day for a call or interview, you need to drop everything you are doing and accommodate his/her schedule.

→ Along with your contact information, also include the contact information of your advocate or family member on the outside they can get a hold of (if you have someone).[29]

NOTE:
Also consider writing to radio shows and podcasts. There are many across the nation that focus on prisons and criminal justice reform and will allow space for prisoners or their families to call in.

Lily Gonzalez advocating for the Governor of California to grant David Diaz clemency.

Members of Congress (State or Federal): There was a time when members of Congress wanted to demonstrate that they were the most punitive and unforgiving of those involved in our criminal justice system. This is not the case anymore for a great majority of our elected officials. They have come to the realization that incarceration actually hurts a community rather than helping it.

Indeed, there are some Congress members who are more sympathetic than others and some who have very little sympathy at all, but it is pretty easy to determine where they stand by researching them. But regardless of their position on criminal justice, you should still take the steps to contact them and formulate a letter in accordance to their ideology and what will appeal them. Even when you reach out to a member of Congress whose views align with yours on criminal justice, they still might not know of the injustice that is occurring with the person or persons you are advocating for. Therefore, you need to educate them by explaining the issue: why this issue aligns with their core beliefs; the importance and history of clemency; and why clemency would undo the injustice. *Appendix X, Letter to Congressmember Bobby Scott by Crack Open The Door, Appendix Y, Letter to Congressmember Sheila Jackson by Crack Open The Door*

NOTE: In Josephine Ledesma and David Barron's case, we were able to get support letters from Congress members in both of their states. Ultimately, they both received clemency under President Obama

High Profile Individuals: This part could probably be better termed the Kim Kardashian Effect, which is based on Kim Kardashian seeing the story of Alice Maria Johnson on social media, who was sentenced to life without parole. Kim Kardashian reached out to the president to release Johnson, which he ultimately did.

Entertainers and athletes are currently a part of the movement to end mass incarceration and change the criminal justice system. They're not only using their platform to speak out against these injustices but also launching their own organizations and movements: such as John Legend, Jay Z, Meek Mills, Colin Kaepernick, Malcom Jenkins of the Philadelphia Eagles, Alyssa Milano, and many more.

YOU KNOW WHO YOUR TARGETS ARE: NOW WHAT DO YOU SEND THEM?

Once you have your mailing list, the next important question is, *What do you say to them?* What should and shouldn't you mail them?

A. Introduction Letter

The first document you want to create is an introduction letter. With this letter, you are basically introducing yourself and your cause to the outside world. Some of the people you send it to will be well versed on the basis for why you are seeking clemency; some will be lightly educated on it; some will have no idea at all about it; and, quite frankly, some won't care about it and you'll have to show them why they should.

Your introduction letter should contain the following:

- → *Who you are, the cause you are advocating for, and your overall mission (whether that be for yourself or a group of individuals).*
- → *The reason that made you reach out to this particular person or organization.*
- → *Grounds that led you to seek clemency and initiate a campaign (and, if possible, support with statistics or studies).*
- → *Citing other people or organizations that are supporting causes similar to yours in your state or other states and/or people who support the basis on which you seek clemency.*
- → *What you are seeking from the person/organization you are reaching out to (e.g., to sign a petition, to offer support for clemency, to simply connect and make them aware you exist and you are willing to collaborate and/or be of assistance).*

When your introduction letter is done it shouldn't be more than a page (and, really, neither should a majority of what you send out). You have to remember these individuals receive mail, emails, and text all day, so you want to make things as simple and short as possible for them. *Appendix Z, Letters Mailed Out to Organizations by Crack Open The Door*

> **NOTE:** Your introductory letters will share most of the same passages word for word. However, you want to be sure to specify what made you reach out to a particular person/organization and why they should take an interest in your cause. As well, what you are seeking or requesting will vary from person to person, so make sure you set forth what you are requesting from them specifically.

B. Profiles

If there is anything that has advanced criminal justice reform and the increase of clemency it is the ability to put faces to statistics. It's important to demonstrate that the person behind bars is more than a prisoner but also a father, mother, son, daughter, husband, wife.

Social media has played a huge part in the narrative of humanizing people behind bars and also the challenges their families encounter while they are incarcerated. But, being behind bars, how does one overcome the obstacle of not having access to social media? You should do what I did: create your own profiles. *Appendix AA, Profile Prison Template*

What is a profile? The simplest way to understand it is to think of a resume that one would create to get a job, but in your case it's a resume that humanizes you and shows why your sentence should be commuted.

All you need is a typewriter, glue stick, copy machine, pictures, and a little bit of imagination. If you don't have imagination, it's okay. Actual examples and a template are included in the Appendix in the back.

Below is information you should consider putting in your profile.

- Name and Prison #
- Age
- Sentence and years in prison
- Where you are currently imprisoned and your release date
- Offense (I would not set out the entire statue here. Keep it short; e.g. conspiracy to distribute marijuana)
- Comment by sentencing judge (if something positive was said)
- Conduct while incarcerated (courses/programs completed, any extracurricular activity you partake in or have created, no incident reports)
- Need/Reason for commutation (e.g., judge disagreed with sentence, a change in the law not rendered retroactive, extraordinary rehabilitation, health issues, personal/family)
- Personal information: number of children, if have a spouse, elderly parents, loss of a loved one, accident or terminal illness in the family
- Contact information: your address and Fed. No. (if you have support on the outside, include either their phone number or email address and any social media handle they are using for you)

The list of factors you want to set forth on the profile are up to you. But remember that whatever you include must be as direct and concise as possible; space will be limited. You don't want it to look cluttered and, in addition, you will want to make sure you have room to include a photo.

For example, instead of listing out every course or program you completed, you can say, *"He/She/I has completed over two dozen courses and programs since being incarcerated; most notably an associates degree in business."* Name one or two courses specifically but only if they are a course/program that is pretty significant.

THE PROFILE PICTURE

As just mentioned, you want to leave room for a photo to place on your profile. And I cannot tell you enough how important a picture is for your profile and how many times I see one and say to myself, *"What were you thinking? Wearing a gold chain, muscle shirt, squatting, Versace shades and to top it off no smile?"*

Think of this picture of your interview to the world. Those who don't know you and those who do. Your picture should be one that makes an employer say, *"I would hire him,"* a homeowner say, *"I wouldn't mind having him/her as a neighbor."* But more importantly, make the pardon attorney and president think, *"He doesn't look like a bad person."*

David Diaz and family – In prison over twenty years on a sentence of 37-to-life.

Things to consider when taking a picture:

DO'S:

- **Smile:** A HUGE smile (cannot stress enough how important this is)
- **Attire:** Clothes ironed, shirt tucked in, khakis
- **Posture:** Standing up, shoulders back
- **Position:** Waist or chest high (refrain from full body picture if possible)
- **Family:** You can include family and/or spouse, but I would keep it minimal to three or four people in the picture to get the best clarity

DONT'S:

- **Tattoos:** Cover up as many as you can. Though they are socially acceptable, I would recommend not displaying them
- **Squatting:** Never do! I'm referring to the typical squatting prison picture that everyone takes. That pose is strictly something prisoners do. Nobody out here does that. And I can't tell you how not friendly it makes you look
- **Shades and jewelry:** Don't do it! The objective of the photo is to humanize you, not to demonstrate you are cool even in prison and everything is fine.

If not done correctly, I cannot tell you how negatively a picture can impact your campaign and others that are incarcerated. *Appendix BB, Profile of Evelyn Made in Prison; Appendix CC, Profile of Jason Made in Prison; Appendix DD, Profile of Tonie Made in Prison*

 TIP: Picture what you will look like the day you receive clemency or the day you are released. That is the face you want everyone to see. That is how you want to appear in your profile picture: as if you have already obtained your freedom.

C. Additional Documents You Can Create and Mail Out

Fact Sheet: When you are seeking clemency, there is going to have to be an extraordinary factor or factors you are relying on to support your claim for a commutation of sentence. As previously mentioned, they can include a number of things such as age, sentencing disparity, or nonretroactivity of a changed law/guideline. There will more than likely be court decisions, extensive studies, and literature on these factors or related thereto. Review those documents, find the most important and relevant facts to your cause, and create a document that supports either the statute or guideline you were sentenced under or stating that your actual sentence is unjust or cruel and unusual. *Appendix EE, Crack Open The Door's Facts and Statistics Sheet on Crack Cocaine Disparity*

Seeking to Change a Statute: This suggestion is not applicable to everyone, but if your basis or one of your basis for seeking clemency as a result of a statute that is unfair for some reason then you can draft your own revision of this statute that would make it fair and equitable.

Petitioning the United States Sentencing Commission To Change A Guideline: Under Title 28 U.S.C. Code 994(s): Duties of The Commission—The Commission shall give due consideration to any petition filed by a defendant requesting modification of the guidelines utilized in the sentencing of such defendant, on the basis of changed circumstances unrelated to the defendant, including changes in–(1) the community view of the gravity of the offense; (2) the public concern generated by the offense; and (3) the deterrent effect particular sentences may have on the commission of the offense by others. *Appendix FF, Jason's Comment and Recommendation to USSC; Appendix GG, Jason's Petition under Section 994(s) to Commission pertaining to Level 43*[30]

Facts and Questions About Your Organization (FAQ): The goal of this document is to make people aware and clarify the most relevant aspects of your campaign: (a) the reason for your campaign and your mission, (b) who are the founders and organizers of your campaign and organization, (c) what you do and don't do, (d) how people can help and support your cause, and (e) any other information you think will be helpful. *Appendix HH, Crack Open The Door FAQ Sheet*

Solutions Sheet: Once you've established the basis for your release and/or others, then what is the solution? Of course clemency is one, but it should not be the only avenue you are pursing. Think about the statute you were convicted under or the guideline your sentence was based on and how they could be changed or amended to be fairer. It could be the way the sentence is being carried out and that the parole process needs to be reevaluated or implemented all together. *Appendix II, Crack Open The Door Solutions*

Petitions: Petitions are usually created to show that one's position or cause is reasonable, just, and supported by a majority of people. And, admittedly, they can be effective. There really is no need to create more than one petition unless you are trying to gain support for clemency and a change in the law. You can create your own, or if you have outside help you can create the petition online (which will be discussed later). *Appendix JJ, Petition To President From Crack Open The Door*

Op-eds: Everyday we are reading something through email or in the newspaper that's being written about the criminal justice system. A lot of this content is being produced by formerly incarcerated people. Some even from people who are currently incarcerated. So write about your case, others people's cases, topics relating to clemency, mass incarceration, and any other injustices relating to the criminal justice system.[31] *Appendix KK, Crack Open The Door Op-ed*

NOTE: In creating these documents you will need statistics. Statistics play a vital role in helping demonstrate an injustice or a need for action. However, using too many statistics can be counterproductive wherein you are giving people too much data to remember—resulting in them not remembering any of it at all. Therefore, you will want to identify 2-3 statistics that illustrate why people should be concerned and that help support your campaign, and then consistently repeat them in material you create.

NOTE: I understand the hardships of trying to create things in prison (the copy machine is low on ink, no scissors to cut paper, using toothpaste and not glue to stick the photos on the paper, being on 24-hour lockdowns, etc., etc., etc.), but do everything possible to make whatever it is you send out the best it can be. This includes checking the grammar, spelling, aligning of the pages, corrections, and clarity. It let's people who have never met you know that, *"I'm in prison but I take pride in everything I do and I will continue to do so if released."*

TIP: I would recommend always using an envelope that doesn't require you to fold the documents you are inserting. This would typically be an envelope that is 9x12 to 10x13.

The reason for doing so is that (1) it stands out and appears more important in the stack of letters that the intended target always receives; and (2) sometimes documents that are folded (especially several pages) are difficult to keep open when reading. You don't want to do anything that is going to burden the reader or make it difficult for him/her to stay focused on what you have written.

When you do begin mailing out documents, be sure to limit how much material you send out to people, especially to those who respond back. You don't want to come off as obsessive or demanding, which is easy to do. What I mean is that time in prison moves extremely slowly as opposed to out in the free world. Remember that the people you're seeking help from have their own people and causes they're advocating for...and not to mention their own personal problems. As well, advocates/organizations think on a much larger scale than helping out one person or two—they are bringing awareness and advocating for thousands or tens of thousands and cover a range of issues.

I'm free, and I even have to wait weeks, sometimes months, to get someone on the phone or a response to an email. Very seldom do I get an actual face-to-face visit. So just relax if no one responds as quickly as you'd like. Last thing you want to do is establish a contact and then get blocked—or worse yet, blocked before you even make the contact.

As well, people may not respond back but don't take that as someone who has no interest in your cause. Just keep sending them documents if you think they can help. By sending them information you have put a topic on their radar that they could look into later in their work or pass along to a colleague who might be in a better position to help you. So, don't look at a non-response as a negative or not having an impact on what you are advocating for.

THE MOST IMPORTANT RESPONSE CAN COME FROM SOMEONE WHO YOU HAD NO IDEA ACTUALLY RECEIVED YOUR LETTER(S).
I sent my letter to President Obama on Sept 24, 2011. It took him 26 months to respond back on December 19, 2013. I did not find out he had read my letter until 2017. Was it the petition that I filed that got the ball rolling on my clemency or the letter I sent to Obama and the follow-ups? I may never know, but I knew I had nothing to lose and everything to gain by trying. And now I'm free. So, send those letters and don't stop.

Staying Organized

Your campaign will take months to prepare and it could be years until you actually get the result you are seeking. During this period you will create numerous documents, make countless attempts to contact people and/or organizations, and you will either (1) receive no response, (2) receive a response that states they can't assist you, or (3) receive a response that states they are interesting in learning more and/or can assist you.

In order to stay organized and not get confused about who you have sent documents to, you will have to keep track of everything related to your advocacy from the inside. You can do this by documenting everything in a folder or notebook of some sort.

You will want to keep track of the following:

→ *List of contacts:* (a) Name, (b) who they work for, (c) address/email/phone/social media handle, (d) how you became aware of them, (e) why you have put them as a contact, and (f) the manner in which you have contacted them (e.g., phone call, email, direct mail, or through a family member)

→ *List of documents:* (a) What you have created, (b) what you will need to create, (c) responses you have received back, and (d) documents you are relying upon for research and stats

→ *Mailed documents:* (a) What has been mailed, (b) who it was mailed to, (c) when was it mailed, (d) response/no response, and (e) who has agreed to support and in what way

A spreadsheet would be ideal to keep track of all contact information. *Appendix LL, Clemency Contact List*

> **NOTE:** If you have family or someone on the outside, I would strongly recommend sending them copies of everything you create relating to your advocacy. This will be necessary if they are assisting in your campaign so that you both know what has been done, what hasn't been done, and what will be done, and also so they can educate themselves on everything they need to know about the issue(s). But more importantly, if your paperwork is lost in a shakedown, an unexpected transfer, or a trip to the SHU, you will be able to re-obtain those documents. If you have no support on the outside, give copies to someone you trust and have that person mail the documents to their loved ones on the outside to hold for you.

Gaining Support From The Outside

I think a good way to determine if you are being effective can be judged by how many people you have on the outside supporting you, joining with you, or allowing you to join with what they already have in progress: whether it be a family member, friend(s), or someone you made contact with through your advocacy.

Do you necessarily need someone on the outside assisting you? No. Will it help tremendously if you do? Without a doubt. Especially if that person is as passionate about your release and/or the release of other prisoners who are similarly situated as you.

If you have people on the outside wanting to help, or if you are already fortunate to have someone on the outside able to help, you must be acknowledgeable and accepting of certain factors and realities:

> Though I do state that how much outside support you gain over time is a good indicator as to how effective your advocacy is going, don't always translate a lack of support as an indicator that you are doing something wrong. It could mean you just need to be more aggressive/creative in your outreach. Remember, it took over a year after my brother and I created Crack Open The Door to get support–and when we got it, it was at the most powerful level: *Michelle Alexander.*

→ *Time:* Phone calls, typing letters, creating material, visiting with people, etc., takes a substantial amount of time. A person helping you will not be able to dedicate their entire day and night to you, they may be only able to help a few hours out of the week or on weekends—and there may be weeks when they can't help at all. Be prepared for it and be accepting and understanding of it.

→ *Skillset:* To implement every aspect set out in this Guidebook, a person needs to be a very efficient writer, tech savvy, and comfortable communicating with others. It will be very unlikely you will know someone who possesses all of the skillset or knowledge to carry out everything in this book. You need to be able to work with what they can do. Don't pressure them to do things they can't or may be uncomfortable doing.

→ *Financial:* Printing, creating certain social media outlets, traveling, phone calls with you, and other items cost money. From my experience, families of the incarcerated and people who volunteer are sometimes not the most financially wealthy people and the amount of money they can put into advocating for you is limited; they probably will not tell you how much the things they're doing for you cost, but nothing is free. So keep that in mind when you ask someone to do something for you. If they do it on their own, be sure to ask what the cost was and send them money (whatever you can) to assist them.

From the outset, when a person is helping you or wants to help, you should determine their strengths and weaknesses in correlation to the factors stated above to determine how he/she can be most effective.

> REMINDER: Part Three has other considerations and questions you should have for people who want to assist you.

YOU HAVE TO BE REASONABLE AND UNDERSTANDING

When I started my advocacy from prison I was fortunate to have my brother assist me. But from the very beginning until the end we had disagreements and arguments on what should be done and what shouldn't. He would get upset with me sometimes and I would get upset with him sometimes. But regardless, we always worked it out and I never let my feelings get in the way. I knew how lucky I was to have someone outside fighting for me. The reason I mention this is because you are going to disagree sometimes with certain decisions or things not done by the person you have on the outside advocating for you. If you know their intentions and heart are in the right place, you can't get lost in your feelings when it happens. Work it out!

WHAT NEXT?

The way I look at clemency is that you are always working to attain it even when you aren't actually working on something to attain it. What I mean by that boils down to two questions. Are you working on yourself? What have you done to better yourself since you've been incarcerated?

When I do clemency petitions for people, I tell them: *"How good your petition comes out is based entirely on you. I can only put into the petition what you give me to put in it. I can't make things up."*

Certificates, programing, degrees, creating your own classes to help others, clear conduct, etc., etc.–things that are out of everyone's control but your own. Experience has shown me the more the merrier. As well, I have learned you can have all the support in the world and have the gravest injustice in your case or sentence but if your conduct is not the best it can be the factor that keeps you from being shown mercy–and receiving clemency.

FINAL NOTE

The great thing about clemency is that it is still an option when there are none left for those incarcerated. The other great thing about clemency is, unlike other appeals and motions, you are not limited to only one chance. There is no limit on how many times you can file. With that said, and with all the hope and belief that your first petition is granted, you need to stay focused and not stray off your goal even for a second, no matter how much time goes by or how many times you are denied. Continue to work on bettering yourself and others around you. That way, if you are denied, the next time you file you will have more material to demonstrate how you have grown and changed since your conviction or time of the offense. *Appendix J, Correspondence and Educational Courses*

PART THREE
Advocating From the Outside for Someone on the Inside

"*Never doubt that a small group of thoughtful, committed citizens, can change the world. Indeed, it is the only thing that ever has.*"

– Margaret Mead

Note: Sections you read in Part Three will either be presented in a way that addresses advocating for a group of people incarcerated or for a single person who is incarcerated. Regardless of the way it is presented, you should assume it applies to either/or.

Families of the incarcerated advocating for clemency in front of the Department of Justice in Washington, DC.

Photo Credit Malik King

We have learned over time, especially in the past few years, that it doesn't matter if you are a single parent, still in high school, a college student, have no degree, or whatever your circumstances or situation may be, that if you're passionate about a cause, are willing to go above and beyond, assure that your voice and the voices you represent are heard, and are relentless day-after-day to seek change, then change will come.[32]

Just about every social justice movement you can name today has started at the grass-roots level from #BlackLivesMatter, to #MarchForOurLives, to the #MeToo Movement, and many more. These grassroots initiated movements have resulted in saving lives, changing laws, getting people elected/getting people out of office, and, as well, getting people out of prison. You name it, there is someone, somewhere, fighting against a social injustice, regardless of their position, social/economic status, education, or age.

Questions to Ask Yourself Before Making a Commitment to Advocate

Advocating for clemency requires action in a lot of different areas, many of which you will probably have no experience with and most of which you will have to learn by teaching yourself.

Whether you are an immediate family member or someone who wants to initiate a clemency campaign you should ask yourself these questions:

→ *Do you have the time?* Working on a clemency campaign is a timely process depending on your level of advocacy. Assuming you want to do everything set out in this Guidebook and more, it will require you to take time not only out of your day but time that you spend with your family, loved ones, and friends.

→ *Are you in it for as long as it takes?* Clemency is not a fast process. In the federal system and in many states, there is no set time period for a response. It can take years to hear something back. In addition, you may go months and years without getting the support you are looking for in the community and from others. For those who are doing this for a loved one, I have no doubt you will be there for as long as it takes. If you are an organization, part of a college program, or someone who just wants to help but can only be involved for a limited time, that is more than okay. Just be sure to make the person or persons you are advocating for aware of this.

→ *Can you deal with the stigma?* In order to bring awareness and gain support for those incarcerated, you'll have to use your social media outlets, speak about it in the open, and possibly attend forums related to the topic. This will mean your immediate family, friends, co-workers, and people in the community will know you have a loved one incarcerated and/or you are advocating to free people who may have committed a crime.

→ *Are you willing to spend your own money?* Though advocating for clemency ain't expensive, it ain't free either. Depending on the extent you want to carry out the campaign, things such as a website, business cards, stamps, copy machine, gas, etc., won't be donated to you and the person(s) on the inside probably won't have any money to give you. It could become costly, which is something to take into consideration.

The reason for these questions is to make you aware of all that comes with advocating for clemency for a person or a group of people, and to help you decide how involved you want to be, if at all. And, again, everything presented in this Guidebook are just ideas and suggestions: everything set forth does not have to be carried out and there is no set time limit on when everything should be completed. Maybe you don't have the time, or you feel uncomfortable talking around people, or you are not social media savvy, etc., etc. If so, it doesn't mean you shouldn't do anything at all. Even if you were to only do one or two of the things that are suggested in this Guidebook, then that is more than one can ask for.

As well, if you do want to play a substantial part in advocating for a person or group of people behind bars but there are certain things preventing you from doing so effectively, such as being an introvert, not a good talker, time constraints, or not tech or social media savvy, you can seek the assistance of volunteers who can help in ways you are unable to.

In any event, you can't do everything by yourself and you are going to want to get people involved, whether it be your family and friends, the friends/family of those you're advocating for, or from people who just want to be part of a worthy and just cause.

HONESTLY, HOW MUCH IMPACT CAN A LOVED ONE OF SOMEONE IN PRISON REALLY HAVE?

To give you an illustration of the impact a family can have through advocacy look at the case of David Diaz. A person who is in his twentieth year of incarceration on a sentence of 38 years to life for shooting someone in Los Angeles. In 2018 his wife Lidia Perez contacted me explaining David was innocent and that no one would help. Myself along with Kriti Sharma (at the time a law student at Texas A&M) prepared a petition of clemency for David, asking the Governor of California to commute his sentence on the basis that David was actually innocent. I informed Lidia and David's mom while we prepared the clemency petition, and after it was filed, they would have to try and accomplish certain task in order to bring awareness, public support and sentiment to David's case. Below are a few things I suggested and that the Diaz Family carried out.

Yolanda Diaz, Mother of David Diaz

1. **Create a Facebook and Instagram page:** Done—you can find it on the Facebook page Free David Diaz
2. **Create t-shirts and banners:** Both done—Banners posted on store walls and 18-wheelers
3. **Contact radio stations and ask to be interview:** Done—his family appeared on a local radio show
4. **Reach out to newspapers, reporters, news media:** Done—the story was spotlighted by Univision, Primer Impacto and Young Turks
5. **Change.org petition:** Done—Nearly 57,000 signatures: *www.change.org/p/free-david-diaz-an-innocent-man-who-has-served-20-years-in-prison*
6. **Deliver all 57,000 signatures to the governor's office:** Done
7. **Go to Sentencing Reform Conference and make connections with certain advocates:** Done—met with Jason Flom, founding member of the Innocence Project, and Scott Budnick, former Hollywood producer and founder of Anti-Recidivism Coalition (ARC), who are both now advocating for David's release
8. **Ask mother of victim to write a letter stating that her son was not shot by David, be interviewed by a reporter and say the same, and go with David's mother to personally deliver petition of clemency to the governor's office.** Done. Done. And done.
9. **See:** *www.facebook.com/freedaviddiaz*

And there is more I could add to this list. Admittedly, what David's wife and mother have been able to accomplish is astounding and every families dream. Indeed, anyone advocating for a loved one should aim as high as David's family has and if you don't achieve the success they have don't be discouraged. Their story is illustrated to show what is possible when a family fights for their loved one in prison when no one else will.

Things to Consider When Seeking Assistance or When Someone Offers Assistance

When you start just about anything in life you are usually by yourself. That will probably be the case when you begin advocating for someone's clemency. Therefore, you will want to seek the assistance from friends or family to help with things you aren't familiar with or have them teach you how to do them yourself.

Eventually, as you begin to grow your advocacy for clemency, more people will become aware of who you are, what you are doing, and will want to help. When they do, you will want to ask them the questions set forth in the previous section on page 68 to gauge their level of commitment and how they may be able to help.

I encourage you to ask the following questions as well:

→ What has inspired them to help you?

→ Why are they passionate about this cause?

→ What is their skillset or a talent they possess?

→ How do they feel they can help? Be sure to also tell them how you believe they can help.

→ How much time can they commit on a weekly or monthly basis?

FROM MY EXPERIENCE

When someone reaches out to me and wants to volunteer, I always ask them, *"What is your skillset, specialized trade, or job?"* I also ask them, *"What do you believe your gift or talent is?" "What do you love doing?"* The reason I do this is because I have learned that just because a person has a job in a certain profession doesn't necessarily mean they love doing it. For example, it may seem natural that if a person is, say, a computer graphic designer you would ask them to assist in creating a website or something else social media related. However, you want to first ask the person what it is they *"want to do?"* or *"how do they feel they can help in a way they want?"* They may be a graphic designer by trade but that might be the last thing they want to do when not working or they might love doing it. I have found that when a person is able to contribute to a cause through a skillset or talent they have and love doing they are more likely to continue to contribute to your cause.

WHAT TO DO FIRST?

Social Media and Using It to Bring Awareness and Freedom

If you are going to have success in bringing awareness to your Clemency Campaign you are more than likely going to have to utilize social media. Social media outlets like Facebook, Instagram, and Twitter, allow you to share your advocacy relatively easy to a large number of networks and gain support rather quickly.[33]

You can utilize social media to tell stories of those incarcerated, your own story, or stories of the families of those incarcerated; recruit supporters and volunteers; and invite people to events you are having or that other organizations are having.

FROM MY EXPERIENCE

I would probably not be out today had it not been for the Internet and social media; President Obama's clemency Initiative may not have ever began, and the sentencing reform that has taken place over the past decade across the country would have never passed. This was the result of images shared across social media of families of those who were incarcerated holding vigils and rallies in front of the White House, lobbying and sitting down with members of Congress, having panel discussions at colleges and Capital Hill, documentaries of those in prison, being released from prison, and of the families who still had a loved one in prison. All of which was shown and shared across the United States on social media, making people aware that these people in prison serving these unjust punishments were more than a statistic. They were someone's mother, father, sister, brother, grandmother, grandfather. Social media made it possible for us to be humanized.

Facebook

Facebook is structured in a way that allows you to use different features and post material and information that other social media sites don't. All of which not only allows you to demonstrate what your campaign is about but also how people can help.

A Facebook page that is used to advocate for someone or a group of people incarcerated will include the following:

→ *Type of page:* Facebook allows you to do a personal page or a business page. I don't think you can go wrong with either approach, though a business page does offer tools you can use to reach larger audiences, view activity within the page, and has other additional features you can use to market and network.

→ *Homepage:* Facebook's homepage will allow you to have two pictures: a profile picture and a profile cover photo. The type of campaign you're doing (for one person or a group of people) will determine what type of photo you put up in each section.

NOTE: Photos and images are overwhelmingly the most engaging type of content on Facebook, generating an 87 percent interaction rate from page followers.

→ *About section:* Use this section to set forth your mission statement, state that you are looking for volunteers, list your email, and include any social media links you have associated with the campaign.

→ *Actual posts:* Here you will want to post pictures of the person or persons who you are advocating for and relevant information to your cause, and charts and statistics that show disparities or injustices relating to your cause (which you can find from other Facebook pages you are following).

→ *Facebook Live:* Use this feature to give updates on the campaign progress or to let your followers know something very important is about to happen, such as a meeting with an organization, members of Congress; etc., or if the opportunity arises where you are at an event or some type of forum where you are speaking.

> **NOTE:** You will also want to share actual content from other Facebook pages, such as stories and documentaries of prisoners granted clemency and becoming successful; articles where very prominent people such as entertainers, politicians, and church officials are commenting about criminal justice reform; actual petitions people can sign (which will be addressed a little later); and any other way people can be involved.

There are different ways to bring awareness to your campaign through Facebook, but try to be strategic and not oversaturate the page with comments or materials daily. People will start to become numb and overlook what you are posting and when the time comes to post something that is very important, or something you need volunteers for, it could get overlooked.

Examples of Facebook Pages:

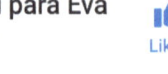
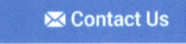

TIP: Be sure to create a hashtag and use it on all social media (e.g., #clemencyforevelynpappa). This is important, because hashtags allow a follower to express their support and sentiment for a cause and, more importantly, by adding this simple hashtag you connect all related social media that everyone posts–as long as they use the hashtag, which they normally would.

Instagram

Instagram is also one of the most popular social media outlets right now and provides a good platform to get your campaign's word out. It's does not have all the options of Facebook, but it is trendier and used more by younger people.

Your Instagram page will almost be a duplicate of your Facebook page, using the same cover photo, name, mission statement/who you are, and contact info. Instagram doesn't let you put as much technical information as Facebook, but it does allow you to put enough. To make up for that omission, you can put a link to your Facebook and/or to your webpage if you have one.

The Buried Alive Project Instagram page[34] is a good example to look at when creating your cover page:

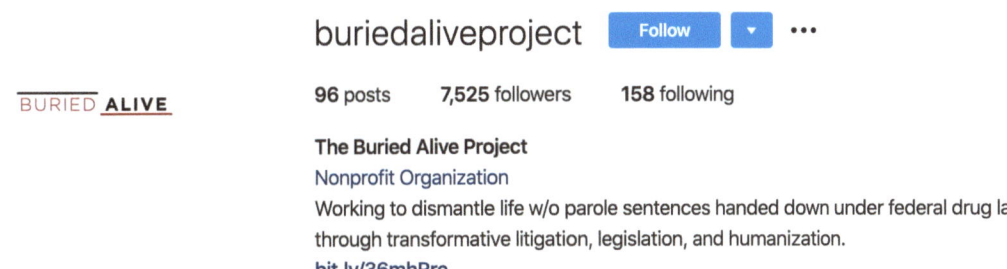

 TIP: Simply Measured did two studies and found that Instagram posts with both hashtags and a location tag get the highest average engagement. *In other words, hashtags could be your best bet for growing a fast following on Instagram and other social media outlets.*

Twitter[35]

With over a billion visitors a month, Twitter can help in many different ways and is useful for keeping up with events in real-time. But most importantly, nearly every elected official has a Twitter account, from advocates, governors, and senators to the President of The United States.

Important tips for using Twitter:

→ Retweet content from advocates and organizations you are following

→ Follow certain accounts related to your advocacy: people in politics, reporters who write about criminal justice reform, and criminal justice reform advocates

→ Tweet to a specific person by commenting on their tweets and using their Twitter handle in your tweets

→ Follow hashtags related to criminal justice reform and clemency

Additional Ways To Advocate Using Social Media:

- **Post interesting images:** In addition to sharing graphs and images that other's post, you can create your own with relatively easy-to-use tools like Canva.com or Adobe Spark. Graphs, images, and other material are very effective in getting people's attention.

- **Create videos:** Live stream events, ask supporters and those impacted by the criminal justice system to share their stories, and conduct your own interviews live.

- **Logo and brand:** Always use the same logo, name, and imagery across all social media outlets. When you post on one media outlet, be sure to post to *all* your media outlets.

- **Engage your audience:** Ask questions, and comment on other people's and organization's posts you are following.

Advice and Reminders:

- Be careful and strategic with what you post about the person(s) you are advocating for. Rants asserting to be a victim and blaming others should never happen.

- There will be people who will vehemently disagree with you advocating for the release of people in prison. If they comment in a rude manner, do not respond: delete comments and then block them.

- Be fair and balanced as much as possible. You don't want to post material that targets a certain political party or organization as the bad guys.

- Get permission from people before you use their name or post their photos on social media (specifically people who are incarcerated and families of the incarcerated).

- Make a determination if a social media campaign is the right choice. Sometimes it could work against the person or persons you are advocating for.

- Before you post or hit send, make sure it will not backfire on you. You could ruin the entire credibility and movement of the work you have done.

Desmond Meade

FROM INCARCERATION TO NOW FIGHTING FOR THOSE INCARCERATED

Desmond Meade, President of the Florida Rights Restoration Coalition (FRRC) and named one of Time Magazine's 100 most influential people and whom the Mayor of Orlando (Desmond's hometown) made September 10 "Desmond Meade Day." Desmond, who was formerly incarcerated and formerly homeless, led the FRRC to a historic victory in 2018 with the successful passage of Amendment 4, a grassroots citizen's initiative which restored voting rights to over 1.4 million Floridians with past felony convictions.

Website

When you have a webpage, it makes everything you are doing sound so much more real, so much more serious, so much more important. But the reality is, unless you are Amazon, eBay or offering some type of service, not many people are going to see your website. On top of that, they cost money to set-up and take hours upon hours to create if you are doing it yourself.

Nevertheless, if you are capable of creating a website, I would recommend doing it for the reasons I stated above: it makes you look professional, serious, and makes your cause seem important. In addition, it acts as a hub for everything surrounding your campaign—the basis for your cause, profiles, proposed laws that can be supported, ways to help, who to contact, a section with media, and links to your social media. And though your average visitor spends only a few seconds on a webpage, the key is to get that person or two on there a little longer and to educate them on an injustice they otherwise did not know existed.[36] That person could be the key to spring-boarding your campaign and spring-boarding you out of prison.

> **NOTE:** A cool aspect about a website is it allows you to see how many people visit your page and the average time they are on there. From this tool, we were able to determine the weeks before I received clemency that the daily visits to our Crack Open The Door website had increased substantially (from 3-4 visits a day up to 20-30 visits a day). We don't actually know who those visitors were, but we strongly believe it was someone in the Obama Administration determining who would be the first to receive clemency.

Components of an effective website:

- → *Domain:* Your domain name should be the same as the name of your organization or name of your campaign.

- → *Homepage:* This is basically your cover page. It should set forth: who you are/what you are about; why you started this campaign; and what you are seeking to accomplish. You will want to use the same exact language you've used in the letters you have been sending out. You should include a photo or photo of you and the people you are representing.

- → *About Us:* Give details on who you are as a person or an organization—the people who are part of the campaign and why they are involved.

- → *The Problem/Issue:* Educate people on what's going on in the case or cases you are advocating for. Who's affected? What impact it is having on families, the community, taxpayers, etc.?

- → *Profiles:* If the campaign is focused strictly on one person, then there will be no need to do a separate profile page since that person will be on the homepage and in the bio section as well. If the campaign focuses on a group of people, then you definitely want to put a profile section and basically mimic the profiles I have set forth in the Appendix. Appendix BB, CC, DD.

- → *Solution Page*: Clemency is the obvious focal point, but if there is another way to achieve this same outcome you should list it (e.g., retroactive application of a law, legislation, etc.).

- → *How To Help*: This page needs to be clear and to set forth the most simplistic way to help you or those you are advocating for. If it's a petition that needs to be signed, set it out clearly and have a link to the petition. If you want actual letters sent to a judicial or elected official, have a template the person can use and the address to where you want the letter sent.

Again, I don't think a webpage is necessary, but it is helpful. Although I would wait to create one until every other aspect of your social media is in place.[37]

CREATING A PETITION FOR SUPPORT

Online petitions are a great way to get the word out, to gain support, and to bring awareness to excessive sentencing in the United States.[38] There are many platforms you can utilize, but Change.org has become the world's largest petition platform, with nearly 100 million users in 196 countries.

FROM MY EXPERIENCE
When I first started my advocacy from prison, one of the first things my brother Stevie suggested I do was start an online petition through Change.org. I received a little less than 400 signatures on my personal petition (which to me was an enormous amount). However, over the years and working with others we were able to perfect petitions asking for the release of prisoners and would see signature amounts increase from 50,000, as in David Diaz's case, to over 250,000, as we did in Josephine Ledesma's case.

The content for your Change.org petition will basically mimic the main points of your campaign thus far, but in a micro-manner. Whether your Change.org petition is solely for one person or a class of people incarcerated, the format is basically going to be the same.

MY BROTHER AND I DID TWO PETITIONS
One for the President to grant me clemency and the other for the United States Sentencing Commission to change how life without parole sentences were determined by the Sentencing Guidelines.

The following are 9 tips to consider when creating a petition for people to sign:[39]

- → *Determine the Mission of Petition:* What are you asking for?
- → *Set A Reasonable Goal:* Yes, everyone would love 100,000 signatures like Josephine Ledesma or David Diaz, but that is extremely rare. 500-1000 is a good goal.
- → *Identify the Decision Maker:* Who can grant what you need? For federal clemency it's a president (in the state it's the governor).
- → *Write a Compelling Petition:* You should have this part down pretty well by now. If the petition is for a body of individuals or to change a law, include a small, personal story.

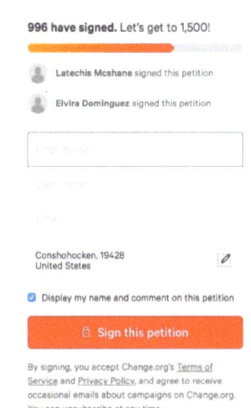

→ *Get The Word Out:* Email, Facebook, Instagram, Twitter. Post it and tell friends to share it. Kind of like knocking on doors, but you are doing it virtually.

→ *The Delivery:* Print out the page that has the number of signatures and include it with the petition for clemency and also mail to the president. You can also take pictures and livestream it when you mail it off to the White House or if you deliver it personally to a governor's office.

→ Studies show that a petition is seven times more likely to succeed when it features a photo or video.

→ If you can't summarize the 'ask' of your petition in one clear and concise sentence, it's probably too broad

Appendix MM, Change.org Profile of Elisa Castillo; Appendix NN, Change.org Profile of Evelyn Pappa

WAYS TO GAIN SUPPORT AND WHO TO REACH OUT TO

At this point, your campaign should have a sound social media presence. But it's time to take it a step further by using other tactics and getting into the trenches, as I like to say. There is a whole other world out there that you are unaware of and who are unaware of you. Indeed, there might actually be an organization or politician looking for a cause just like yours to demonstrate the injustice of the criminal justice system and mass incarceration. And there are those who don't know an injustice is occurring and would no doubt support and advocate with you once they learn of your campaign.

How to find and connect with people

To find names of people and organizations to connect with, I would start with asking those you are advocating for who are incarcerated. I'm sure they can compile or already have a list of everyone on the outside who would have interest in the campaign and who is advocating for criminal justice reform on a state and national level.

Next, the Internet. Your searches should initially focus on clemency campaigns or reform surrounding the cause you are advocating for—then expand from there.

For example, if you are advocating for women to be released who may have committed murder relating to sex trafficking or battered women's syndrome, you would go to Google and do a search with the following words and others in different patterns:

- [Your state/or no specific state]/sex trafficking/murder/sentencing reform
- [Your state]/sex trafficking/clemency
- Battered women syndrome/commutation/advocacy

If you are advocating for a person/persons sentenced under 924(c) who did not receive relief because the changes under The First Step Act were not retroactive, you would Google search words such as:

- 924(c)/Clemency/President
- 924(c)/commutations/advocate
- 924(c)/retroactivity/senator

FROM MY EXPERIENCE
Admittedly, my brother was unable to find any organization that was advocating for prisoners such as myself. But by keying in other patterns such as: *clemency/criminal justice reform; life without parole/abolishing/cruel and unusual*, we were able to connect with organizations that didn't specifically advocate for crack cocaine offenders serving life but that were also pushing for the president to exercise his clemency powers on drug offenders.

When you do find an organization or individual advocating for your same cause, add them to the mailing list, reach out to them, link up with them, see what their tactics are, share your tactics with them, and see how you can help them and how they can help you. Even if you don't find anyone associated with your cause but who are involved in clemency or any type of criminal justice reform, send an email making them aware of your campaign and requesting to speak.

If the people you sent emails to don't respond or you are unable to get them on the phone or if there is no email or phone number to contact them don't get discouraged. There are still other methods to possibly reach out to them and get their attention.

Nearly all apps provide a forum to contact any person who has a social media page. I'm not saying everyone reads the messages they receive, but nonetheless you can send one. It's not very orthodox or maybe even unprofessional or out-of-the-ordinary to message someone through their social media, but there is nothing ordinary about your loved one being in prison for decades or their whole life. So, as they say, *"extraordinary times call for extraordinary measures."* With that said, it has never stopped me from reaching out when all else fails, and I have been successful in connecting with my target and achieving my objective more than once by doing so. Again, I would not pursue this avenue until mail, email, and phone calls are unanswered or none of those other avenues are pursuable.

NOTE: Meeting face-to-face with the advocates you do locate is always best but not always an option. There is distance involved, scheduling, and some of these people just don't have the time to meet on a one-on-one basis. With that said, however, many of these individuals are most likely having speaking engagements, panel discussions, live Facebook interviews, and are on other forums in which you can speak with them in person or directly. These events are usually scheduled and made public on their social media. You need to find out when these events are being held, be present, and make contact with these individuals and present your cause to them.

Who You Should Contact

- → *Criminal Justice and Civil Rights Organizations*
- → *Colleges (Professors, Students, Clubs)*
- → *High Profile Individuals*
- → *Media and News Outlets*
- → *Radio Stations, Podcasts*
- → *Churches*
- → *Members of Congress (State or Federal)*
- → *Former Correctional Officers (officers at the prison for those you are advocating for or from other facilities)*

NOTE: Page 61 & 62 instructs those incarcerated to create a folder or spreadsheet to keep track of all contacts and actions taken in furtherance of the clemency campaign; you should do the same. If the person or persons you are advocating for are also assisting in the campaign, careful attention must be given to who is being contacted by whom and what is sent to them. You don't want to overlap. How I approached it when I was in prison, since I was the lead and my brother was assisting, is that I would mail out everything from prison. My brother would have a copy and he would then do a follow up email asking if they received my mail. If they did not respond to his email after seven days, then he would email them a copy of what I originally sent to assure they received it.

This approach may not work for everyone.

ADVANCED ADVOCACY TACTICS

Since my release, I have had the benefit of advocating with some pretty amazing people and organizations when it comes to clemency. This has given me the unique experience of lobbying before members of Congress, having rallies/vigils in front of the White House, being a part of panel discussions at Capital Hill, and other similar events. All of which were extremely powerful, empowering, and effective.

These advanced grass-roots tactics are primarily used once you are well-established, organized, well-informed of the areas of the law surrounding your cause, and when the objectives of the campaign are clear.

It is one thing to advocate through emails, make phone calls, or post on social media, but it is an entirely different thing to do so in the public. For some it comes naturally, and for others it is a very uncomfortable feeling. But no worries, I will explain how to carry out these different tools with ease and effectiveness.

LOBBYING

Lobbying is defined as, *"a form of advocacy with the attention to influence government leaders to create legislation or conduct an activity that will help a particular organization."* Thus it is natural to think of lobbying as being done by big time corporations or organizations using their power and money to influence politicians to pass laws or policies that would benefit them. With that perception, one might ask: *"Can I, or a group of people, really get a member of Congress to support the release of a person from prison?"* The answer to that is: *"Hell yeah you can!"*

To dial back your doubts, in the campaigns to free Josephine Ledesma and David Barron (as I mentioned earlier) we were able to get members of Congress to send a letter to President Obama asking for him to release them.

Jason at Capitol Hill in Washington DC meeting with Congressman Beto O'Rourke

FROM MY EXPERIENCE
When I was lobbying in DC, I knew I wouldn't have much time to speak and that there was a chance the actual Congress member might not be present. To make sure I left an impression, I created business cards that were extremely unique that I passed out to everyone who was in the room (*for design of business cards see page 211*). I also brought copies of the actual clemency petitions of some of the people I was advocating for and left a couple of those for them to view as well. My goal was to leave an impression and to keep them talking about our cause after we left.

THE FIRST THING YOU SHOULD DO WHEN YOU WANT TO SET UP A MEETING WITH A MEMBER OF CONGRESS IS:

Assemble your Advocacy Team

Your group should range between 4-5 people and can consist of a local lawyer or representative from a civil rights/criminal justice reform group, a representative of a family member of the person incarcerated (if you are not one), a person who has received clemency (or formerly incarcerated who has transitioned successfully), a representative of a church, and correctional staff or someone connected with the judicial system (former or current).

Schedule a meeting

Select the representative or senator based in your hometown (on the state and federal level). Once you are ready, call weeks in advance to arrange meetings with the desired Congress members.

When you contact the representative's or senator's office, inform the scheduler that you are or aren't a constituent (if they live in an area that the member represents) or that you are representing a constituent of their area (the person incarcerated), and the topic you want to discuss with them (i.e., clemency).

If your representative or senator is not available, you can ask for a meeting with one of their staff members.

Prepare

Your Advocacy Team should:

- → Google and research the member of Congress you are meeting with and determine their position on criminal justice reform and clemency. Also meet with local groups such as the ACLU or other organizations to get advice and input on meeting with the legislatures.

- → Review current news related to clemency or situations similar to yours.

- → Compile data, character references, and rebuttals to any potential concerns you think your representative or senator may have.

- → Meet with the Team to make an agenda and plan who will say what.

- → Think of what the policymaker's reasons would be for not supporting clemency and address those points. If there is something you can't answer, just say, "I'm not sure, but I will give you a response through email."

Meeting

The meeting needs to start with introductions and gratitude. Everyone should then explain why and how you got involved with advocating for clemency for the person or persons you are representing. Someone should explain the purpose and meaning behind clemency and how it is being used in other states and on the federal level.

Before the meeting concludes, you should make your ask clear: *"Will you support our campaign to grant [person's name] or [a group of prisoners] clemency?"*

If the senator or representative hesitates or says no, ask him or her to give specific reasons for their decision and offer to provide additional information or resources if that would be helpful. You can humbly express your disappointment and urge them to reconsider their decision. Be assertive but respectful.

The meeting should end by thanking the representative or senator (and all staff) again for their time and leaving behind any printed materials (e.g., fact sheets and business cards).

Follow-up

You should send a thank you card or email immediately after the meeting. In the weeks following, you can follow up with whomever you met with and offer again to provide additional information. Keep in mind that representatives and senators have packed schedules and receive countless requests in a given day. Patience and thoughtful persistence are key.

Leyla Martinez

FROM INCARCERATION TO NOW FIGHTING FOR THOSE INCARCERATED

Leyla Martinez, formerly incarcerated, is a graduate of Columbia University, where she received her BA in Human Rights and is currently the Executive Director/Founder of the Beyond the Box Initiative (BTB), which is an organization that assists formerly incarcerated people overcome barriers by providing supportive services that are essential to achieving their academic goals (e.g., housing, employment, scholarships, mentorship, counseling, tutoring, etc.).

PANEL DISCUSSION

A panel discussion involves a group of individuals discussing a certain issue and giving different viewpoints and expert opinions. Over the years, I have been on panels to discuss clemency at criminal justice reform conferences held by organizations and colleges. These panels can be very effective in demonstrating the need to grant clemency to a single person, but more importantly for a wider body of individuals incarcerated.

Overall the panel should be informative, compelling, and offer a variety of different perspectives. The components for an effective panel discussion include but are not limited to:

- → *Time:* 60 to 90 minutes. Within that time frame leave 15-20 minutes for questions from the audience. Make sure panelists and guests know the length of the discussion. Also be sure not to extend the discussion past the set time.

- → *Moderator:* The moderator is like the referee. They keep the discussion moving and keep a panelist from taking over and keep the audience engaged. They should also be familiar with clemency and a supporter of it. They typically should speak with the panelists days in advance to determine what questions are best to ask each individual and to get background information on them.

- → *Panelists:* A panel can have anywhere from 3-5 people on it. I have found no more than four works best. On a clemency panel, I would suggest (1) someone who has received clemency or someone who was released from prison who can talk about their accomplishments since release; (2) a loved one of someone incarcerated to speak of the hardship of having a loved one incarcerated (parent, spouse, or a child); (3) an advocate for clemency or professor who can talk about how clemency is being used in other areas, its purpose, and the need to implement it more; and (4) someone from the criminal justice side, such as a prosecutor, judge, parole officer, correctional officer, etc., who agrees that reform is needed in the system and clemency can contribute to doing so.

- → *Location:* A college, church, or rotary club would work great. If no one is willing to volunteer a place you will have to rent a location.

ORGANIZING A VIGIL OR RALLY

Everything set forth so far is extremely important and none of it to be overlooked. But during my entire experience in advocating for clemency, I witnessed and participated in nothing more empowering than campaigning in front of the White House or Department of Justice and seeing dozens and sometimes hundreds of people who had loved ones incarcerated or were formerly incarcerated holding up poster boards and wearing t-shirts with the face of a person who deserved clemency, chanting, "What do we want??!! Clemency!!! When do we want it??!! Now!!!"

Vigils and Rallies aren't easy to organize. The following will help you plan yours.[40]

- → Choose a location that supporters can easily get to, and where your presence will be felt— such as outside your senator's district office, a government building, the White House, etc..

- → Send out invites and call families of those impacted, advocacy groups, and people in public office.

- → Make sure to check weeks in advance with the local police, city hall, and local government to see if you need a permit to hold the event. If so, get the permit and closely follow the regulations regarding bullhorns, picket signs/posters, unobstructed space for pedestrians, not interfering with traffic, etc.

Families of the Incarcerated advocating for clemency in front of The White House.

Photo Credit: Malik King

→ Before the vigil/rally, make sure that you and your supporters have a clear understanding about what you want to achieve with the action.

→ Gather supporters to make posters and picket signs. Think of the visuals you want for press photographs or social media.

→ Think of ideas the crowd can do together such as (a) a moment of silence; (b) singing songs related to issue; (c) reading names; (d) lighting candles; (e) chants related to issue.

→ Make leaflets with your demands, social media handles and hashtags, and upcoming events to hand out so people know how to stay involved.

→ Notify the media about your event, and prepare someone to be the official media contact and/or the spokesperson. Make sure the press can easily find them.

→ Ask four to five speakers to deliver a short speech and recommend a topic for each to address. Also choose someone to emcee the event to keep the program on message and on time. Keep the action to about an hour.

→ Define the end of the action. Always have something that people at the action can do right then. Ask them to volunteer to circulate petitions, coordinate phone-banking, or even sign a postcard.

→ Follow-up with organizations and members who attended and showed visible support for your issue. Remember to thank organizations for participating.

→ Let your target know about your action and how many people showed up, signed petitions, and/or got involved (send pictures along with email or letter).

CAN VIGILS AND RALLIES REALLY MAKE A DIFFERENCE?
IT COULD BE ALL THE DIFFERENCE IN THE WORLD.

In 2015, I would attend my first rally in DC that was held for families who had a loved one incarcerated and who were asking for President Obama to grant their loved one clemency. It was orchestrated by Amy Povah of Cando Clemency, who had herself received clemency from President Clinton in 2001. It was at this event that I saw a poster board of Josephine Ledesma that Amy Povah was holding up and learned that a lady who basically had limited-to-no-involvement with drugs had been in prison nearly 24 years on a sentence of life without parole for a nonviolent drug offense. When I asked Amy to tell me more about her and learned of the amazing stuff she was doing for others while incarcerated, but more importantly that no one was helping her with a clemency petition, I told Amy to put me in contact with her and I would do her clemency petition for her and advocate on the outside. With the assistance of a school administrator named Tracey King we filed a petition for clemency on her behalf. On August 3rd, 2016 (eight months after speaking with Amy at the rally), President Obama granted her clemency. Josephine, at the age of 58 was released from prison in August of 2017. She spent nearly 25 years in prison.

Items You Will Need to Create to Make the Most Out of Every Engagement

To make the most out of every opportunity you encounter, whether you are being interviewed or on a radio show or having a vigil in front of the White House or your state capital, you are going to need to do a couple things to ensure that people see you, that they know what you are doing, and what your purpose is.

Most of what you can do to draw attention to your cause is pretty simple and cheap, yet effective.

Poster Boards and Banners

Poster Boards and Banners make people in public places (close and far away) stop and take notice of what is going on when they otherwise wouldn't. They also look powerful when images or video of crowds of people are holding them and are posted on social media.

Poster boards and banners can be used in a number of ways: standing them on a table near or next to you while doing an interview, at conferences if you have a table or booth, if you are doing a video on social media, or during a vigil or rally.

Consider the following when creating a poster board or banner:

- → Name, logo (if you have one) and picture of the person or persons you are advocating for (picture should be the same you have used for social media).

- → State what your mission is (remember, less is more). Avoid trying to clutter things to get more across—otherwise the result will be getting nothing across.

- → At the bottom you should have a Facebook link, website or hashtag that people can like and follow to get involved.

- → Make sure to check if permits are required to put up displays (e.g., courthouses, state capital).

Appendix OO, Poster Board of David Diaz; Appendix PP, Poster Board of Elisa Castillo; Appendix QQ, Poster Board for Evelyn Pappa

T-Shirts

T-shirts are always on the list of basic things I tell people to consider creating throughout their campaign because it's such an attention getter and immediately makes people aware of what your cause is. You would definitely want to wear them whenever you are advocating or doing something on social media, at a rally, vigil, interview, etc., and have others wear them as well.

A t-shirt should replicate everything you have done up until this point with key messages and images you have used for your campaign.

Business/Advocacy Cards

You know it isn't official until you get a business card, right? Well, honestly, many believe business cards are not as important as they once were and not a necessity. And I'll admit, maybe they aren't. However, if used innovatively, I think a business card can be an extremely effective way to leave a memorable impression on someone. Remember that some of the people you meet may never see you again and, on top of that, you may only be in their presence for a couple of minutes. Therefore, you need to do all you can in a normalized way to stand out.

This might sound odd, but I think the key to an impactful business card is making it appear more like a billboard than an actual business card.

Consider adding the following to your business card:

- → A photo of a person or persons you are advocating for; be consistent with what you already have on social media.

- → Use a QR code that links to further material.

- → Use the back side of the card for advocating.

- → Consider adding a call for action.[41]

Imagine the card being a smaller version of your poster board and create it with the same considerations in mind: make sure the images are clear and it doesn't look cluttered.

Appendix UU, Three Business Cards of Jason Hernandez Front and Back

Clemency Petition(s)

When you are meeting with community leaders, members of Congress, the media, and other people of significant importance, you will want to have in your possession a couple of clemency petitions and profiles of the person or people you are advocating for. If you meet with members of Congress, I would recommend leaving them a copy of a petition for clemency in the hope that they look at it more thoroughly.

FROM MY EXPERIENCE

When I was invited by organizations to attend White House events or lobby to members of Congress, I was asked to only advocate for prisoners as a whole and not limit it to one person or a group of people. Which I agreed with and totally understood and which I did...well, kind of.

Knowing I would be in rooms with people who were close to President Obama's Clemency Initiative, what I did was create business cards that not only set forth my information but also the information of those I was advocating for. For example, one of the cards basically was a replica of what the poster board of Josie looked like with the addition of a QR code that linked to Josie's entire clemency petition. On the back of another business card I had an entire list of people (with their prison number) serving life without parole who I was advocating for. Before I left their presence, I would thank them for the work they were doing and then say, *"If you don't mind, let me give you my card. If you need any more information or if I can help in any way, please contact me. Oh, by the way, on the back is a list of people I am advocating for as well. If you want to speak with them or their loved one's, I can arrange it."*

FINAL NOTE

I've set forth tactics and strategies that I've used and that I have found to be effective, but by no means is this a do-all-end-all list. I believe just as we are creative and innovative with technology, we have to be the same when it comes to educating people about clemency and the necessity for it to be utilized more. Your passion will drive you in the direction of what you need to do and how to do it young and old. The only question now is, **will you do it?**

Gloria Pappa, 96 year old mother of Evelyn Bozon Pappa who has been in prison 25 years serving 8 life sentences without parole for nonviolent drug offenders.

PART FOUR

The Last But Most Important Steps You Must Take In Order To Obtain Your Freedom

"*I never lost faith in the end of the story...I never doubted not only that I would get out, but also that I would prevail in the end and turn the experience into the defining event of my life, which, in retrospect, I would not trade.*"

– Admiral Jim Stockdale, prisoner of war

Families of the Incarcerated during a vigil in front of The White House.

We have learned over time, especially in the past few years, that it doesn't matter if you are a single parent, still in high school, a college student, have no degrees, or whatever your circumstances or situation may be, that if you're passionate about a cause, are willing to go above and beyond, assure that your voice and the voices you represent are heard, and are relentless day-after-day to seek change, then change will come.

Just about every social justice movement you can name today has started at the grass-roots level from #BlackLivesMatter, to #MarchForOurLives, to the #MeToo Movement, and many more. These grassroots initiated movements have resulted in saving lives, changing laws, getting people elected/getting people out of office, and, as well, getting people out of prison. You name it, there is someone, somewhere, fighting against a social injustice, regardless of their position, social/economic status, education, or age.

You can also make change: from your prison cell or from your living room. But it's going to take everything you've got day after day, year after year.

Following are the steps I took to attain my freedom — I believe you must take them as well to gain yours.

PERSONAL STEPS

GET MAD

"From passion there is action and from action there is change.

What do we know about change?

We know you will never change that which you tolerate.

And you will only change when you get angry."

- George C. Fraser

I believe that if you are going to make a major impact in your life, others' lives, or society as a whole, you must first get mad—angry. Because what we know is that when one gets mad they fight. And not only do they fight but they will take drastic measures to assure victory. I don't suggest in any way that you fight with your fist or with any acts of violence. What I am asking is that you fight with your persistence, your heart, your words, your mind, and with the knowledge that you have and will soon attain.

In this journey, you will encounter a lot of setbacks and denials. And when those times come (and they will come), you will feel like giving up, giving in, and not wanting to continue. You must have a reason that'll get you out of bed every morning, you must have a reason that will prevent you from acting out negatively, you must have a reason that will keep you fighting day after day, week after week, year after year, and maybe even decade after decade.

Find what it is or who it is you are fighting for: freedom, family, redemption. Then you need to make a commitment, a declaration to yourself, to a loved one, and fight every day, every hour until you reach it, no matter how long it takes.

When my brother was murdered in 2002, I became upset with the system and I also became upset with myself for contributing to the system. However, I was able to turn that anger into passion, to drive myself, and to turn it into something positive. I had made a commitment, a declaration that I was not going to let his death be in vain. His death would serve a purpose. It would result in me getting my life back and to help better, change, and save other lives as well.

DECIDE

"If not us then who?"

If not now then when?"

- John Lewis, Civil Rights Activist and Congressman

You have to next make a decision, a commitment that from this day forward you will live as if you are going home tomorrow. That you will not take any action that is not in furtherance of your freedom or that could also jeopardize your freedom. That you will do whatever it takes, for however long it takes until it happens. You cannot have one foot in the door and one foot out because it will not work. You have to make this commitment regardless of the situation you are currently in, regardless of the prison you are in, regardless if you are on 23-hour lockdown, regardless of your sentence. You can't wait for the circumstances to be right. They will never be right. There will always be something that can hold you back. Don't look at what you don't have, but at what you do have. George Bernard Shaw, a playwriter and political activist, said, *"Those who make it in life look around for the things they need to succeed and if they don't exist they create them."*

Had I not made the decision that I was going to do whatever it took to attain my freedom, had I not decided it was possible, everything that followed would not have happened.

The day I made my declaration, I was in my prison cell on lockdown. It took place days after my brother was murdered and after I considered taking my own life. But instead of taking my own life, I decided I was going to get my life back. And looking into the dull, scratched up metal mirror with red, teary eyes, I told myself, *"Today, today is the day that I make a commitment to myself, to the person in the mirror who is looking at me right now–That through the loss of my brother's life, I will get my life back and make his death have meaning, a purpose. I am going to do everything possible everyday, all day to attain my freedom. I won't give up, I won't give in and whatever adversity or setbacks that I encounter will only make me stronger and more determined to attain my freedom. I will live everyday as if I am going home tomorrow, because I know that if I follow through on my commitment to myself and to my brother, then it will happen."*

OBSESSED

"I have learned from years of experience with men that when a man truly desires a thing so deeply that he is willing to stake his entire future on a single turn of the wheel in order to get it, he is sure to win."

- Thomas Edison

If you are not thinking about your freedom and how you are going to attain your freedom from the moment you wake up until you go to bed, it's probably not going to happen. You have to become obsessed with obtaining your freedom, even when you aren't actually working on something or doing something that you think pertains to clemency, because the reality is everything you do or don't do relates to obtaining your freedom one day.

Before you go to bed, you should be asking yourself: *"What did I do today? Is everything I did in furtherance of my goal of attaining my freedom and keeping it? If there was something I did that was not in furtherance of that goal, why did I do it? Regardless, I will make sure I will not repeat it. That which I did in furtherance of my goal, could I have done it better? And if so, when the opportunity or action happens again, how I can maximize it?"*

In the morning when you wake up you should be asking yourself: *"What am I going to do today in furtherance of my goal to attain my freedom and keep it? What will I be doing tomorrow, the next day, next week? A month from now, where will I be at this exact moment in my fight for freedom?"* You should have a clear road map drawn out in your head of all you are going to do for that week and the next: every minute of it, everyday.

> Throughout the day at any given time, whether I was walking in the yard, leaving the chow-hall, in the Unit, wherever I was, I would ask myself, "What am I doing right now? Is it in furtherance of my goal to get out of prison and giving my brother's death meaning? Wherever I was previously, wherever I am headed to next, is it in furtherance of my goal for freedom? If I did do something in furtherance of my freedom, did I make the most of it? If not, why didn't I and what can I do differently next time?"

VISUALIZING AND BELIEVING

"Great people have a vision of their lives which they practice emulating each and every day. Their lives are spent living out the vision they have of their future in the present."

- <u>The E Myth: Why Most Small Businesses Don't Work and What To Do About It,</u> by Michael E. Gerber

They say, *"Seeing is believing."* But for me, the reality was reversed. I believed in my freedom so much that I began to see it. And when I tell you I could see it, I literally mean that. I could see myself back in my city, in my community, at my parents' house, speaking in schools and jails that I'd been in, and even places I'd never been like Capitol Hill, speaking with members of Congress, at White House events, but most importantly, walking out of prison. All things I have since done.

Visualize yourself carrying out the steps I have set out in this book and what your life will look like today, tomorrow, next week, next month, next year and so on.

Visualize the day you receive clemency, how it will happen, what you will say, how you will feel. Visualize your first day of freedom, your first week, first month, first year, and every year thereafter.

And when I say visualize it, I am not just talking about conjuring up vague images in your mind. Picture the steps it's going to take to attain your freedom and how your life will look thereafter. Picture it as clearly as your current immediate surroundings, as if it has already happened.

Once I believed it could happen, I knew I could make it happen. You gotta believe.

It was in prison that I learned how to do yoga and mindful meditation, which taught me how to breathe and focus. Learning how to do so helped me focus and visualize my path to freedom and what freedom would look like. I was able to practice meditating and visualizing no matter where I was at in the prison (track, TV Room, weight pile, etc.). I even went as far as visualizing what the room looked like that held all the clemency petitions at the Pardon Attorney's Office and what I would need to do to make my petition stand out in the pile of thousands that were in there. What would my petition need to look like and have inside it to get their attention and keep their attention once they grabbed it and opened it up.

BE GREAT AT EVERYTHING YOU DO

"[O]nce I had a picture of how IBM would look when the dream was in place and how such a company would act, I then realized that, unless we began to act that way from the very beginning, we would never get there…In other words I realized that for IBM to become a great company it would have to act like a great company long before it ever became one."

- Tom Watson, Founder of IBM

I've never been the smartest or most physically gifted person but, regardless of that, no matter what I did in life I always did it the best I felt it could possibly be done. I just didn't limit this mindset of *"doing the best I can"* to things that I considered important. I applied it to everything in my life. Whether it was running Crack Open The Door, creating a prisoner profile with toothpaste, working on my clemency petition with a broken type writer, buffing a floor, or cleaning my cell or my toilet—and even the prison staff's toilet.

You have to have the mindset that everything you do in life is important and that it is a direct reflection of who you are. If you do something in a sloppy manner it means you are a sloppy person inside. If you cut corners on a job or project, it means you are a person who cuts corners in life and one who seeks the easy (not right) way out. How you do something (no matter how small) is a direct reflection of who you are and who you aren't. When you approach everything in life in this manner it will become a habit over time.

I was not the smartest person in prison by far. I was not the best writer or jailhouse attorney. But I told myself when it came to research and preparing legal documents, especially my clemency petition, and advocating from prison, that no one would do it as consistently, intensely, or meticulously as I was going to do. And I did it that way from day one and everyday after: as if my life depended on it—because in fact it did, and yours does too.

Now, in hindsight, I can see the mindset of "No matter what you do, you do the best you can," started at a young age in the streets and it resulted in me getting a life sentence. But I also used this same determination and commitment in prison to get my life sentence off. Now I'm using it to get life sentences off others in the system.

POSITIVE MENTAL ATTITUDE

"A man's mind may be likened to a garden, which may be intelligently cultivated or allowed to run wild; but whether cultivated or neglected, it must, and will, bring forth. If no useful seeds are put into it, then an abundance of useless weed seeds will fall therein, and will continue to produce their kind."

- As A Man Thinketh, by James Allen

I didn't know exactly how I was going to get out of prison when I made the declaration to my brother and myself that day in my prison cell. I just knew that if I stayed focused on that goal, stayed positive and surrounded myself with as much positivity that I possibly could, that the universe would bring into my life what I needed. To not only get out but to help others as well.

Albert Einstein would say you can't solve a problem with the same mind that created it and discussed the need to decide if we want to live in a friendly universe or a hostile universe. If you choose to see the world as hostile, everything will seem hostile to you. But if you choose to see the world as a friendly place, you will experience things this way. This was hard to do in prison, but I found it a necessity to do so.

So everyday, all day, when I wasn't doing legal work I would be reading or watching something that bettered me educationally, mentally, emotionally, physically, and spiritually. If it didn't improve my life in some way, I wasn't wasting my time with it. And, ultimately, life put me where I needed to be and brought into my life what I ultimately needed in order to attain my freedom when the time came.

CHANGE YOUR FRIENDS

"You want to change your life, you have to start by changing your friends. People who have nothing want you to have nothing with them. People who are going nowhere want you to go nowhere with them. You have to get all the toxic people out of your life."

- George Frasier

When I made the decision that I was going to commit my life to pursuing my freedom, there was another decision I made as well. That was changing who I was friends and associates with at the prison. Because I knew that no matter what other positive steps I took, if I didn't pull totally away from my current friends it would eventually result in me staying in prison for the rest of my life and/or even losing my life.

Once you pull away from your circle, you must then be careful about who you let in. Ask yourself, *"Do they have the same goals as me (e.g., self-enrichment, betterment of themselves/other, getting out of prison, staying out of prison)? Are they a positive force in my life? Is my life better in some way as a result of knowing them?"*

If you want to change your life, gain your freedom—you will have to start by changing your friends. But more importantly, you most also change who you are and do it now.

I knew that pulling away from the clique I was hanging with and rolling by myself put me at greater risk of danger. But I told myself, "If I die in prison it will be for something I believe in: my freedom and making sure my brother didn't die for nothing."

TAKE CONTROL OF YOUR LIFE

*"[E]verything can be taken from a man but one thing: **the last of the human freedoms—to choose one's attitude in any given set of circumstances, to choose one's own way...**And there are always choices to make. Every day, every hour, offers the opportunity to make a decision, a decision which determines whether you will or will not submit to those powers which threaten to rob you or your very self, your inner freedom, which determines whether or not you will become the plaything of circumstance, renouncing freedom and dignity to become molded into the form of the typical inmate."*

- paraphrased from Man's Search For Meaning, by Viktor E. Frankl.

You must decide that you are tired of the life you are currently living. You must take full responsibility for where you are today and what you will ultimately become. Change does not take a week, a year, or a decade. It starts the moment you decide, and you set forth a plan of action, and you tell yourself that if you don't succeed or accomplish your goals then it is no one's fault but your own.

I lived every day in prison as if I were going home tomorrow. And I had that mindset with a life without parole sentence and with the realization that it was going to take years, if not decades, for that day to finally come—if ever. But I also knew that if I slipped up once, that if I let another person in prison or a guard get inside my head and get me out of my element, regardless of all the other good things I was accomplishing that action alone could be the deciding factor if I were ever to obtain freedom again or die in prison. I was not going to let that happen. I was not going to let another person impact my freedom. **You, can not let that happen.**

Photo Credit: Natalie Michelle Photo

IN CONCLUSION

This Guidebook is not an end-all-be-all for those behind the walls or for those who have a loved one locked up. Indeed, there may be aspects of this book you may not want to apply and think that in doing so might hurt your cause rather than support it. And that definitely could be true. And in all honesty, one shouldn't have to rally and make t-shirts or seek out Hollywood celebrities to make people aware that an injustice is happening in the hopes of convincing a president or governor that justice would be served by releasing a person from prison rather than letting them perish there.

It is hoped, however, that through numerous campaigns for clemency initiated from those incarcerated, by their families and people in the community, that the president and governors will begin to use this extraordinary power of mercy on a mass scale to reduce sentences that cause more harm than good to the individual, families, and to society. And to give second chances to people who made mistakes at one point in their life but have grown up, changed the way they think and view life, and have been redeemed.

And it will happen, because we—those incarcerated, formerly incarcerated, and families of the incarcerated—will make it happen:

"It will be hard, but you come from sturdy peasant stock, men who picked cotton and dammed rivers and built railroads, and in the teeth of the most terrifying odds, achieved an unassailable and monumental dignity. You come from a long line of great poets since Homer. One of them said, **The very time I thought I was lost, My dungeon shook and my chains fell off. . .***"*

- <u>The Fire Next Time</u>, by the Great James Baldwin

Acknowledgments

We have all had someone to lean on, to assist us, and to guide us. This could be a family member, a friend, someone we know, or someone who's inspired us with their writing, words, or accomplished an extraordinary feat that pushed us to want more, to do more, to be more. Here are a few of the people who did so for me:

The amazingly, wonderful, and beautiful God Mother of Criminal Justice Reform, **The Michelle Alexander.** Who "made my dungeon shake and my chains fall off." I owe you…We owe you.

Joe Jessie (JJ) Hernandez, my brother who lost his life in prison but in doing so saved mine. All was not lost brother. Will see you in the next life. Miss you, bro.

Stevie Hernandez, my brother, my best friend. Little did I know his annoying trait of never shutting up as a kid would one day be used to get people to listen and help free me and others from prison. Love you, bro.

The quiet, yet powerful, **Vanita Gupta, Zeke Edwards,** and **Jennifer Turner** of the ACLU, and **Nkechi Taifa** and **Anthony Underwood** (#freeunderwood) who were ahead of the curb when it came to advocating for clemency for drug offenders serving life without parole and so much more.

And to those who helped put this very important Guidebook together. It could not have happened without all of you:

The entire **Open Society Foundation Family** and especially **Adam Culbreath** and **Crissy Voight**, two of the kindest and compassionate souls I have ever met.

Courtney M. Oliva, NYU School of Law Executive Director, who's expertise, wisdom, and desire to help those incarcerated played an integral part in making possible my vision of a Clemency Guidebook for prisoners and their families.

Professor Mark Osler, leading expert and advocate for clemency, who's wisdom went not only into this Guidebook but also into hundreds of petitions that have freed so many from prison.

Thanks to **Jessica Sandoval** of the ACLU for her overview and insight in assuring that the tools needed for prisoners and their families' voices to be heard are within this book.

Huge shout out to **Natalie Michelle Photography** for the amazing cover photo.

Graphic designer **Blake Boring** who somehow, someway, was able to take all of my material and give it life, turning it into something beautiful and powerful.

And last, but definitely not least, **President of the United States, Barack Obama,** who gave life to the power of clemency. Not only did he give it to those most in need, but he recognized those who are most often overlooked (prisoners of color, prisoners doing life). His actions have resulted in other presidents and governors exercising this extraordinary power in an extraordinary way. May God continue to bless him and his family.

RECOMMENDED READING

The New Jim Crow: Mass Incarceration in The Age of Colorblindness, by Michelle Alexander

Just Mercy: A Story of Justice and Redemption, by Bryan Stevenson

Slavery By Another Name: The Re-Enslavement of Black-Americans From the Civil War to War World II, by Douglas A. Blackmon

Man's Search For Meaning, by Viktor Frankl

As A Man Thinketh, by James Allen

Think And Grow Rich, by Napoleon Hill

The E-Myth, Why Most Small Businesses Don't Work and What to Do About It, by Michael Gerber

Becoming Ms. Burton: From Prison to Recovery to Leading the Fight for Incarcerated Women, by Susan Burton

The Change Agent, How a Former College QB Sentenced to Life in Prison Transformed His World, by Damon West

The Fire Next Time, by James Baldwin

The Autobiography of Malcolm X, by Alex Haley

Between The World and Me, by Ta-Nehesi Coates

Are Prisons Obsolete? By Angela Y. Davis

The Prisoner's Wife, by Asha Bandele

The Audacity of Hope, By President Obama

Good to Great; and Built To Last by Jim Collins

APPENDIX

APPENDIX A. Petition for Commutation of Sentence	102
APPENDIX B. DOJ Commutation Instructions and Governing Rules	108
APPENDIX C. DOJ Standards for Consideration of Clemency Petitioners	115
APPENDIX D. DOJ Frequently Asked Questions of Clemency	119
APPENDIX E. BOP Clemency Program Statement 1330.15	123
APPENDIX F. Clemency Checklist	129
APPENDIX G. Jason's Memorandum in Support of Petition for Commutation	130
APPENDIX H. Eva Palma's Answer to Question Seven of Petition for Commutation	141
APPENDIX I. Evelyn Pappa's Answer to Question Seven of Petition for Commutation	142
APPENDIX J. Correspondence and Educational Courses	143
APPENDIX K. Eva Palma's Memorandum in Support of Her Petition for Commutation	145
APPENDIX L. Evelyn Pappa's Memorandum in Support of Petition for Commutation	153
APPENDIX M. Letter to President by Eva Palma's Daughter	160
APPENDIX N. Letter to President by David Barren's Son	161
APPENDIX O. Letter to President by David Barren's Mother	162
APPENDIX P. Letter to President by Church Official for David Barren	164
APPENDIX Q. Letter to President by Community Member for David Barren	165
APPENDIX R. Letter to Governor by Homeboys Ind. for David Diaz	166
APPENDIX S. Letter to Sentencing Judge by Jason	167
APPENDIX T. Letter to Investigating Narcotics Officer by Jason	169
APPENDIX U. Letter to President by Jason	171
APPENDIX V. Letter to President by Evelyn Pappa	173
APPENDIX W. Letter to Michelle Alexander by Crack Open the Door	175
APPENDIX X. Letter to Congressmember Bobby Scott by Crack Open the Door	176
APPENDIX Y. Letter to Congressmember Sheila Jackson by Crack Open the Door	177
APPENDIX Z. Letters Mailed Out to Organizations by Crack Open the Door	178
APPENDIX AA. Profile Prison Template	181
APPENDIX BB. Profile of Evelyn Made in Prison	182
APPENDIX CC. Profile of Jason Made in Prison	183
APPENDIX DD. Profile of Tonie Douglas Made in Prison	184
APPENDIX EE. Crack Open the Door's Facts and Statistics Sheet on Crack Cocaine Disparity	185
APPENDIX FF. Jason's Comment and Recommendation to USSC	186
APPENDIX GG. Jason's Petition under Section 994(s) to Commission pertaining to Level 43	195
APPENDIX HH. Crack Open the Door FAQ Sheet	196
APPENDIX II. Crack Open the Door Solutions	198
APPENDIX JJ. Petition to President from Crack Open the Door	200
APPENDIX KK. Crack Open the Door Op-ed	201
APPENDIX LL. Clemency Contact List	202
APPENDIX MM. Change.org Profile of Elisa Castillo	203
APPENDIX NN. Change.org Profile of Evelyn Pappa	204
APPENDIX OO. Poster Board of David Diaz	205
APPENDIX PP. Poster board of Elisa Castillo	206
APPENDIX QQ. Poster board for Evelyn Pappa	207
APPENDIX RR. Eva Palma's Cover to Petition for Commutation	208
APPENDIX SS. Eva Palma's Cover to Memorandum in Support of Petition for Commutation	209
APPENDIX TT. Evelyn Pappa's Cover for Petition and Memorandum	210
APPENDIX UU. Three Business Cards of Jason Hernandez Front and Back	211

APPENDIX A: PETITION FOR COMMUTATION OF SENTENCE

Petition for Commutation of Sentence

Please read the accompanying instructions carefully before completing the application. Type or print the answers in ink. Each question must be answered fully, truthfully and accurately. If the space for any answer is insufficient, you may complete the answer on a separate sheet of paper and attach it to the petition. You may attach any additional documentation that you believe is relevant to your petition. The submission of any material, false information is punishable by up to five years' imprisonment and a fine of not more than $250,000. 18 U.S.C. §§ 1001 and 3571.

Relief sought: *(check one)*

☐ Reduction of Prison Sentence Only
☐ Remission of Fine and/or Restitution Only
☐ Reduction of Prison Sentence and Remission
☐ Other _____

To The President of the United States:

The undersigned petitioner, a Federal prisoner, prays for commutation of sentence and in support thereof states as follows:

1. Full name: _____
                  First   *Middle*   *Last*

   Reg. No. _____ Social Security No. _____

   Confined in the Federal Institution at _____

   Date and place of birth: _____

   Are you a United States citizen?   ☐ yes ☐ no
   If you are not a U.S. citizen, indicate your country of citizenship
   _____

   Have you ever applied for commutation of sentence before?   ☐ yes ☐ no
   If yes, state the date(s) on which you applied, and the date(s) when you were notified of the final decision on your petition(s).
   _____
   _____

Offense(s) For Which Commutation Is Sought

2. I was convicted on a plea of _____ in the United States District Court
                             (guilty, not guilty, nolo contendere)

   for the _____ District of _____ of the crime of:
          (Northern, Western, etc.)   *(identify state)*

United States Department of Justice   *January 2002*
Office of the Pardon Attorney
Washington, D.C. 20530

Offense(s) For Which Commutation Is Sought

(State specific offense(s); provide citation of statute(s) violated, if known)

_____

_____

_____

_____

I was sentenced on _____, _____ to imprisonment for _____, to pay
                           (month/day)   *(year)*   *(length of sentence)*

☐ a fine of $ _____, ☐ restitution of $ _____, and to
             (do not include special assessment)

☐ supervised release or ☐ special parole for _____, and/or to probation for

_____. I was _____ years of age when the offense was committed.
   (length of sentence)

3.   I began service of the sentence of imprisonment on _____, _____, and I am projected to
                                                          (month/day) *(year)*

    be released from confinement on _____, _____.
                                       (month/day) *(year)*

    Are you eligible for parole?   ☐ yes ☐ no

    If yes, indicate the date when you became eligible for release, and state whether your application for parole was granted or denied

    _____

    Have you paid in full any fine or restitution imposed on you?   ☐ yes ☐ no

    If the fine or restitution has not been paid in full, state the remaining balance.

4.   **Did you appeal your conviction or sentence to the United States Court of Appeals?**   ☐ yes ☐ no

    Is your appeal concluded?   ☐ yes ☐ no

    If yes, indicate whether your conviction or sentence was affirmed or reversed, the date of the decision, and the citation(s) to any published court opinions. Provide copies of any unpublished court decisions concerning such appeals, if they are available to you.

    _____

    _____

    Did you seek review by the Supreme Court?   ☐ yes ☐ no

    Is your appeal concluded?   ☐ yes ☐ no

    If yes, indicate whether your petition was granted or denied and the date of the decision.

    _____

    _____

Offense(s) For Which Commutation Is Sought

Have you filed a challenge to your conviction or sentence under 28 U.S.C. § 2255 (habeas corpus)? ☐ yes ☐ no

Is your challenge concluded? ☐ yes ☐ no

If yes, indicate whether your motion was granted or denied, the date of the decision, and the citation(s) to any published court opinions, if known. Provide copies of any unpublished court decisions concerning such motions, if they are available to you. If you have filed more than one post-conviction motion, provide the requested information for each such motion.

_____
_____
_____

5. Provide a complete and detailed account of the offense for which you seek commutation, including the full extent of your involvement. If you need more space, you may complete your answer on a separate sheet of paper and attach it to the petition.

Petition for Commutation of Sentence

Other Criminal Record

6. **Aside from the offense for which commutation is sought, have you ever been arrested or taken into custody by any law enforcement authority, or convicted in any court, either as a juvenile or an adult, for any other incident?** ☐ yes ☐ no

   For each such incident, provide: the date, the nature of charge, the law enforcement authority involved, and the final disposition of the incident. You must list every violation, including traffic violations that resulted arrest or in an criminal charge, such as driving under the influence.

Arrests:

_____
_____
_____
_____
_____
_____
_____
_____
_____
_____
_____
_____

Convictions:

_____
_____
_____
_____
_____
_____
_____
_____
_____
_____
_____
_____

Reasons for Seeking Clemency

7. State your reasons for seeking commutation of sentence. If you need more space, you may complete your answer on a separate sheet of paper and attach it to the petition.

Certification and Personal Oath

I hereby certify that all answers to the above questions and all statement contained herein are true and correct to the best of my knowledge, information, and belief. I understand that any intentional misstatements of material facts contained in this application form may cause adverse action on my petition for executive clemency and may subject me to criminal prosecution.

Respectfully submitted this _____ day of _____, _____.
(month)   (year)

_____
Signature of Petitioner

APPENDIX B: DOJ COMMUTATION INSTRUCTIONS AND GOVERNING RULES

COMMUTATION INSTRUCTIONS

Information and Instructions on Commutations and Remissions
Please Read Carefully Before Completing Commutation Form

1. Submit the petition to the Office of the Pardon Attorney

To be considered for commutation (reduction) of sentence, an eligible inmate should submit a completed Petition for Commutation of Sentence to the Office of the Pardon Attorney, preferably through the warden in accordance with BOP Program Statement 1330.15. Commutation petitions that are not submitted through the warden may be emailed to us directly at USPARDON.Attorney@usdoj.gov. If email is not available, petitions may be mailed to the Office of the Pardon Attorney, U.S. Department of Justice, 950 Pennsylvania Avenue, Washington, D.C. 20530. The completed commutation petition must be entirely legible; therefore, please type or print in ink. The form must be completed fully and accurately and signed by the applicant in order to be considered. You may attach to the petition additional pages and documents that amplify or clarify your answer to any question. **Please do not staple, glue, bind or tape any portion of your petition or supplemental documents. We also will not accept pictures of documents, so they must be scanned on a flatbed scanner and submitted in PDF format if sent electronically.**

2. Federal convictions only

Under the Constitution, the President has the authority to commute sentences for federal criminal convictions, which are those adjudicated in the United States District Courts. In addition, the President's clemency power extends to convictions adjudicated in the Superior Court of the District of Columbia. However, the President cannot commute a state criminal sentence. Accordingly, if you are seeking clemency for a state criminal conviction, you should not complete and submit this petition. Instead, you should contact the Governor or other appropriate authorities of the state where you were convicted (such as the state board of pardons and paroles) to determine whether any relief is available to you under state law.

3. Reduction of sentence only

The President's clemency power includes the authority to commute, or reduce, a sentence imposed upon conviction of a federal offense, including the authority to remit, or reduce, the amount of a fine or restitution order that has not already been paid. This form of clemency is different from a pardon after completion of sentence. Under the current regulations governing petitions for executive clemency, a person may not apply for a full pardon until at least five years after his or her release from incarceration. Accordingly, the commutation form should be used only for the purpose of seeking a reduction of sentence.

4. Completion of court challenges

A request for a commutation of a prison sentence generally is not accepted unless and until a person has begun serving that sentence. In addition, a commutation request generally is not accepted from a person who is currently challenging his or her conviction or sentence through appeal or other court proceeding. Accordingly, you should not complete and submit this petition until you have concluded all judicial challenges to your conviction and sentence and you have begun serving your sentence. You should also be aware that, in evaluating the merits of a commutation petition, clemency authorities take into consideration the amount of time the petitioner has already served and the availability of other remedies to secure the relief sought (such as parole or judicial action).

5. Special assessment

Requests for the remission of a special assessment are not accepted. The special assessment is not considered to be a fine, and should not be included in describing any fine that might have been imposed upon you.

6. Commutation of probation, supervised release, or special parole.

If you are seeking reduction of a period of probation, supervised release, or special parole, you should state that fact specifically on the form and set forth the particular reasons why this portion of your sentence should be reduced, including the reasons why you believe serving probation, supervised release, or special parole would be an unusual hardship for you. You should also explain why requesting the sentencing court or the U.S. Parole Commission to grant early termination of a term of supervision, pursuant to 18 U.S.C. § 3583(e)(1) or former 18 U.S.C. § 4211, is not an adequate remedy.

7. Immigration status

If you are not a citizen of the United States, you should be aware that commutation of your sentence only shortens the prison sentence and will not result in a change of your immigration status. A full pardon is the only form of executive clemency that might affect a person's immigration status; however, as noted in paragraph 3 above, a person who is currently serving a prison term is not eligible to apply for that form of relief. Accordingly, if a detainer has been lodged against you for deportation or removal, commutation of sentence, if granted, will not prevent your deportation or removal from the United States and may actually hasten the process. You may wish to contact U.S. Immigration and Customs Enforcement in the Department of Homeland Security, which is the agency responsible for decisions regarding a person's immigration status, to determine whether any other relief from deportation or removal is available to you.

8. Additional criminal record

In response to question 6, you must disclose all additional arrests or charges by any civilian or military law enforcement authority, including any federal, state, local, or foreign authority, whether they occurred before or after the offense for which you are seeking commutation. Your answer should list every violation, including traffic violations that resulted in an arrest or criminal charge, such as driving under the influence. You should also include all convictions, including convictions that may have been expunged, whether or not they were counted in computing your criminal history category under the Sentencing Guidelines. Your failure to disclose any arrest, whether or not it resulted in a conviction, and every conviction may be considered a false statement.

9. Penalty for false statements

The failure to fully and accurately complete the application form may be construed as a falsification of the petition, which may provide a reason for denying your petition. In addition, the knowing and willful falsification of a document submitted to the government may subject you to criminal punishment, including up to five years' imprisonment and a $250,000 fine. *See* 18 U.S.C. §§ 1001 and 3571.

10. Exclusive Presidential authority

The power to commute a sentence for a federal offense is vested in the President alone. It is an extraordinary remedy that is very rarely granted. No hearing is held on the commutation application by either the Department of Justice or the White House. You will be notified when a final decision is made on your petition, and there is no appeal from the President's decision to deny a clemency request. The Office of the Pardon Attorney does not disclose information regarding the nature or results of any investigation that may have been undertaken in a particular case, or the exact point in the clemency process at which a particular petition is pending at a given time. As a matter of well-established policy, the specific reasons for the President's decision to grant or deny a petition are generally not disclosed by either the White House or the Department of Justice. In addition, documents reflecting deliberative communications pertaining to presidential decision-making, such as the Department's recommendation to the President in a clemency matter, are confidential and not available under the Freedom of Information Act. If your petition is denied, you may reapply one year after the date of denial.

11. Remission of Restitution or Fine

If you are seeking remission of restitution or fine, you should state that fact specifically on the application and set forth the particular reasons why you believe that this portion of your sentence should be reduced, including the reasons why you believe that paying your restitution or fine would present an unusual hardship for you.

PRIVACY STATEMENT FOR COMMUTATION OF SENTENCE

IMPORTANT NOTICE
To Applicants for Commutation of Sentence

The following notice is provided pursuant to the Privacy Act of 1974 to help you to understand what is involved in petitioning for executive clemency and why we need to obtain certain information about you.

The information that we request from you on the accompanying commutation of sentence application form, and in the event of a background investigation, is needed to help provide the basis for an informed judgment about whether you should be granted clemency. This is our only purpose in asking you to complete and sign the application. You are under no obligation to furnish any information. However, if you do not provide all the information requested, we may be unable to process your application. Failure to provide your Social Security number will not prejudice your case.

Our authority for requesting the information solicited in the accompanying commutation of sentence application form is the United States Constitution, Article II, Section 2 (the pardon clause); Orders of the Attorney General Nos. 1798-93, 58 Fed. Reg. 53658 and 53659 (1993), 2317-2000, 65 Fed. Reg. 48381 (2000), and 2323-2000, 65 Fed. Reg. 58223 and 58224 (2000), codified in 28 C.F.R. §§ 1.1 *et seq.* (the rules governing petitions for executive clemency); and Order of the Attorney General No. 1012-83, 48 Fed. Reg. 22290 (1983), as codified in 28 C.F.R. §§ 0.35 and 0.36 (the authority of the Office of the Pardon Attorney).

After the President has taken favorable final action on an application, a public affairs notice is prepared describing each grant of clemency (such a notice also may be prepared for a denial of clemency in cases of substantial public interest). A copy of each warrant of clemency is maintained in this office as a public and official record. Copies of the public affairs notices, clemency warrants, and lists of recent clemency recipients are routinely made available to the public upon request.

Executive clemency files are compiled and maintained to assist the President in exercising his constitutional clemency power and are routinely made available to him, members of his staff, and other government officials concerned with clemency proceedings. The Pardon Attorney may disclose the contents of executive clemency files to anyone when the disclosure is required by law or the ends of justice. In particular, public record documents that may be compiled in the course of processing a clemency application, such as the judgment order from the criminal case for which commutation is sought, trial or sentencing transcripts, court opinions, and newspaper articles, are generally made available upon request by third-parties (including representatives of the news media) pursuant to the Freedom of Information Act, unless such disclosure could reasonably be expected to constitute an unwarranted invasion of the petitioner's personal privacy. In addition, unsolicited Congressional correspondence is treated in the same manner. On the other hand, non-public documents that may be compiled in the course of processing a clemency application, such as the petition and supporting documents, the presentence investigation report, the results of any background investigation, and the report and recommendation of the Department of Justice to the President, are not generally available under the Freedom of Information Act.

The foregoing rules apply to the disclosure of documents in the possession of the Department of Justice. However, the President and his immediate staff are not subject to the constraints of the Freedom of Information and Privacy Acts. Accordingly, while clemency-related documents in the possession of the White House traditionally have not been made public, they may be legally disclosed at the discretion of the President. In addition, clemency-related documents retained by the White House at the end of a presidential administration will become part of the President's official library, where they become subject to the disclosure provisions of the Presidential Records Act.

Moreover, in accordance with the ruling by the federal court of the District of Columbia in Lardner v. Department of Justice, 638 F.Supp.2d 14 (D.D.C. 2009), affirmed, Lardner v. United States Department of Justice, No. 09-5337, 2010 WL 4366062 (D.C. Cir. Oct. 28, 2010) (unpublished), the Office of the Pardon Attorney is obliged to release existing lists of the names of persons who have been denied executive clemency by the President to anyone who requests such records pursuant to the Freedom of Information Act. Given the frequency of such requests, the Office of the Pardon Attorney has started to proactively disclose the names of persons who have been denied executive clemency by the President on our website, in accordance with our Freedom of Information Act obligations.

RULES GOVERNING PETITIONS FOR EXECUTIVE CLEMENCY

PART I - EXECUTIVE CLEMENCY

Sec.

1.1 Submission of petition; form to be used; contents of petition.
1.2 Eligibility for filing petition for pardon.
1.3 Eligibility for filing petition for commutation of sentence.
1.4 Offenses against the laws of possessions or territories of the United States.
1.5 Disclosure of files.
1.6 Consideration of petitions; notification of victims; recommendations to the President.
1.7 Notification of grant of clemency.
1.8 Notification of denial of clemency.
1.9 Delegation of authority.
1.10 Procedures applicable to prisoners under a sentence of death imposed by a United States Court.
1.11 Advisory nature of regulations.

Authority: U.S. Const., Art. II, Sec. 2; authority of the President as Chief Executive; and 28 C.F.R. §§ 0.35, 0.36.

§ 1.1 Submission of petition; form to be used; contents of petition.

A person seeking executive clemency by pardon, reprieve, commutation of sentence, or remission of fine shall execute a formal petition. The petition shall be addressed to the President of the United States and shall be submitted to the Pardon Attorney, Department of Justice, Washington, D.C. 20530, except for petitions relating to military offenses. Petitions and other required forms may be obtained from the Pardon Attorney. Petition forms for commutation of sentence also may be obtained from the wardens of federal penal institutions. A petitioner applying for executive clemency with respect to military offenses should submit his or her petition directly to the Secretary of the military department that had original jurisdiction over the court-martial trial and conviction of the petitioner. In such a case, a form furnished by the Pardon Attorney may be used but should be modified to meet the needs of the particular case. Each petition for executive clemency should include the information required in the form prescribed by the Attorney General.

§ 1.2 Eligibility for filing petition for pardon.

No petition for pardon should be filed until the expiration of a waiting period of at least five years after the date of the release of the petitioner from confinement or, in case no prison sentence was imposed, until the expiration of a period of at least five years after the date of the conviction of the petitioner. Generally, no petition should be submitted by a person who is on probation, parole, or supervised release.

§ 1.3 Eligibility for filing petition for commutation of sentence.

No petition for commutation of sentence, including remission of fine, should be filed if other forms of judicial or administrative relief are available, except upon a showing of exceptional circumstances.

§ 1.4 Offenses against the laws of possessions or territories of the United States.

Petitions for executive clemency shall relate only to violations of laws of the United States. Petitions relating to violations of laws of the possessions of the United States or territories subject to the jurisdiction of the United States should be submitted to the appropriate official or agency of the possession or territory concerned.

§ 1.5 Disclosure of files.

Petitions, reports, memoranda, and communications submitted or furnished in connection with the consideration of a petition for executive clemency generally shall be available only to the officials concerned with the consideration of the petition. However, they may be made available for inspection, in whole or in part, when in the judgment of the Attorney General their disclosure is required by law or the ends of justice.

§ 1.6 Consideration of petitions; notification of victims; recommendations to the President.

(a) Upon receipt of a petition for executive clemency, the Attorney General shall cause such investigation to be made of the matter as he or she may deem necessary and appropriate, using the services of, or obtaining reports from, appropriate officials and agencies of the Government, including the Federal Bureau of Investigation.

(b)(1) When a person requests clemency (in the form of either a commutation of a sentence or a pardon after serving a sentence) for a conviction of a felony offense for which there was a victim, and the Attorney General concludes from the information developed in the clemency case that investigation of the clemency case warrants contacting the victim, the Attorney General shall cause reasonable effort to be made to notify the victim or victims of the crime for which clemency is sought:

(i) That a clemency petition has been filed;
(ii) That the victim may submit comments regarding clemency; and
(iii) Whether the clemency request ultimately is granted or denied by the President.

(2) In determining whether contacting the victim is warranted, the Attorney General shall consider the seriousness and recency of the offense, the nature and extent of the harm to the victim, the defendant's overall criminal history and history of violent behavior, and the likelihood that clemency could be recommended in the case.

(3) For the purposes of this paragraph (b), "victim" means an individual who:

(i) Has suffered direct or threatened physical, emotional, or pecuniary harm as a result of the commission of the crime for which clemency is sought (or, in the case of an individual who dies or was rendered incompetent as a direct and proximate result of the commission of the crime for which clemency is sought, one of the following relatives of the victim (in order of preference): the spouse; an adult offspring; or a parent); and
(ii) Has on file with the Federal Bureau of Prisons a request to be notified pursuant to 28 CFR § 551.152 of the offender's release from custody.

(4) For the purposes of this paragraph (b), "reasonable effort" is satisfied by mailing to the last-known address reported by the victim to the Federal Bureau of Prisons under 28 CFR § 551.152.

(5) The provisions of this paragraph (b) apply to clemency cases filed on or after September 28, 2000.

(c) The Attorney General shall review each petition and all pertinent information developed by the investigation and shall determine whether the request for clemency is of sufficient merit to warrant favorable action by the President. The Attorney General shall report in writing his or her recommendation to the President, stating whether in his or her judgment, the President should grant or deny the petition.

§ 1.7 Notification of grant of clemency.

When a petition for pardon is granted, the petitioner or his or her attorney shall be notified of such action and the warrant of pardon shall be mailed to the petitioner. When commutation of sentence is granted, the petitioner shall be notified of such action and the warrant of commutation shall be sent to the petitioner through the officer in charge of his or her place of confinement, or directly to the petitioner if he/she is on parole, probation, or supervised release.

§ 1.8 Notification of denial of clemency.

(a) Whenever the President notifies the Attorney General that he has denied a request for clemency, the Attorney General shall so advise the petitioner and close the case.

(b) Except in cases in which a sentence of death has been imposed, whenever the Attorney General recommends that the President deny a request for clemency and the President does not disapprove or take other action with respect to that adverse recommendation within 30 days after the date of its submission to him, it shall be presumed that the President concurs in that adverse recommendation of the Attorney General, and the Attorney General shall so advise the petitioner and close the case.

§ 1.9 Delegation of authority.

The Attorney General may delegate to any officer of the Department of Justice any of his or her duties or responsibilities under §§ 1.1 through 1.8.

§ 1.10 Procedures applicable to prisoners under a sentence of death imposed by a United States District Court.

The following procedures shall apply with respect to any request for clemency by a person under a sentence of death imposed by a United States District Court for an offense against the United States. Other provisions set forth in this part shall also apply to the extent they are not inconsistent with this section.

(a) Clemency in the form of reprieve or commutation of a death sentence imposed by a United States District Court shall be requested by the person under the sentence of death or by the person's attorney acting with the person's written and signed authorization.

(b) No petition for reprieve or commutation of a death sentence should be filed before proceedings on the petitioner's direct appeal of the judgment of conviction and first petition under 28 U.S.C. § 2255 have terminated. A petition for commutation of sentence should be filed no later than 30 days after the petitioner has received notification from the Bureau of Prisons of the scheduled date of execution. All papers in support of a petition for commutation of sentence should be filed no later than 15 days after the filing of the petition itself. Papers filed by the petitioner more than 15 days after the commutation petition has been filed may be excluded from consideration.

(c) The petitioner's clemency counsel may request to make an oral presentation of reasonable duration to the Office of the Pardon Attorney in support of the clemency petition. The presentation should be requested at the time the clemency petition is filed. The family or families of any victim of an offense for which the petitioner was sentenced to death may, with the assistance of the prosecuting office, request to make an oral presentation of reasonable duration to the Office of the Pardon Attorney.

(d) Clemency proceedings may be suspended if a court orders a stay of execution for any reason other than to allow completion of the clemency proceeding.

(e) Only one request for commutation of a death sentence will be processed to completion, absent a clear showing of exceptional circumstances.

(f) The provisions of this § 1.10 apply to any person under a sentence of death imposed by a United States District Court for whom an execution date is set on or after August 1, 2000.

§ 1.11 Advisory nature of regulations.

The regulations contained in this part are advisory only and for the internal guidance of Department of Justice personnel. They create no enforceable rights in persons applying for executive clemency, nor do they restrict the authority granted to the President under Article II, Section 2 of the Constitution.

Published in the FEDERAL REGISTER of the National Archives and Records Administration of the United States, October 18, 1993, Vol. 58, No. 199, at pages 53658 and 53659; as amended by a publication in the FEDERAL REGISTER of the National Archives and Records Administration of the United States, August 8, 2000, Vol. 65, No. 153, at page 48381; and as amended by a publication in the FEDERAL REGISTER of the National Archives and Records Administration of the United States, September 28, 2000, Vol. 65, No. 189, at pages 58223 and 58224, 28 CFR §§ 1.1 et seq. See also 28 CFR § 0.35

Updated November 23, 2018

APPENDIX C: DOJ STANDARDS FOR CONSIDERATION OF CLEMENCY PETITIONERS

STANDARDS FOR CONSIDERATION OF CLEMENCY PETITIONERS

Reproduced from the Justice Manual, last updated April 2018.

Section 9-140.110 - Pardon Attorney
Section 9-140.111 - Role of the Prosecuting Component in Clemency Matters
Section 9-140.112 - Standards for Considering Pardon Petitions
Section 9-140.113 - Standards for Considering Commutation Petitions

SECTION 9-140.110 - OFFICE OF THE PARDON ATTORNEY

The Pardon Attorney assists the President in the exercise of his power under Article II, Section 2, clause 1 of the Constitution (the pardon clause). See Executive Order dated June 16, 1893 (transferring clemency petition processing and advisory functions to the Justice Department), the Rules Governing the Processing of Petitions for Executive Clemency (codified in 28 CFR Sections 1.1 et seq.), and 28 CFR Sections 0.35 and 0.36 (relating to the authority of the Pardon Attorney). The Pardon Attorney, under the direction of the Deputy Attorney General, receives and reviews all petitions for Executive Clemency (which includes pardon after completion of sentence, commutation of sentence, remission of fine or restitution and reprieve), initiates and directs the necessary investigations, and prepares a report and recommendation for submission to the President in every case. In addition, the Office of the Pardon Attorney acts as a liaison with the public during the pendency of a clemency petition, responding to correspondence and answering inquiries about clemency cases and issues. The following sets forth guidance on clemency matters.

SECTION 9-140.111 - ROLE OF THE PROSECUTING COMPONENT IN CLEMENCY MATTERS

The Pardon Attorney routinely requests the United States Attorney in the district of conviction or if a Department litigating component was responsible for the case, the Assistant Attorney General in charge of the component to provide comments and recommendations on clemency cases that appear to have some merit, as well as on cases that raise issues of fact about which the United States Attorney or Assistant Attorney General may be in a position to provide information. Occasionally, the United States Attorney in the district in which a petitioner currently resides also may be contacted. In addition, in cases in which the petitioner seeks clemency based on cooperation with the government, the Pardon Attorney may solicit the views of the United States Attorney in the district(s) in which the petitioner cooperated, if different from the district of conviction, or the views of the Assistant Attorney General in charge of the Department litigating component with which the petitioner cooperated, if different from the prosecuting component. When a particular Main Justice component has jurisdiction over or involvement in a case, such as approving charges or participating in the prosecution of the defendant, the Pardon Attorney will also solicit comments and recommendations from that component. For example, the Tax Division, which authorizes and supervises nearly all charges arising under the internal revenue laws, will be consulted when a defendant convicted of such a charge seeks clemency, whether or not a Division attorney was directly involved in prosecuting the case While the decision to grant clemency generally is driven by considerations that differ from those that dictate the decision to prosecute, the United States Attorney's or Assistant Attorney's General prosecutive perspective lends valuable insights to the clemency process.

The views of the United States Attorney or Assistant Attorney General are given considerable weight in determining what recommendations the Department should make to the President. For this reason, and in order to ensure consistency, it is important that each request sent to the district or litigating component receive the personal attention of the United States Attorney or Assistant Attorney General . Each petition is presented for action to the President with a report and recommendation from the Department, and the substance of the recommendation by the United States Attorney or Assistant Attorney General is included in this report.

The United States Attorney or Assistant Attorney General can contribute significantly to the clemency process by providing factual information and perspectives about the offense of conviction that may not be reflected in the presentence or background investigation reports or other sources, e.g., the extent of the petitioner's wrongdoing and the attendant circumstances, the amount of money involved or losses sustained, the petitioner's involvement in other criminal activity, the petitioner's reputation in the community and, when appropriate, the victim impact of the petitioner's crime. On occasion, the Pardon Attorney may request information from prosecution records that may not be readily available from other sources.

As a general matter, in clemency cases the correctness of the underlying conviction is assumed, and the question of guilt or innocence is not generally at issue. However, if a petitioner refuses to accept guilt, minimizes culpability, or raises a claim of innocence or miscarriage of justice, the United States Attorney or Assistant Attorney General should address these issues.

In cases involving pardon after completion of sentence, the United States Attorney or Assistant Attorney General is expected to comment on the petitioner's post-conviction rehabilitation, particularly any actions that may evidence a desire to atone for the offense, in light of the standards generally applicable in pardon cases as discussed in the following section. Similarly, in commutation cases, comments may be sought on developments after sentencing that are relevant to the merits of a petitioner's request for mercy.

In pardon cases, the Pardon Attorney will forward to the United States Attorney or Assistant Attorney General copies of the pardon petition and relevant investigative reports. These records should be destroyed by the United States Attorney or Assistant Attorney General (if in electronic form) or returned (if in hard copy) to the Pardon Attorney along with the response. In cases involving requests for other forms of executive clemency (i.e., commutation of sentence or remission of fine), copies of the clemency petition and such related records as may be useful (e.g., presentence report, judgment of conviction, prison progress reports, and completed statement of debtor forms) will be provided.

The Pardon Attorney also routinely requests the United States Attorney or Assistant Attorney General to solicit the views and recommendation of the sentencing judge. If the sentencing judge is retired, deceased, or otherwise unavailable for comment, the United States Attorney's or Assistant Attorney's General report should so advise. In the event the United States Attorney or Assistant Attorney General does not wish to contact the sentencing judge, the Pardon Attorney should be advised accordingly so that the judge's views may be solicited directly. Absent an express request for confidentiality, the Pardon Attorney may share the comments of the United States Attorney or Assistant Attorney General with the sentencing judge or other concerned officials whose views are solicited.

The United States Attorney or Assistant Attorney General may support, oppose or take no position on a pardon request. In this regard, it is helpful to have a clear expression of the office's position. The Pardon Attorney generally asks for a response within 30 days. If an unusual delay is anticipated, the Pardon Attorney should be advised when a response may be expected. If desired, the official views of the United States Attorney or Assistant Attorney General may be supplemented by separate reports from present or former officials involved in the prosecution of the case. The United States Attorney or Assistant Attorney General may of course submit a recommendation for or against clemency even if the Pardon Attorney has not yet solicited comments from the district or component. The Pardon Attorney informs the United States Attorney or Assistant Attorney General of the final disposition of any clemency application on which he or she has commented.

Should a president leave office without acting on a particular clemency petition, that petition will remain open and active until the incoming president reaches a decision.

SECTION 9-140.112 - STANDARDS FOR CONSIDERING PARDON PETITIONS

In general, a pardon is granted on the basis of the petitioner's demonstrated good conduct for a substantial period of time after conviction and service of sentence. The Department's regulations require a petitioner to wait a period of at least five years after conviction or release from confinement (whichever is later) before filing a pardon application (28 CFR Section 1.2). The Department may grant a waiver of the five-year requirement. In determining whether a particular petitioner should be recommended for a pardon, the following are the principal factors taken into account.

A. **Post-conviction conduct, character, and reputation.** An individual's demonstrated ability to lead a responsible and productive life for a significant period after conviction or release from confinement is strong evidence of rehabilitation and worthiness for pardon. The background investigation customarily conducted by the FBI in pardon cases focuses on the petitioner's financial and employment stability, responsibility toward family, reputation in the community, participation in community service, charitable or other meritorious activities and, if applicable, military record. The investigation also serves to verify the petitioner's responses in the pardon application. In assessing post-conviction accomplishments, each petitioner's life circumstances are considered in their totality: it may not be appropriate or realistic to expect "extraordinary" post-conviction achievements from individuals who are less fortunately situated in terms of cultural, educational, or economic background.

B. **Seriousness and relative recentness of the offense.** When an offense is very serious, (e.g., a violent crime, major drug trafficking, breach of public trust, or white collar fraud involving substantial sums of money), a suitable length of time should have elapsed in order to avoid denigrating the seriousness of the offense or undermining the deterrent effect of the conviction. In the case of a prominent individual or notorious crime, the likely effect of a pardon on law enforcement interests or upon the general public should be taken into account. Victim impact may also be a relevant consideration. When an offense is very old and relatively minor, the equities may weigh more heavily in favor of forgiveness, provided the petitioner is otherwise a suitable candidate for pardon.

C. **Acceptance of responsibility, remorse, and atonement.** The extent to which a petitioner has accepted responsibility for his or her criminal conduct and made restitution to its victims are important considerations. A petitioner should be genuinely desirous of forgiveness rather than vindication. While the absence of expressions of remorse should not preclude favorable consideration, a petitioner's attempt to minimize or rationalize culpability does not advance the case for pardon. In this regard, statements made in mitigation (e.g., "everybody was doing it," or I didn't realize it was illegal") should be judged in context. Persons seeking a pardon on grounds of innocence or miscarriage of justice bear a formidable burden of persuasion.

D. **Need for Relief.** The purpose for which pardon is sought may influence disposition of the petition. A felony conviction may result in a wide variety of legal disabilities under state or federal law, some of which can provide persuasive grounds for recommending a pardon. For example, a specific employment-related need for pardon, such as removal of a bar to licensure or bonding, may make an otherwise marginal case sufficiently compelling to warrant a grant in aid of the individual's continuing rehabilitation. On the other hand, the absence of a specific need should not be held against an otherwise deserving applicant, who may understandably be motivated solely by a strong personal desire for a sign of forgiveness.

E. **Official recommendations and reports.** The comments and recommendations of concerned and knowledgeable officials, particularly the United States Attorney or Assistant Attorney General whose office prosecuted the case and the sentencing judge, are carefully considered. The likely impact of favorable action in the district or nationally, particularly on current law enforcement priorities, will always be relevant to the President's decision. Apart from their significance to the individuals who seek them, pardons can play an important part in defining and furthering the rehabilitative goals of the criminal justice system.

SECTION 9-140.113 - STANDARDS FOR CONSIDERING COMMUTATION PETITIONS

A commutation of sentence reduces the period of incarceration; it does not imply forgiveness of the underlying offense, but simply remits a portion of the punishment. It has no effect upon the underlying conviction and does not necessarily reflect upon the fairness of the sentence originally imposed. Requests for commutation generally are not accepted unless and until a person has begun serving that sentence. Nor are commutation requests generally accepted from persons who are presently challenging their convictions or sentences through appeal or other court proceeding.

In the case of a petitioner seeking relief from a sentence of death, the petitioner must have exhausted only the first motion for relief under 18 U.S.C. § 2255 before applying for clemency. In such a case, the Bureau of Prisons generally will set a date of execution upon denial of the first Section 2255 motion. Thereafter, the petitioner has a limited amount of time to submit clemency applications and materials. *See* 28 C.F.R. § 1.10.

The President may commute a sentence to time served or he may reduce a sentence to achieve the inmate's release after a specified period of time. Commutation may be granted upon conditions similar to those imposed pursuant to parole or supervised release or, in the case of an alien, upon condition of deportation.

Commutation of sentence is an extraordinary remedy. Appropriate grounds for considering commutation have traditionally included disparity or undue severity of sentence, critical illness or old age, and meritorious service rendered to the government by the petitioner, e.g., cooperation with investigative or prosecutive efforts that has not been adequately rewarded by other official action. A combination of these and/or other equitable factors (such as demonstrated rehabilitation while in custody or exigent circumstances unforeseen by the court at the time of sentencing) may also provide a basis for recommending commutation in the context of a particular case.

The amount of time already served and the availability of other remedies are taken into account in deciding whether to recommend clemency. The possibility that the Department itself could accomplish the same result by petitioning the sentencing court, through a motion to reward substantial assistance under Rule 35 of the Federal Rules of Criminal Procedure, a motion for modification or remission of fine under 18 U.S.C. Section 3573, or a request for compassionate reduction in sentence under 18 U.S.C. Section 3582(c)(1), will also bear on the decision whether to recommend Presidential intervention in the form of clemency. When a commutation request is based on the serious illness of the petitioner, an expedited response from the United States Attorney or Assistant Attorney General is always appreciated. If the request involves a sentence of death, an expedited response from the United States Attorney or Assistant Attorney General is essential.

When a petitioner seeks remission of fine or restitution, the ability to pay and any good faith efforts to discharge the obligation are important considerations. Petitioners for remission also should demonstrate satisfactory post-conviction conduct.

On January 21, 1977, the President by Proclamation 4483 granted pardon to persons who committed nonviolent violations of the Selective Service Act between August 4, 1964 and March 28, 1973 and who were not Selective Service employees. Although a person who comes within the described class was immediately pardoned by the proclamation, the Pardon Attorney issues certificates of pardon to those within the class who were actually convicted of a draft violation and who make written application to the Department on official forms. When these applications are received by the Pardon Attorney, they are forwarded to the United States Attorney for the district in which the applicant was convicted to verify the facts of the case. The verification should be returned to the Pardon Attorney promptly.

Updated September 21, 2018

APPENDIX D: DOJ FREQUENTLY ASKED QUESTIONS OF CLEMENCY

THE UNITED STATES DEPARTMENT of JUSTICE

Search form

Search [   ]

[Search]

FREQUENTLY ASKED QUESTIONS

What is your physical mailing address if I want to mail you something, have items hand-delivered, or want to stop by for an unscheduled meeting?

We prefer email, but if you don't have access to email, you can send records to us at U.S. Department of Justice, Office of the Pardon Attorney, 950 Pennsylvania Avenue, Washington, DC 20530. All of our mail is now processed through the RFK-Main Justice Building. We do not accept visitors or hand delivered packages to ensure the safety of our staff.

If I submit a new clemency petition, how long should it take for me to be able to use the Clemency Lookup Feature to confirm my clemency casefile number?

We update the Clemency Lookup Feature once per month, but it could take up to 8 weeks before your case will show up on the lookup feature. In addition to pending cases, as of December 2019 you can also confirm the status of all cases accepted for review since January 1989 at https://www.justice.gov/pardon/search-clemency-case-status-since-1989. Therefore, we will not respond to requests for confirmation of receipt or status updates if your petition was submitted to us within the past 8 weeks because we deem your request premature and the only publicly available information about a pending case is already proactively disclosed through this feature of our website. **We will also refrain from providing status updates on cases that you can now use our Clemency Lookup Feature to confirm the status of. Due to longstanding policy, we will not provide any additional information about the status of a pending case, outside of what is available on our website, and we also cannot rush or expedite the President's decision making process.**

Can an inmate who is currently in litigation challenging his/her conviction apply for clemency while waiting for the court case to be resolved?

No. Under well-established procedures, this office will not process a clemency application while litigation concerning the case is pending. Should the inmate's case be resolved adversely to the inmate and should no other litigation follow, the inmate may submit a new commutation of sentence petition to this Office, through the case manager, along with the standard reports detailed in the Bureau of Prisons Program Statement No. 1330.15, effective August 23, 2001 (28 C.F.R. §§ 571.40 - 571.41).

If Pardon Attorney screens my petition and comes back to me requesting additional information or documentation, am I required to provide it? How will refusing to provide such information affect my clemency case?

Clemency officials conduct a very thorough review in determining a petitioner's worthiness for relief. Accordingly, you should be prepared for a detailed inquiry into your personal and criminal background as well as current activities. If you choose not to respond or refuse to provide requested information and/or documentation that would be helpful in analyzing your clemency request, it is possible that your case will be administratively closed without presidential action.

How does an inmate apply for compassionate release?

A request for a motion under 18 USC 4205(g) or 3582(c)(1)(A) *(otherwise known as compassionate release)* should be submitted to the Warden of the Bureau of Prisons institution that houses the inmate. Compassionate release requests cannot be accepted by the Pardon Attorney because a commutation by the President must be a last resort remedy. Therefore, if an inmate is currently being considered for compassionate release, the Pardon Attorney will close any pending commutation of sentence petition until a decision is made by the court on the request for compassionate release and the inmate will have to reapply through the Pardon Attorney for clemency at a later date.

What is the difference between a commutation of sentence and a pardon?

In the federal system, commutation of sentence and pardon are different forms of executive clemency, which is a broad term that applies to the President's constitutional power to exercise leniency toward persons who have committed federal crimes.

A commutation of sentence reduces a sentence, either totally or partially, that is then being served, but it does not change the fact of conviction, imply innocence, or remove civil disabilities that apply to the convicted person as a result of the criminal conviction. A commutation may include remission (release) of the financial obligations that are imposed as part of a sentence, such as payment of a fine or restitution. A remission applies only to the part of the financial obligation that has not already been paid. A commutation of sentence has no effect on a person's immigration status and will not prevent removal or deportation from the United States. To be eligible to apply for commutation of sentence, a person must have reported to prison to begin serving his sentence and may not be challenging his conviction in the courts.

A pardon is an expression of the President's forgiveness and ordinarily is granted in recognition of the applicant's acceptance of responsibility for the crime and established good conduct for a significant period of time after conviction or completion of sentence. It does not signify innocence. It does, however, remove civil disabilities – e.g., restrictions on the right to vote, hold state or local office, or sit on a jury – imposed because of the conviction for which pardon is sought, and should lessen the stigma arising from the conviction. It may also be helpful in obtaining licenses, bonding, or employment. Under some – but not all – circumstances, a pardon will eliminate the legal basis for removal or deportation from the United States. Pursuant to the Rules Governing Petitions for Executive Clemency, which are available on this website, a person is not eligible to apply for a presidential pardon until a minimum of five years has elapsed since his release from any form of confinement imposed upon him as part of a sentence for his most recent criminal conviction, whether or not that is the conviction for which he is seeking the pardon.

Do you have to pay a fee to file an application for pardon or commutation of sentence with the Office of the Pardon Attorney?

No. There is no fee for applying for any form of executive clemency.

Do you have to hire a lawyer to apply for a pardon or a commutation of sentence?

No. The executive clemency process is intended to be accessible to ALL eligible applicants, whether or not they are represented by counsel, and is begun by filing the appropriate clemency petition. In fact, most clemency applications are submitted by persons who are not represented by counsel. Application forms are available on this website. If you have questions about the application as you are completing it or helping someone else to complete it, you may contact the Pardon Attorney at USPardon.Attorney@usdoj.gov to ask for clarification, but please be aware that we are unable to provide legal advice. If a pardon applicant submits an application that is incomplete or does not sufficiently answer the questions posed, the Pardon Attorney will contact the applicant through whatever communication mode we were contacted through and explain what additional information is required.

Is a hearing held on an application for pardon or commutation of sentence?

No. The executive clemency process is a written process. There is no hearing held by Pardon Attorney on any commutation or pardon application. However, in the processing of a pardon application, a thorough investigation is made of the applicant's post-conviction life, which may include a background investigation conducted by the Federal Bureau of Investigation. As a general matter, if an applicant wishes to have specific information considered in connection with his clemency request, he should submit that information in writing to the Pardon Attorney. He may do this at any time while the application is pending.

Is there any limit to the kinds of information an applicant may submit in support of his clemency application?

A clemency applicant – or any third party – is free to send any documentation or other written information he believes has a bearing on the applicant's suitability for clemency so that it may be considered in connection with the application. We recommend that a person desiring to submit a document to the Pardon Attorney send a copy of the record rather than the original document, since the record will be made part of the applicant's executive clemency file. Because of the nature of its case tracking system, the Pardon Attorney cannot make information recorded on digital media part of an applicant's file. The office therefore does not accept information presented in such formats.

How are applications for commutation of sentence evaluated?

As a general matter, commutation of sentence has long been considered to be an extraordinary remedy that is rarely granted. The merit of a commutation request is evaluated by considering the standards contained in Section 9-140.113 of the Justice Manual, which is available on this website. Appropriate standards for considering commutation relief traditionally have included such factors as disparity or undue severity of sentence, critical illness or old age, and meritorious service to the government by the applicant that has not been adequately rewarded by other official actions, as well as other equitable factors that may be present in a given case. The seriousness of the offense of conviction, the applicant's overall criminal record, the nature of the applicant's adjustment to prison supervision, the length of time the applicant has already served, and the availability of other remedies are also considered in evaluating the merit of an application. Finally, as with a pardon request, the applicant's candor in the commutation application is an important consideration.

How long does it take for a clemency application to be decided?

The executive clemency process can be lengthy, and the Pardon Attorney is not able to estimate for any particular applicant when he may expect to receive a decision on his application. The Pardon Attorney reviews each application and conducts the appropriate investigation of the case. In many instances, this process requires the Pardon Attorney to obtain information or comments from other agencies, which in turn may have to obtain records from off-site storage in order to respond to the Pardon Attorney's inquiry. After all relevant information has been received, the Pardon Attorney prepares a proposed recommendation for disposition of the case that is submitted to the Deputy Attorney General, who makes the final determination of the Justice Department's recommendation to the President. The Deputy Attorney General's signed recommendation is then transmitted to the White House, and the President acts on each case when he believes it is appropriate to do so. As a matter of long-standing policy, the Pardon Attorney does not disclose to applicants or third parties the stage at which a clemency application is pending at any given time. After the President decides to grant or deny a particular clemency request, the Pardon Attorney notifies the applicant of the decision in writing. Because the written notification is sent to the last address an applicant has provided to the Pardon Attorney, it is important that an applicant notify the Pardon Attorney if his address changes while the application is under consideration.

If the President does not make a decision on my case before he leaves office, do I need to submit another petition for the new President?

No. Except for situations in which an application must be closed administratively because an applicant withdraws the application from consideration, repeatedly fails to respond to a request by the Pardon Attorney for required information, dies during processing of the application, is no longer a resident of the United States, or is released from prison during the processing of a commutation application that seeks only the reduction of his prison sentence, every clemency application submitted to the Pardon Attorney is decided by the President. Accordingly, if the outgoing President does not reach a decision before the end of his elected term, the application will remain open until resolved by a later President. While both the Department of Justice and the President make every effort to resolve clemency applications in a timely manner, there is no guarantee that an application submitted during an administration will be decided by that President. If an applicant has not received a denial notification from the Pardon Attorney, then the applicant may assume that the application remains pending and will extend into the next administration.

If the President denies a clemency request, is the applicant told why?

As a general matter, Presidents in recent times have rarely announced their reasons for granting or denying clemency, although the President may choose to do so in a given case. Consistent with long-standing policy, if the President does not issue a public statement concerning his action in a clemency matter, no explanation is provided by the Department of Justice. Moreover, deliberative communications pertaining to agency and presidential decision-making are confidential and not available under existing case law interpreting the Freedom of Information Act and Privacy Act.

If I apply for executive clemency from the President and my request is denied, may I reapply?

Yes. A person whose request for a commutation of sentence is turned down may reapply anytime after one year from the date of the President's denial of the request. A person whose request for a pardon is denied may reapply anytime after two years from the date of the President's denial of the request. To reapply for a pardon or commutation, a person must complete and submit a new application form that contains current information in response to all questions. Resubmitting the prior application form that was previously denied is not an acceptable form of reapplication.

I was convicted of an offense by military court martial and I am still incarcerated. May I apply for Commutation (reduction) of Sentence?

No. The Office of the Pardon Attorney does not process requests for commutation (reduction) of sentences from persons convicted of offenses in military courts-martial. Military commutation requests are handled by the military branch that handled the conviction and sentencing.

I am in federal prison, but I'd like to have my sentence commuted to time-served to speed up my deportation from the United States and return to my country of citizenship.

Deportation is not a remedy available through the executive clemency process. Decisions regarding deportation status are within the authority of the Department of Homeland Security. However, to the extent that you are seeking reduction of sentence to advance the date of your deportation, you may apply for commutation (reduction) of sentence if you are not presently challenging your conviction or sentence through appeal or other court proceeding.

How can I find out the status of a clemency petition has been submitted and accepted for processing from 1989 to Present?

Members of the public who wish to confirm whether an executive clemency case is currently in "pending" status, either for themselves or a third party, may use the Pardon Attorney's clemency Lookup Feature to search by clemency casefile number, BOP register number or by the name of the petitioner.

Updated December 14, 2019

APPENDIX E: BOP CLEMENCY PROGRAM STATEMENT 1330.15

U.S. Department of Justice
Federal Bureau of Prisons

CHANGE NOTICE
OPI: CPD/CPB
NUMBER: 1330.15, CN-1
DATE: 05/02/2014

Commutation of Sentence, Petition for

/s/
Approved: Charles E. Samuels, Jr.
Director, Federal Bureau of Prisons

This Change Notice (CN) implements the following changes to Program Statement 1330.15, **Petition for Commutation of Sentence**, dated August 23, 2001:

1. On p. 3, the following paragraph is deleted:

To expedite the Pardon Attorney's consideration of an inmate's petition for commutation of sentence, the inmate **must** send the petition through the Warden to the U.S. Pardon Attorney.

2. On p. 3, the U.S. Pardon Attorney's telephone number is deleted.

3. On p. 5, the address of the U.S. Pardon Attorney is changed as follows:

   U.S. Pardon Attorney
   1425 New York Avenue, NW.
   Suite 11000
   Washington, DC 20530

U.S. Department of Justice
Federal Bureau of Prisons

Program Statement

OPI: CPD
NUMBER: 1330.15
DATE: 8/23/2001
SUBJECT: Commutation of Sentence, Petition for

1. [**PURPOSE AND SCOPE** §571.40. An inmate may file a petition for commutation of sentence in accordance with the provisions of 28 CFR Part 1.

   a. An inmate may request from the inmate's case manager the appropriate forms (and instructions) for filing a petition for commutation of sentence.

   b. When specifically requested by the U.S. Pardon Attorney, the Director, Bureau of Prisons will forward a recommendation on the inmate's petition for commutation of sentence.]

   Article II, Section 2 of the U.S. Constitution empowers the President of the United States to grant Executive Clemency, including pardon, commutation (reduction) of sentence, remission of time and reprieve. Commutation of the term of a prison sentence is considered only in the most exceptional circumstances.

   Rules governing petitions for Executive Clemency such as commutation of sentence, are published in 28 CFR Part 1 (§1.1-1.10).

   In accordance with 28 CFR 1.3, a petition for commutation of sentence, including remission of fine, should be filed only if no other form of relief is available, such as from a court of the United States, U.S. Parole Commission, or upon motions under 18 U.S.C. §§ 3582(c) and 4205(g), or if unusual circumstances exist, such as:

   ! critical illness,
   ! severity of sentence,

[Bracketed Bold - Rules]
Regular Type - Implementing Information

- ineligibility for parole, or
- meritorious service rendered by the petitioner.

2. **SUMMARY OF CHANGES.** This revision:

    - Requires inmates to submit petitions through their Wardens if they wish expedited consideration by the U.S. Pardon Attorney.

    - Clarifies what documents staff must send to the U.S. Pardon Attorney with an inmate's petition for commutation of sentence.

    - Establishes procedures by which the inmate's petition is receipted and further processed.

3. **PROGRAM OBJECTIVE.** The expected result of this program is:

All inmates will have access to the U.S. Pardon Attorney to request a petition for commutation of sentence.

4. **DIRECTIVES AFFECTED**

    a. **Directive Rescinded**

    PS 1330.14   Petition for Commutation of Sentence (11/24/97)

    b. **Directives Referenced**

    PS 5803.07   Progress Reports (2/18/98)
    PS 6000.05   Health Services Manual (10/28/97)

    c. Rules cited in this Program Statement are contained in 28 CFR 571.40-41.

5. **STANDARDS REFERENCED.** None

6. **PRETRIAL/HOLDOVER/DETAINEE PROCEDURES.** The procedures contained in this Program Statement apply only to sentenced inmates.

7. [**PROCEDURES** §571.41

    a. Staff shall suggest that an inmate who wishes to submit a petition for commutation of sentence do so through the Warden to the U.S. Pardon Attorney. This procedure allows institution staff to forward with the application the necessary supplemental

information (for example, sentencing information, presentence report, progress report, pertinent medical records if the petition involves the inmate's health, etc.). Except as provided in paragraph (b) of this section, no Bureau of Prisons recommendation is to be forwarded with the package of material submitted to the U.S. Pardon Attorney.]

To expedite the Pardon Attorney's consideration of an inmate's petition for commutation of sentence, the inmate **must** send the petition through the Warden to the U.S. Pardon Attorney.

Staff may not refuse to process an inmate's petition for commutation of sentence, even when it appears that the inmate is not eligible. When an inmate submits the petition for commutation of sentence, the Case Manager will document the petition's receipt with a complete entry on the Inmate Activity Record in the Inmate Central File.

Once the petition is received, the Case Manager will have 30 calendar days to compile the required documents and route for the Warden's signature.

When referring an inmate's petition for commutation of sentence, staff **must** include:

- Petition for Commutation of Sentence (Form OPA-6);
- Pre-sentence Investigation Report (if available);
- Judgment in a Criminal Case; and,
- The inmate's most recent **already existing** Progress Report (**staff need not create or update a Progress Report**);

If available, staff should also include any other pertinent, documented information.

The Pardon Attorney may later request the following, if necessary:

- All pertinent medical records if the petition involves the inmate's health; and
- An updated Progress Report.

In the event of a medical emergency certified by the physician at the institution where the inmate is confined, staff must expedite the petition at all levels. In such cases, the documents cited above may be transmitted to the U.S. Pardon Attorney's office via BOPNet Mail ID or Facsimile (Commercial (202) 616-6069). The telephone number is (202) 616-6070.

The U.S. Pardon Attorney may delay and/or return petitions received without proper documentation pending the remaining documentation's receipt.

When the U.S. Pardon Attorney needs **additional** information, a request will be forwarded directly to the Warden of the institution housing the inmate, with a copy to the Assistant Director, Correctional Programs Division, Central Office, Washington DC. In these cases, the Warden must ensure the requested documents are forwarded to the U.S. Pardon Attorney within 15 working days and a copy of the transmittal memorandum provided to the Assistant Director, Correctional Programs Division.

[b. **When specifically requested by the U.S. Pardon Attorney, the Director, Bureau of Prisons shall submit a recommendation on the petition. Prior to making a recommendation, the Director may request comments from the Warden at the institution where the inmate is confined. Upon review of those comments, the Director will forward a recommendation on the petition to the U.S. Pardon Attorney.**]

(1) The Director, through the Assistant Director, Correctional Programs Division, will contact (ordinarily via BOPNet) the Warden for comments, with an information copy sent to the Regional Director.

(2) The Warden must submit a written response to the Assistant Director, Correctional Programs Division (Attention: Administrator, Correctional Programs Branch) within 10 days of receiving the request, and forward an information copy to the Regional Director.

(3) The Director, upon review of all available information, forwards the Bureau's recommendation to the U.S. Pardon Attorney, with a copy to the Warden and Regional Director.

The Director's recommendation is ordinarily one of several reviewed by the U.S. Pardon Attorney and others concerned with the disposition of Clemency Petitions. The Attorney General, or designee, will provide a recommendation to the President on each petition for commutation of sentence.

[c. **When a petition for commutation of sentence is granted by the President of the United States, the U.S. Pardon Attorney will forward the original of the signed and sealed warrant of clemency evidencing the President's action to the Warden at the detaining** institution, with a copy to the Director, Bureau of Prisons. The Warden shall deliver the original warrant to the affected inmate, and obtain a signed receipt for return to the U.S. Pardon Attorney. The Warden shall take such action as is indicated in the warrant of clemency.]

The Warden is to forward a copy of the warrant of clemency to the Regional Director.

[(1) If a petition for commutation of sentence is granted, institutional staff shall recalculate the inmate's sentence in accordance with the terms of the commutation order.

(2) If the commutation grants parole eligibility, the inmate is to be placed on the appropriate parole docket.

d. When a petition for commutation of sentence is denied, the U.S. Pardon Attorney ordinarily notifies the Warden, requesting that the Warden notify the inmate of the denial.]

The Warden is to forward a copy of the denial to the Regional Director.

8. **FORMS**. The Case Management Coordinator or Executive Assistant may obtain the necessary forms from the:

> U.S. Pardon Attorney
> 500 First Street NW, 4th Floor
> Washington DC 20530.

These forms shall also be available on BOPDOCS.

/s/
Kathleen Hawk Sawyer
Director

APPENDIX F: CLEMENCY CHECKLIST

CLEMENCY CHECKLIST

Being prepared before and during the filing of your clemency petition is crucial to increasing your likelihood of being granted a commutation of sentence. The checklist below is to give you an idea of actions you need to take and information/documents you will want to obtain or will need when preparing your petition.

Documents and Information that Will Be Needed.

- Social Security Number
- Charges you were convicted of and information pertaining to balance of fine/restitution
- Indictment, Sentencing Transcript, PSR, Judgement of Conviction (relevant information)
- Arrest and conviction records for state and federal (adult and juvenile)
- Case number and date of any published or unpublished decisions on appeal or habeas pertaining to your case.
- Inmate Skills Development Plan Progress Report (Updated)
- Documentation of significant courses, certificates, degrees you have obtained
- Documentation and Information pertaining to serious medical condition you have or family (if this is the basis for your request for clemency or offered as one of the reasons in support)

Things to Do

- Make sure you have no pending litigation in the courts or that there is a process through the courts that is available that could possibly provide you relief.
- Write a list of extraordinary circumstances or reasons that justify a commutation of sentence
- A draft of your life prior to incarceration (family background, education, employment, health issues, addiction/no addiction, abuse, etc.,)
- A draft of your life during incarceration (programs completed, education, work duties, behavior, etc.,)
- A draft of what your life would look like if released (where will you work or what work will you do, where will you live, with whom will you live, car or no car, mentor or support group, etc.)
- List of contacts for support, including people and organization; include phone numbers, addresses, and emails if possible.
- Request to Special Investigative Services (SIS) to determine if you are a Confirmed Gang Member. If you are confirmed but not a gang-member then provide documentation you had this designation removed.
- A picture by yourself and one with family (wife, fiancé, kids,) of the best clarity possible
- Letters of Support from immediate friends, family, and organizations in the community
- Letter from individual of whom you will be staying with when released (if available)
- Letter from employer for whom you will or could work for when released (if known)
- Letter to Sentencing Judge asking for Support
- Letter to Prosecutor asking for Support
- Letter to The President
- Speak with Case Manager and inform them you will be filing a clemency petition soon and ask if there is anything you need to know about before handing them the petition

APPENDIX G: JASON'S MEMORANDUM IN SUPPORT OF PETITION FOR COMMUTATION

1. <u>REASON FOR ADDENDUM TO PETITION FOR COMMUTATION OF SENTENCE</u>

Federal Inmate Jason Hernandez ("Jason"), Federal Number 07031-078, serving a sentence of LIFE WITHOUT PAROLE for violating federal drug laws respectfully asks the Pardon Attorney for the United States to consider the information enclosed in considering to recommend whether said Petition for Commutation of Sentence be granted or denied.

This addendum is necessary due to the space provided in the Petition was insufficient to list all information that need be provided. Furthermore, the addendum contains important information, such as Bureau of Prison Progress Reports, family history and other matters that will expedite and assist this agency in making it's recommendation to the President of the United States.

Respectfully, the following is submitted.

2. <u>FACTS, CIRCUMSTANCES AND REASONS FOR SEEKING COMMUTATION OF SENTENCE</u>

A. <u>THE NATURE AND CIRCUMSTANCES OF THE OFFENSE</u>:

In 1992 Jason, at the early age of 15, began selling marijuana joints and dime bags on the street corners of Eastern McKinney, Texas. At around the age of 17 the amounts of marijuana Jason distributed increased to ounces, quarter-pounds, half-pounds, and ultimately pounds. Because Jason could obtain drugs from Dallas, Texas at discount prices he ended up being a wholesale drug distributor in McKinney of crack cocaine and methamphetamine.

Eventually friends of Jason joined him to assist in his drug dealing. They assisted by either storing, delivering, or picking up narcotics/money for Jason. Jason's drug distribution activities spanned a little over five years and involved a number of people. Nearly all the individuals who bought controlled substances from Jason would purchase amounts of crack cocaine or methamphetamines in amounts ranging between a quarter-ounce to an ounce. As for Jason's character or demeanor during the five year period he distributed drugs there was no evidence that demonstrated or represented to a serious extent that he nor those associated with him engaged in the typical dangers and violence associated with the distribution of narcotics, especially that of crack cocaine (e.g. gang activity, weapons use, turf wars, employment of children, etc.,).

On March 16, 1998, Jason, a little over a month after turning the age of 21, was arrested and placed in federal custody for conspiracy to distribute drugs and for violating other federal drug statutes. Following his arrest Jason sought to enter a guilty plea, but was advised by his attorney ▄▄▄ ▄▄▄ that the only way the government would allow him to plead guilty is if he cooperated. Based on reasons non-related to arrogance or stubborness Jason did not cooperate and proceeded to trial.

On June 4th, 1998, Jason was found guilty.

The Pre-Sentence Report determined that over a five year period Jason distributed 32.5 kilos of crack cocaine, 7 lbs. of methamphetamines, 200 lbs. of marijuana, was the leader organizer of the conspiracy and distributed drugs within 1,000 feet of a school zone. Combined with a Criminal History Category I the Sentencing Guideline range called for Life imprisonment.[1/] At sentencing the now retired United States Senior District Judge Paul Brown stated the

---

[1.] If the amount of crack cocaine attributed to Jason by the Presentence Report were converted to cocaine powder his total base offense level would be reduced from level 43 to level 39. With a Criminal History Category I Jason's imprisonment of LIFE would have been anywhere from 24 to 27 years under the Guidelines.

following:

> "...Well, in response to that last argument, Mr. Hikel, the Congress has been urged to do something about that disparity and various judges, including this judge have urged to do something about it because I think -- I frankly think it's too great a disparity, I mean, insofar as the penalty for crack as opposed to powder."

See U.S. v. Jason Hernandez, 4:98cr14(2) Docket #776 10/02/98. The Sentencing Judge also stated, "Well the Court will not repeat what I had to say with respect to ▬▬▬ [Jason's co-defendant who also received LIFE], but I think a great deal of it applies to Mr. Hernandez. He's even younger than Mr. ▬▬. And it certainly is sad an regrettable that he became involved with drugs at such a young age." When the Sentencing Judge referred to Mr. ▬▬ we was speaking of the following passage:

> "...Well, I certainly take no pleasure in sentencing a 25-year-old man to life imprisonment; you can believe me when I say that. And I have thought about this a good deal...Congress has enacted these laws. They are very punitive, and have determined that punishment should be established in accordance with these Sentencing Guidelines...And I don't have anything, [], to work with insofar as a downward departure..."

See U.S. v. ▬▬▬▬▬, ▬▬▬▬ Docket #____, 10/02/98. Jason was then sentenced to a sentence of life imprisonment in addition to other terms of years all to run concurrent.[2]

B. THE HISTORY AND CHARACTER OF JASON HERNANDEZ

(i) Prior to Incarceration

Jason is a 34-year-old mexican-american who has lived in Mckinney, Texas his entire life. He had the benefit of being raised by both his parents and

---

[2] Jason's drug supplier ▬▬▬▬▬ was also indicted and convicted at trial. The Presentence Report attributed the same amount of controlled substances to ▬▬ as it did Jason. However, being that ▬▬ was attributed 32.5 kilograms of powder cocaine and not crack cocaine he was sentenced to a term of only twelve years.

lived a relatively normal childhood. During his school years he was a consistent A-B Honor Roll Student who was never considered a trouble maker. It was not until after Jason began high school that his life took a drastic turn for the worst; wherein he began associating with the neighborhood drug dealers and, ultimately, became a dealer himself.

Jason does not deny he distributed drugs. See Jason's Letter to President of the United States. He also acknowledges the harm his conduct had on the community as a whole and that he deserves to be imprisoned as a result thereof. Id. As far as drug addiction or alcohol abuse Jason has never suffered from either or. He did, however, drink and smoke marijuana from time to time. See Presentence Report.

Jason's character and current situation is better captured by two highly respected individuals from his community: Former McKinney High School Teacher Charlotte Jaguours and Former McKinney Narcotics Officer ███████. See Exhibit A, Charlotte Jagours Support Letter, and Exhibit B, ███). 3/

As former McKinney High School Teacher Charlotte Jaguors expressed, Jason, with the changes that he has made in his life, is a person that could get other people in the lower-income parts of McKinney, Texas to take steps that would have a positive effect on their lives. Former McKinney Narcotics Officer ███████ comments are more illustrative. This is because Mr. ███████ new Jason throughout the whole period he distributed drugs. In fact, it was Mr. ███████ investigative efforts which basically led to Jason being

---

3/ ███

prosecuted by the federal government and his current incarceration. Nevertheless, despite spending years on ensuring that Jason ended up in prison for his involvement in drugs, even Mr. ▅▅▅▅ would attest that a life sentence without parole is far to severe a punishment for Jason to serve.

(ii) <u>During Incarceration</u>:

Nearly fifteen years of incarceration can negatively impact a man's life in several ways. Thus it is reasonable to question Jason's state of mind, his attitude towards criminal conduct, whether or not he can function in society and, if so, can he obtain gainful employment? In the instant case not only are these concerns nonexistent, there is good reason to believe that not only would Jason be a productive member of society if released, he will thrive if ever given the opportunity.

Despite the very realistic liklihood of never being released from prison Jason has become an extraordinary man since his imprisonment. He has done everything possible to better himself, and others, mentally, emotionally and educationally. From 1999 to 2008 Jason served his sentence at a United States Penitentiary in Beaumont, Texas (Beaumont USP). Unfortunately, during this period Beaumont USP was considered the most violent, drug and gang infested prison in the entire federal system. Nevertheless, Jason did not conform to the behavior of such an environment.

Jason's behavior while at Beaumont USP was remarkable. As the Bureau of Prison's Progress Report details Jason has never received an incident report, tested positive for drug/alcohol usage, or had any connection with the gang activity that is so prevalent in the prison system. See Exhibit C

Progress Report from Beaumont USP; Exhibit D, Bureau of Prison Administrative Response.[4/] The Report from Beaumont further states that Jason "was not considered a management concern", "he maintain[ed] a good rapport with staff and inmates alike", and his work performance was "above average to outstanding." Id. p.1-2. Though programming was limited at Beaumont USP, because of its high security, Jason completed as many classes as he was capable of:

* Micro-Computer Applications (360 clock hours), Lamar State College, Division of Technical Programs;

* Culinary Arts (180 clock hours), Lamar State College, Division of Technical Programs;

* Business Management (360 clock hours), Lamar State College, Division of Technical Programs

* Legal Assistant/Paralegal Program (915 clock hours), Blackstone Career Institute;

* General Equivalence Diploma (G.E.D.); and

* Vocational Training Welding (over 1200 clock hours), obtained at El Reno F.C.I. not Beaumont USP).

See Exhibit C, Beaumont USP Progress Report at p.3; and Exhibit E, Educational Certificates Obtained Throughout Incarceration.

Based on Jason's exemplary behavior at Beaumont USP his custody level was reduced and he was allowed to transfer to a lesser security facility (El Reno FCI) on June of 2008. Upon entering El Reno's Federal Facility Jason continued with his path of rehabilitation and staff at the prison took notice.

4.
    Being that a majority of hispanics in prison are gang-related it is common for the B.O.P. to mistakenly classify mexicans as being a part of a gang. Throughout Jason's inccarceration he has been mistakenly associated with prison gangs on more than one occassion. In each instance, however, Jason proved he had no ties with said gang. In addition, while Jason was at Beaumont USP there was another individual there with the same exact first and last name, shared the same body build and height, who was a gang member, and lived in the same unit with Jason. Unfortunately, these strikingly identical similarities between the two caused much confusion and hardships for Jason with staff and inmates.

-6-

As such, Jason was one of six inmates selected out of the entire prison population by Chief Psychologist Eddie Scott to participate in the program "A Better Path." A program that allowed troubled youth in the community to enter the prison and communicate with the selected inmates about the consequences of living a life of crime, doing/selling drugs, resorting to violence, and the hardships of being in prison. The kids would also be given advice on how to change their lives around. In addition, Jason was selected to serve on El Reno's Prison Suicide Watch Companion Program.

Moreover, with the knowledge Jason has obtained in the law he has went on to assist his fellow inmates in obtaining reduced sentences, dismissal of state charges, parental rights, divorces, etc.,. As well Jason, along with his brother (Stevie Hernandez), are initiating a website designed to make the public and lawmakers aware of the collateral consequences and problems caused by the federal sentencing system, along with suggesting alternatives to mitigate these effects. The site is also designed to educate the youth on the consequences they face if they choose to distribute drugs. See www.crackopenthedoor.com (still under construction).

Jason has matured greatly since his arrest. Indeed, he was never considered a bad kid, just a kid who made bad decisions growing up. But for whatever reasons led Jason towards dealing drugs it appears such reasoning is no longer apart of his mind set.

C. FAMILY TIES AND SUPPORT

If released the home of Jason's Parents would provide an excellent residence for him to make his transition back into society. Mr. and Mrs. Hernandez, who've been married for over 40 years, have been by Jason's side the last past 14½ years of his incarceration; providing attorney fees, money for commissary, assisting in raising his child, and visiting at the prison.

Jason's conduct which led to his imprisonment is not a reflection of the manner in which his Parent's raised him.[5] Mr. and Mrs. Hernandez, age 65 and 64, have been hard workers and devoted christians their entire life. They have never been arrested, let alone a criminal conviction, and are well respected within their community. See Exhibit F, Letters in Support of Mr. and Mrs. Hernandez' Character. Being that Mr. Hernandez is about to retire for the third time, the Hernandez family is financially stable and secure.[6] They currently live in a residential area of McKinney, Texas that is void of violence, gangs and other negative elements that plagued their last residence where Jason was raised. Additionally, the Hernandez' residence has two empty bedrooms where Jason would be able to reside if his sentence was commuted and released from prison.

The Hernandez family is more than capable and willing of providing assistance and a setting that will greatly increase Jason's chances of succeeding on the outside and achieving his goals. This is evidenced in the fact that Stevie Hernandez, Jason's brother and co-defendant, resided with his parents upon being released from federal custody and, fortunately, went on to make great strides for himself and the community as well.[7]

---

[5] When Jason's Parents discovered he was involved in drug dealing he was given an ultimatum; either quit selling or move out the house. Jason young, naive and ignorant, left the house.

[6] Father's Work History: ▓▓▓▓▓▓▓▓▓▓▓▓ (1968 to 1992), ▓▓▓▓▓▓▓▓▓▓▓▓ (1992 to 2002), and ▓▓▓▓▓▓▓▓▓▓▓▓ (2002 to now).

[7] For instance, upon release Stevie Hernandez (Stevie) enrolled into Cosmotology school and graduated therefrom. As well, personnel from the McKinney Police Department requested Stevie to appear at certain functions so that he could lecture the youth about the downfalls of committing

Furthermore, Jason has a 14 year old son named Jason Estevan Hernandez (Estevan), who was only eight months at the time of his arrest. Jason stays in constant contact with him and despite Jason's absence from his life Estevan acknowledges him as his father and cares for him. Being that Estevan is entering his high school years Jason's guidance and support is necessary and vital to his up bringing.[8/]

Fortunately, unlike many prisoners who are released, Jason has a stable home where he can reside, and a family that will assist him in making his transition back into society if released.

D. EMPLOYABLE JOB SKILLS

Since incarceration Jason has acquired an array of skills and training that will help him earn a satisfactory income and living outside of prison. For example, he has obtained college accrediation in culinary arts, business management and micro-computer applications. He also completed Blackstone's Career Institute Paralegal/Legal Assistant Program. And he is currently a few weeks upon completing El Reno's Vocational Training Welding Program, which will provide him with over 1200 hours of training in Shielded Metal Arc Welding, Gas Metal Arc Welding, Oxyacetylene Welding, and blue-print reading.

---

criminal conduct and being in prison; which Stevie did unhesitantingly. Stevie also combined with other individuals, on more than one ocassion, to orchestrate gatherings that provided free haircuts and clothes to the children of Eastern McKinney that were returning back to school.

Because Stevie's conduct after his release was so remarkable the United States Probation Department via ▮▮▮▮▮▮▮ requested a U.S. District Judge to terminate his supervised release. See U.S. v. Stevie Hernandez, 4:98cr14(14) Docket #1220 (4/20/09) and Docket #1271 (4/26/10).

8.

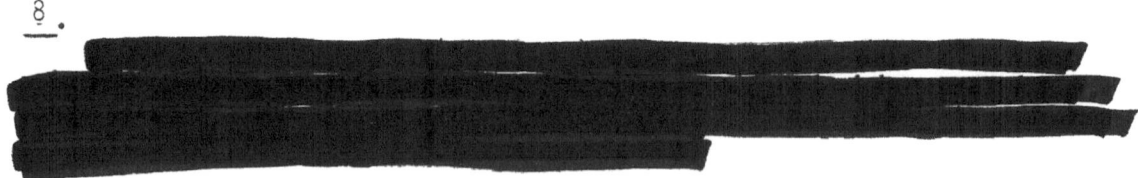

With this job skill, alone, Jason will able to obtain a job at any cite/ business with a starting rate of $24 an hour.⁹/

In all Jason has the skills to make a honest living immediately upon release. But overall he has the drive and determination to succeed and stay out of prison.

E. **CONCLUSION**

Every year over 600,000 inmates are released from prison in the United States. Many of whom, because of no family support, no employable job skills, drug/alcohol addiction, etc., have little to no chance of succeeding on the outside. Admittingly, many inmates do not succeed simply because they choose not to.

Fortunately, none of these concerns are existent with the current Petitioner. In fact, the circumstances surrounding Jason are at such an extraordinary remarkable level it is hard to imagine how he could not succeed. But what makes Jason's situation unique is that in addition to the likelihood

---

9. See www.indeed.com and search national average pay for welders experienced in stick/meg welding capable of reading blueprints.

10.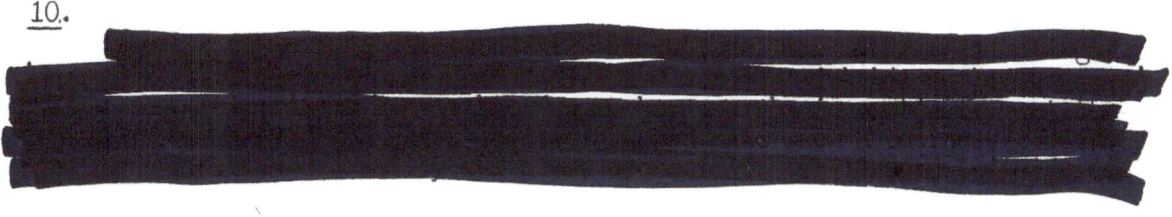

of him succeeding, he also has a desire to right what he has wronged by means of preventing the youths of his community from falling into the many pitfalls that arise while growing up in impoverished neighborhoods. See Exhibit G, Reach for The Stars Mission Statement, (A non-profit organization Jason seeks to initiate fromprison or if released).

There is no question that Jason's past experience provide him with the knowledge of knowing the factors which result in today's youth to use/sell drugs, drop out of school, join gangs, end up in prison, etc., and the insight of knowing the most effective manners to curb such drastic outcomes. There is also no question that Jason, although admittingly in the past not with the best intentions, has the ability to get people to listen to him and believe in what he envisions. But the most important aspect of all is that Jason has exhibited he has changed dramatically from that dumb, misguided, boy who roamed the streets of McKinney, Texas over 15 to 20 years ago.

Jason has many goals in life, which for now can only be viewed as dreams. Jason now respectfully and sincerly asks the Pardon Attorney and the President of the United States to give him a chance to turn those dreams into reality.

WHEREFORE it is requested that Jason Hernandez' federal sentence of LIFE without parole be commuted to a term between 17 to 24 years, with his supervised release extended from 10 years to 20 years, the first two years of which to be served in home confinement under GPS monitoring and any other modifications this agency so desires.[11/]

11.

It is not certain whether the President of the United States has the authority to modify a federal prisoners term of supervised release, and, if not, it could request the district court that sentenced Jason to make such modifications and others. See Title 18 U.S.C. § 3583(e)(2)(statute that allows a district court at any time to extend or add restrictions to a term of supervised release).

APPENDIX H: EVA PALMA'S ANSWER TO QUESTION SEVEN OF PETITION FOR COMMUTATION

Reasons for Seeking Clemency

7. State your reasons for seeking commutation of sentence. If you need more space, you may complete your answer on a separate sheet of paper and attach it to the petition.

(A) NONVIOLENT OFFENSE: Eva does not dispute the seriousness of her Offense and understands collateral consequences drugs have on people and society. It is worth noting, however, there was no testimony or evidence to indicate that Eva partook or was directly responsible for any type of violence. Again, Eva, does not try and suggest that because there was no violence there was nothing wrong with her criminal behavior.

(B) SENTENCED BEFORE BOOKER: Eva was sentenced in 2004 before the Supreme Court ruled Guidelines were unconstitutional. Indeed, because Eva was sentenced to a mandatory life under CCE Booker would be of no benefit. Eva does ask to consider that based on the Guideline Amendment "Reduce By Two" that the threshold amounts stated in 841(a) should be higher than they currently are.

(C) U.S. DISTRICT JUDGE BRUCE D. BLACK DISAGREES WITH EVA'S LIFE SENTENCE: It is noteworthy that U.S. District Judge Black, a fellow judge of Eva's sentencing judge, stated during the sentencing of Loius P. Romero who killed his 71 year old grandmother and burned her body, that it made no sense how she could receive life and Louis Romero no more than 6 and a half years: "By contrast to the relatively short sentence imposed on Romero, Black noted that a fellow federal district judge in New Mexico earlier this week sentenced a 29 year old mother of three, Eva Palma Atencio, to life in prison without parole for being a participant in a marijuana case in which she possed a gun." quoting abqjournal.com "Son Who Murdered His Mother Gets 6 And A Half Years (11/19/04)

(D) EVA HAS BEEN A MODEL INMATE: Despite having no release date Eva has done everything to better herself and others she comes in contact with. She has been a model inmate and has never received an infraction and does everything she is allowed to educate and better herself.

(E) A LIFE SENTENCE DOES NOT PROMOTE REHABILITATION: When a person is sentenced to life without parole in the federal system it severely restricts the access to programs and resources that the prison and society have deemed necessary for rehabilitation. These programs are reserved for those inmates who are subject to release, and rarely, if at all accessible to inmates serving life, like Eva

(F) EVA ASK THAT HER SENTENCE BE COMMUTED TO 30 YEARS RATHER THAN HER HER CURRENT SENTENCE THAT WILL RESULT IN HER DYING IN PRISON: Eva strongly regrets what she did and all the pain she caused her family and others by her actions. She knows she deserves to be punished severely but ask she atleast be given a second chance for her 3 kids.

Petition for Commutation of Sentence

APPENDIX I: EVELYN PAPPA'S ANSWER TO QUESTION SEVEN OF PETITION FOR COMMUTATION

Reasons for Seeking Clemency

7. State your reasons for seeking commutation of sentence. If you need more space, you may complete your answer on a separate sheet of paper and attach it to the petition.

(1) FIRST TIME NONVIOLENT OFFENDER: Evelyn does not dispute the seriousness of the offense and understands the collateral consequences that drugs have on a community. Evelyn would like to point our that she did not partake or was convicted of a violent offense and this is her first conviction.

(2) EVELYN WAS SENTENCED BEFORE BOOKER: Evelyn was sentenced in 1997 before the Guidelines were ruled unconstitutional by the Supreme Court in 2005. Evelyn's life without parole sentences were mandated by the Guidelines not a statute.

(3) EVELYN HAS BEEN A MODEL PRISONER: Evelyn has been in prison since 1997. Since her incarceration she has not recieved an incident report and has lived in the Honor Unit at her prison for 21 years. She also has support letters from staff at the prison praising her for her extraordinary conduct and help for other prisoners.

(4) EVELYN'S HEALTH IS DETERIORATING: Since Evelyn's incarceration she has suffered a stroke (in 2011), tumors on her neck, vaginal tumors, hypothyroidism, and circulatory problems.

(5) EVELYN IS ONE OF FEW FEMALE PRISONERS SERVING LIFE WITHOUT PAROLE FOR A NONVIOLENT OFFENSE: From what information that is available there are around five women serving life without parole for a nonviolent offense in the BOP. The United States is one of few civiliized countries that setences defendant's to lwop for a nonviolent offense.. The commutation of Evelyn's sentence would send a message to other countries lwop should never be a punishment for a woman.

(6) EVELYN HAS BEEN IN PRISON OVER TWENTY-THREE (23) YEARS
Evelyn has been incarcerated for over 23 years. She is currently 57 years old. Evelyn has done wrong. The acknowldges this and deeply regrets for getting involved with her husband and understands the impact on the community and society at large that her conduct and drugs have. She is extremely sorry for what she did and has been trying to make up for it for the past 23 years of incarceration and will continue to do so. She does not blame anyone for her mistakes but herself.

These factors that Evelyn relies upon to demonstrate her sentence should be commuted are further supported by a memorandum and exhibits attached thereto. WHEREFORE IT IS REQUESTED AND PLEADED THAT EVELYN'S SENTENCE OF LIFE BY COMMUTED TO LESS THAN 30 YEARS.

APPENDIX J: CORRESPONDENCE AND EDUCATIONAL COURSES

CORRESPONDENCE AND EDUCATIONAL COURSES

COLLEGE

A large problem for prisoners desiring to further their education is a lack of viable information on what correspondence programs are available to them. After all, American prisoners almost categorically lack access to the internet. As such, they often ask their loved ones and friends to search online for suitable educational offerings. That is where this article comes in.

Below you will find the top five college correspondence programs for prisoners. As a long-time incarcerated student, and holder of a bachelor's degree earned entirely through correspondence education while in prison, I have taken courses from many of these educational providers. These are the college correspondence course providers that I recommend for incarcerated students.

1. Adams State University

Adams State University's Prison College Program is my top pick by far. Regionally accredited by the North Central Association of Colleges and Schools, ASU offers a plethora of certificates, associates and bachelor's degrees, all of which are available entirely through correspondence education. Each course costs around $500 and incarcerated students have 12 months to complete each. Currently certificates are available in paralegal studies and associates and bachelor's degrees are offered in business, business administration, English/liberal arts, history, interdisciplinary studies, political science, and sociology. [Full Disclosure: I received my bachelor's degree from ASU.]

2. Upper Iowa University

Upper Iowa University's Self-Paced Degree Program is a newer player in higher education for prisoners, but they make a bold statement. Regionally accredited by the North Central Association of Colleges and Schools, they offer a large number of certificates, associates and bachelor's degrees. Many of their courses can be completed entirely through the mail. The only draw is that their courses run just shy of $1,000 each. Incarcerated students have six months to complete each course but can request a free six-month extension if needed. Certificates are offered in management and psychology, while associates and bachelor's degrees are available in business, liberal arts, psychology, business administration, management, public administration, and social sciences.

3. Colorado State University at Pueblo

Colorado State University's Distance Education Program is another great option for incarcerated students, though their degree offerings are somewhat limited. Regionally accredited by the North Central Association of Colleges and Schools, they offer bachelor's degrees in social sciences and sociology. Each course runs around $500 and students have six months to complete each. While the offerings aren't as extensive as Adams State University's, Colorado State University is a very well-respected institution of higher education for prisoners.

4. Ohio University

Ohio University's Correctional Education Program is also a great provider of correspondence courses for prisoners. Back in the 1990s, Ohio University was the hottest thing in prison education, but in the past several years they have slimmed down their course offerings. Regionally accredited by the North Central Association of Colleges and Schools, Ohio University offers several associates and bachelor's degrees, though more limited than ASU and CSU. Courses run around $1,000 each and students have eight months to complete each.

5. California Coast University

California Coast University is the wildcard of the batch. Not regionally accredited, which means that their courses might not transfer to other colleges and universities, CCU offers a surprisingly wide range of certificates, associates, bachelors, masters and doctorate degrees through the mail. Courses run around $500 each. While any non-regionally accredited school that offers so many options immediately raises red flags in my mind, California Coast University does appear to be a legitimate university, albeit one with special distance learning focus.

6. Blackstone Paralegal Course

Blackstone's accredited Paralegal Certificate Program enables students to learn about the law and the paralegal field by studying at their own pace and at their facility. It is reasonably priced, can be completed in less than a year and provides information that can be put into practice while incarcerated and once released. No computers, proctors, or facility instructors are required. Soft-covered books and materials are used for ease of entry into most state prisons, federal penitentiaries, county jails, and other institutions. https://blackstone.edu/paralegal-courses-inmate-information/

APPENDIX K: EVA PALMA'S MEMORANDUM IN SUPPORT OF HER PETITION FOR COMMUTATION

EVA PALMA ATENCIO'S MEMORANDUM IN SUPPORT OF HER PETITION TO COMMUTE HER SENTENCE OF LIFE WITHOUT PAROLE

1. **REASON FOR MEMORANDUM**

In 2018, Eva Palma Atencio (Fed No. 21868-051) ("Eva") filed a Petition to Commute her Sentence of Life without Parole for drug-related offenses, which is currently pending before the Pardon Attorney's Office.

In the Petition for Commutation, Eva set forth multiple factors which she believes would support the reduction of her life sentence; however, the petition only briefly touched on the facts and circumstances surrounding each issue. Eva is now in a position to offer facts and information in support of those issues. In addition, other important information and facts have come about that were not available at the time of the filing of the Petition for Commutation.

Therefore, Eva Palma Atencio, Petitioner, asks for the following to be considered in determining whether she should be shown mercy.

2. **PROCEDURAL HISTORY AND BACKGROUND**

On December 2003, a grand jury returned a nine-count indictment against Eva and her husband Edward Atencio for violation of federal drug laws pertaining to marijuana and powder cocaine.

Eva and her husband proceeded to trial and the jury found them guilty on all counts. Eva received life sentences on Counts 1 and 2, 240 months on Counts 3 - 7, and a 60-month sentence on the last Count, all ordered to run concurrently by the district court.

Eva appealed her conviction, and it was affirmed on January 20, 2006. *See U.S. v. Atencio, 435 F.3d 1222 (10th Circuit)*. She then sought a writ of certiorari, which was denied. Thereafter a habeas corpus motion under 28 USC Section 2255 was filed, which was also denied.

A Petition for Commutation was filed and denied in September 2016.

Eva filed another Petition For Commutation in 2018, which is currently pending.

Eva has no pending litigation before any court and there are no changes in laws or remedies that she can pursue to seek relief from the multiple sentences she received, specifically two sentences of life without parole.

Eva currently has an immigration hold on her being she is not a citizen of the United States. If granted clemency Eva would not fight her deportation.

3. <u>**FACTORS IN SUPPORT OF EVA'S REQUEST TO COMMUTE HER SENTENCE OF LIFE WITHOUT PAROLE**</u>

(a) **There Is a National and Global Consensus Against Imprisoning Nonviolent Offenders to Life Without Parole**

The United States is one of the just 20% of countries that issue sentences of life without parole. The vast majority of countries that do allow LWOP have high restrictions on when the sentence can be issued, such as only in cases of murder. *Cruel and Unusual, University of San Francisco School of Law 2012*. In the United States, however, life sentences (or de facto life) can be recommended under the Federal Sentencing Guidelines for non-violent crimes such as drug dealing or even fraud.

A review of the criminal punishments enacted within this country suggests that just two states mandate a sentence of life without parole for certain offenders who have no criminal history and who commit a felony that is not a "crime of violence." However, there are several states that have recidivist statutes that do allow or mandate courts to impose life sentences on defendants for non-violent offenses.

According to the United States Sentencing Commission, "Life imprisonment sentences are rare in the federal criminal justice system. Virtually all offenders convicted of a federal crime are released from prison eventually and return to society or, in the case of illegal aliens, are deported to their country of origin." *Life Sentences in The Federal System, USSC Report 2015*.

Drug trafficking is the most common offense in which a life imprisonment sentence is imposed in the federal system, usually in cases where death or serious bodily injury resulted from the use of the drug, or where the defendant had been convicted previously of a drug trafficking offense. Although many people in the United States continue to serve sentences of life without parole, the federal system and individual states have started to move away from issuing this sentence to nonviolent offenders.

As is the case with imprisonment generally, men comprise the overwhelming majority of people in prison for life: 97% of lifers are men. At the same time, the number of women serving life sentences is rising more quickly than it is for men. The Sentencing Project collected life-imprisonment figures by gender in 2008 and 2016, and found that during this nine-year period the number of women serving life sentences increased by 20% compared to a 15% increase for men. While women represent only 3% of the prisoners sentenced to life imprisonment, they are a growing segment of the lifer population.

Because LWOP forswears altogether the concept of rehabilitation, the penalty rests on a determination that the offender has committed criminal conduct so atrocious that he or she is irredeemable, incapable of rehabilitation, and will be a danger to society for the rest of his or her life. It is a determination that has typically been made by a judge or jury, who can evaluate a sentence based on the individual circumstances.

In Eva's case, on the other hand, the imposition of life without parole was mandated by Congress. Her punishment was implemented during the hysteria surrounding the "War On Drugs" of the 1980s.

(b) Eva's Non-Citizen Status Precluded Her From Being Considered For Clemency Under President Obama's Clemency Initiative

Eva filed a petition for commutation under President Obama's Clemency Initiative, seeking to have her life without parole sentence commuted. Eva's clemency petition was denied.

Unbeknownst to Eva at the time, and to nearly everyone else, prisoners who were non-citizens were not considered as candidates for commutation, even though that was not mentioned as one of the Initiative's criteria. This was a significant criterion, considering the fact that at the time, *"approximately 25 percent of all federal inmates were non-citizens."*

Based on the Inspector General's Office's "Review of the Department's Clemency Initiative" it was learned that the reason for excluding "non-citizens" was because it was *"believed that the [DOJ] should channel its limited resources to inmates who, if granted clemency, would be returning to U.S. communities as opposed to non-citizen inmates, who would instead be immediately deported."*

Despite the exclusion of non-citizens from the Clemency Initiative, the Office of the Pardon Attorney sent a list of 112 non-citizen inmates to the White House for clemency consideration. All were denied. *31 of those non-citizen inmates were serving life sentences. See OIG Report p.32.*

Also, of concern is Latinos made up only 8.7 percent of those granted clemency under the Obama Administration. This was an extremely low percentage considering that 37% of Latinos in federal prison at that time were incarcerated for a drug related offense: 1,716 prisoners granted clemency were incarcerated for a drug offense.

The actual number of Latina women granted clemency is not known, but is estimated to be significantly low, considering that only 6% of those granted clemency were women.

Criminal law makes no distinction between citizens and non-citizens in determining whether to incarcerate. Therefore, this factor should not come into play in determining whether one is entitled to clemency or not. All those who have been subject to the sharp edge of the knife bear the human dignity that merits consideration of forgiveness.

(c) Eva Is a First-Time Nonviolent Offender Who Is Less Likely to Recidivate if Released

In 2017, the United States Sentencing Commission issued its fourth report of an ongoing study of Recidivism. The report found that older offenders who were released from prison were substantially less likely to recidivate, and that those who did recidivate tended to have a less serious recidivism offense. Specifically, among women aged 40-49, like Eva, the reconviction rate was 16.8%.

Age and gender were not the only factors associated with recidivism rates. An offender's Criminal History Category was also closely correlated with recidivism rates. Defendants who were classified as having a CHC of I, who are released in Eva's current age group, have a reconviction rate of 14.0%, far lower than the other Criminal History Categories. Additionally, the higher a Defendant's education level, the lower the likelihood they were to reoffend. For instance, college graduates in Eva's age range have a 12.5% reconviction rate.

When Eva was arrested for the instant offense, she was 29. She is currently 44. She has never been convicted of a violent crime nor has she every committed an violent offense while incarcerated for the past 18 years. As the Memorandum will explain, Eva has taken every opportunity to better herself educationally and spiritually and has sought to help other ladies in the prison do the same.

These factors, in conjunction with Eva's release plan, suggest that she is not only less likely to reoffend, but is also more likely to succeed if released from prison.

4. <u>EVA PALMA ATENCIO THE MOTHER; THE PRISONER; THE PERSON</u>

(a) Eva, Before Prison

Eva is from Parral, Chihuahua in Mexico. Growing up, she suffered extreme abuse from her father. She went back and forth between her grandmother's house and her mother's house. Eva spent most of her time in school while

living with her grandmother. ███████████████████████████████
███████████████ This began when Eva was just five years old.

Eva did not tell the family this had occurred to her until months before she was arrested. She has shared this tragedy with the prison psychologist, in an effort to better deal with the trauma. Eva's experience is tragically common among incarcerated women: 39.9 percent of federally incarcerated women reported suffering prior abuse, including 22.8 percent who were previously sexually abused. *Prior Abuse Reported by Inmates and Probationers, BJS 1999.*

As a teenager Eva graduated from school then enrolled into The Institute of Mexico, where she was certified in accounting and secretarial services. *See Attachment A, Documents Verifying Education Prior To Incarceration*

In 1996 Eva met her husband Edward Atencio (also serving life without parole for same charges) at a McDonald's she was working at in Albuquerque, New Mexico: Eva was age 22, Edward was 37. They were legally married in New Mexico in 1997.

Eva would give birth to three beautiful children (2 live in Mexico and 1 in the U.S.):

- ███████████████████ Ten years old at the time of Eva's arrest; 26 years old now.
- ███████████████████ Five years old at the time of Eva's arrest; 21 years old now.
- ███████████████████ Three years old at the time of Eva's arrest; 19 years old now.

Eva's children have grown up without her being physically there, but she attempts to be the best mother she can through constant phone calls and letters, skype, and she believes she can still be of great support to them in their adulthood. And even though she was not there for their childhood she hopes and prays she can help in the raising of their children when that time comes.

Eva's mother passed away eight years ago. Her father is alive but is severely ill and is expected to pass soon. Her father was abusive, but Eva saw this as a part of growing up in the Mexican culture and never viewed her father as a bad person. Eva has forgiven her father and communicates once a month through phone calls with him.

(b) Eva Has Been a Model Prisoner for The Past 17 Years of Her Incarceration

Eva has been in prison since 2003, serving a sentence of life without parole. This sentence is characterized as being given to individuals who are incorrigible and beyond rehabilitation and is a length of time in prison that would practically drive any person to give up and act out. However, Eva's conduct while in prison is no indication of a person who is incorrigible or a person who has given up and given in to life in prison. In fact, her behavior shows the opposite.

Eva has been in prison nearly 17 years and **she has never received an incident report**. And it would not be a stretch to say she has helped others maintain good behavior or change their behavior from bad to good through her work with the prison Chaplain; where Eva leads the Church Choir and is also a leader for worship services. Most notably, Eva's commitment is shown through her baptism and communion in prison and the numerous courses she has completed that have given her the tools to minister to other women in prison. *See Attachment C, Certificates of Faith Based Courses Eva Has Completed*

Eva's current employment in the prison is as Secretary for the Environmental and Safety Compliance Department: a job given only to those prisoners who are most responsible and trusted. *See Attachment B, Support Letter by BOP Officer John R. Bellhouse*

Eva has made full use of her time, and when she is not working or at church services, she is educating herself by having completed dozens of courses offered at the prison such as forklift license, graphic design, etc. *See BOP Individualized Reentry Plan-Program Review (2019).* Eva has also been recognized by the prison for helping the instructor teach other prisoners. *Id.*

Due to overcrowding at the prison, classes and programs are limited and prisoners who will be released have priority: while prisoners who have extensive sentences (such as Eva) are overlooked. However, as a result of Eva's persistence to educate herself she has been able to participate in many courses.

The most telling of Eva's conduct is illustrated in a support letter by an employee at the prison Eva is incarcerated at: ███

In pertinent part ███████████ states of Eva,

> "In my short time [working] here, I've observed several things about her that I wish to share.....She is very responsible,...her conduct history has been excellent. She is also a woman of deep faith. I ensure that she has the time needed for her religious activities. She has never missed a day at church... She has taken a leadership role within her religious group, the Spanish Protesta Church. She has been the director of the church choir for over 8 years. She serves as a guide for many in her community..... Despite her sentencing, she has unshakeable resolve. It serves as an inspiration to many."

See Attachment B, Support Letter by ████████████████████ The extreme rarity of a Correctional Officer writing a support letter for a prisoner's release speaks to the true change Eva has undertaken.

Eva's conduct the past two decades shows she is not a bad person or one who is motivated by criminal conduct, but rather a person who made very bad decisions in her life when she was younger, some by choice and some by circumstance, but which she fully understands was wrong and which she is terribly sorry for.

(c) Eva's Release Plan

Eva will be deported to Mexico when she is released, which is no detriment to her. She has strong ties with her family in Mexico and communicates with them regularly. Specifically, she is close to her sisters ███████ ███████████████████████████████ If released, she would live with either ███████████████ ███████████

Based on Eva's education and work as a clerk for the prison, if released she would seek employment doing similar work for a faith-based business or a church. Her dream, however, is to ultimately work in ministry and become a Pastor and focus on women who have been abused.

5. CONCLUSION AND PRAYER

In the 1980's the United States was faced with a serious drug epidemic. At that time, we thought the only answer to the problem was to lock people up and throw away the key. Society, judges, Congressmembers, and even Presidents, have learned over time that such policies and practices have not only fueled drug consumption but have also led to the breakdown of families and communities and made a terrible situation worse. As a result, reform is being implemented throughout the criminal justice system on a federal and state level. However, there will be those who will not receive relief though these changes and their only hope will be clemency.

Former Supreme Court Justice Kennedy, in a 2003 speech to the American Bar Association, illustrated the pardon power as one of being extraordinary unique, and a necessity in assuring justice is administered and adjusted over time;

> *A people confident in its laws and institutions should not be ashamed of mercy. The greatest of poets reminds us that mercy is "mightiest in the mightiest. It becomes the throned monarch better than his crown." I hope more lawyers involved in the pardon process will say to Chief Executives,* ***"Mr. President,"*** *or "Your Excellency, the Governor, this young man has not served his full sentence, but he has served long enough.* ***Give him what only you can give him. Give him another chance. Give him a priceless gift. Give him Liberty."***

If the President of The United States, the most powerful man in the world, were to commute Eva's sentence it would send a message to others incarcerated as well as to those who are free that people can change and when they do mercy and forgiveness should be bestowed upon them. **For *"still, the prisoner*** *is a person; still he or she is part of the family of humankind."* Quoting Justice Kennedy, ABA Speech 2003.

WHEREFORE, Eva Palma Atencio, begs the President of the United States to exercise his executive authority and spare her from a sentence that mandates she die in prison and to bestow upon her a second chance at freedom, at life.

APPENDIX L: EVELYN PAPPA'S MEMORANDUM IN SUPPORT OF HER PETITION FOR COMMUTATION

EVELYN BOZON PAPPA'S MEMORANDUM IN SUPPORT OF COMMUTING HER SENTENCE OF LIFE WITHOUT PAROLE

FOR A NONVIOLENT OFFENSE

I. <u>This Memorandum Is Critical To Understanding Evelyn's Plea For Mercy</u>

The following memorandum is being offered in support of Evelyn Bozon Pappa's (Evelyn) request for Commutation of Sentence. The actual application does not provide ample space to present the facts necessary to illustrate that Evelyn has shown that she is worthy of a second chance. In addition, attached are documents and several support letters from prison staff that speak of Evelyn in a very high regard who also are requesting that President Trump show mercy and compassion for Evelyn and release her from prison.

The following is respectfully submitted in support of Evelyn's freedom

II. <u>Facts, Circumstances and Reasons For Granting Evelyn A Commutation of Sentence</u>

(A) <u>Evelyn Is A First-Time Nonviolent Offender</u>

Evelyn, as set forth in her letter to the President, does not dispute her involvement in the drug distribution ring her husband was involved in. Nor does Evelyn downplay the effect that drugs have on a community. She is extremely remorseful for her conduct. Evelyn would ask that consideration be given to the culture and environment she was living in where drugs seemed to be a part of life. She knows, however, this is no excuse for what she did.

(B) <u>Evelyn Would Receive A Lower Punishment If Sentenced Today</u>

At the time of Evelyn's sentencing the Guidelines were mandatory. With an offense level of 43, Criminal History Category One the only applicable punishment was life without parole. In 2005 the Guidelines were ruled unconstitutional by the Supreme Court. Unfortunately for Evelyn the Supreme Court never addressed whether Booker was retroactive or not. However, based on current sentencing practices it is highly unlikely that Evelyn would have received life without parole. In 2014, almost 50% of all individuals sentences in powder cocaine cases were sentenced below the guidelines. In 2015, 71 months was the mean, nationwide, for trafficking offenses. Over 50% of the individuals convicted of drug trafficking were sentenced below the guidelines. 52.7% of all cases received below guideline sentences. In 2015, the Southern District of Florida, over 30% of the individuals sentenced for drug trafficking received Booker below guideline sentences. Sentences imposed regarding trafficking offenses received an average reduction of 35% in their sentences.

(C) <u>Evelyn Has Exhibited Extraordinary Behavior Since Her Incarceration.</u>

Evelyn has been incarcerated nearly 23 years. And it would be natural to assume that this length of incarceration in addition to never having a release date would more likely promote disobedience than obedience to rules of the prison. However, despite the very realistic likelihood of never being released Evelyn has used her situation to become an extraordinary person. She has done everything possible to better herself mentally, physically, emotionally, educationally, and spiritually.

Almost immediately upon her arrival at the federal prison in Tallahassee she was placed in what is called THE HONOR UNIT. Which is for selected prisoners who

who have clear conduct: she has 21 years leaving in the honor unit.

Evelyn has completed dozen of classes including obtaining her GED, High School Diploma, Religious Studies, and Women's Empowerment.

During her entire 23 years of incarceration she has never received a disciplinary report. She has served as a role model for younger and new prisoners coming into the system.

Evelyn was worked for several years at the Chapel in the prison as a librarian and orderly. Evelyn was involved in the spanish general worship and English general Christian worship services. Evelyn also served on the translation ministry team. Evelyn was responsible for the translation of the chaplains sermon from English to Spanish. She participates in various christian workshops, biblical studies and special events.. She is a teacher for the Religious Services reentry faith based classes that equips inmates with skills that will enable them to transition back to their community. Evelyn assisted the Chaplain with assembling a Spanish curriculum for each of the nine Spanish reentry faith based classes, and also participated in the general Christian leadership team, teaching ministry and disciple ministry team See Attachment, A-1. Letter From Bureau of Prisons

Indeed, Evelyn's behavior on paper looks remarkable especially considering behaving in such an impeccable manner can not earn her parole or early release.

However, after being in prison so long many would ask whether a person can function and adapt to society? How is her state of mind? Her views towards law enforcement? Is she filled with rage, hate, mentally stable?

The extraordinary thing about Evelyn is that not only are these questions not a concern, she has become a person of the highest character and integrity not only of that of a person that is incarcerated but even free. All which can be verified by former prison employees:

- " As her pastor, I am in the unique position to have observed her spiritual and emotional growth. I have been a Chaplain for twenty-five years. I have studied criminal behavior, and fairly knowledgeable of criminal thinking. What I have observed about Ms. Bozon, is that she is sincere about he faith in the Lord Jesus and has made tremendous progress in her spiritual transformation. I believe that she should be given a second chance in society. She has taken every effort to learn from her past by participating and teaching classes that has brought about change in her life." See Attachment, A-1: Letter to President Trump by ▓▓▓▓▓▓▓▓ Retired Federal Bureau of Prisons Supervisory Chaplain from 2007-2014

- "Ms Bozon immediately struck me as a strong maternal leader of a family. It was obvious that numerous inmates relied on her advice and guidance while dealing with the often difficult burdens of incarceration. She impressed me with the ways in which she balanced her duties and yet still had time to care for the needs of others. I was also surprised at her avoidance of condemning the system and leaders for the situation she was in. I'm sure that deep in her heart she had resentments, but she was enough of a realist to know that she had to make the best of the situation, and to help others do the same. During those five years many changes occurred, yet she still retained a level of humility and respect which I have rarely observed in my life." See Attachment A-2, Letter to President Trump by ▓▓▓▓▓▓▓▓ Military Veteran and Twenty Year Federal Law Enforcement Officer.

- "I have known Ms. Bozon Pappa for approximately 12 years while at tallahassee and have observed the following: Ms. Bozon Pappa is a conscientious and disciplined person who appears to do the right thing; she effectively communicates with both staff and inmates; she is consistent, dependable, and committed in carrying out her day to day activities in the unit and at her job as a library clerk in the Chapel; extremely cooperative when sanitation tasks have to be completed in the unit; she has established short and long term goals during her incarceration and upon her release from prison; she displays a high degree of emotional maturity; and appears to cope effectively with pressure and tensions. . See Attachment A-3, Letter To President Trump by Bureau of Prisons ███ at Tallahassee, Florida.

It is extremely rare to have prison staff write a letter of recommendation to a President asking for the release of a prisoner. *Amazingly, Evelyn has had a total of 8 prison staff members (some retired some currently working) ask this President to release her.* See Attachment A-4, Letter To President Trump by ███ FCI Tallahassee (*"I will say with confidence and conviction, that she epitomizes true change…."*) See Attachment A-5, Letter to President by ███ Specialist at FCI Tallahassee: See Attachment A-6, Letter To President by Supervisory ███ FCI Tallahassee (*"She serves as a suicide companion, a position of trust where she monitors inmates who were placed on suicide watch"*): See Attachment A-7, Letter to President Trump by ███ at FCI Tallahassee: See Attachment A-8, Letter To President Trump by ███ at FCI Tallahassee (*"Through her experience she has been able to help younger inmates…"*).

As noted by these Evelyn has not only changed her life around but she has also helped women in prison do the same. In fact, this petition or campaign rather would not be possible had it not been for Damaris Ramos who was formerly incarcerated with Evelyn: who owes her current goodwill and fortune to the mentoring of Evelyn while she was in prison with her. See Attachment C, Letter From Damaris Ramos To President.

If there is anything that prison shows it is the true character of a person. If there is a bad bone in a person's body it will be revealed: especially if that person is in prison for decades with a sentence that amounts to the death penalty. The statements of these former and current federal employees clearly show that Evelyn was not a bad person just a person who made bad choices over 24 years ago. One of those choices, though not based on her discretion, is that of the relationship with her husband ███

(D) <u>Evelyn Experienced Abuse As A Kid, Teenager And As a Wife: Known To The Sentencing Judge But Could Not Be Considered Under The Guidelines.</u>

Evelyn married ███ when she was fourteen and he was eighteen. Twenty years later, Evelyn was convicted, after trial, of participation in a cocaine trafficking scheme controlled by her husband, who though indicted, was never actively prosecuted. Evelyn, who did not testify at trial, argued she was subjected to extreme domestic abuse at the hands of her husband. Through cross-examination of the government's witnesses and proffers made outside the presence of the jury, Evelyn attempted to demonstrate her horrific life experience - sexual molestation by a family friend at age eleven, the seduction by ▆▆▆▆▆▆▆ when she was fourteen, forced marriage resulting from mistaken belief she was pregnant, followed by years of physical abuse.

Ms. Bozon Pappa believing she was unclean was forced to marry a violent man who used her at will. The psychological report by the defense expert details the extent of the abuse and the impact on Ms. Bozon Pappa. The evaluation occurring over multiple dates in 1995, details Ms. Bozon Pappa's constant fear. According to the report, Bozon Pappa grew up a religious female in a male dominated culture and was a child when she married. Subjected to the will of the man who was dominant physically, as well as financially, Ms. Bozon Pappa was repeatedly raped – she "had to be available…sexually at any time". She was physically beaten, threatened and alienated from the world. Her world was subjected to his will. When individuals were arrested, the control continued. Ms. Bozon Pappa went to the police, while her husband, the most culpable individual, fled to Columbia taking Ms. Bozon Pappa's children with him. Expert testimony in domestic violence would explain the subservience of Ms. Bozon Pappa, and her mental state.

Ms. Bozon Pappa presented no evidence at the sentencing in 1997, relying instead on evidence heard by the court at trial and argument. The facts stated above, even if it had been presented at sentencing, was irrelevant, under the then, mandatory guidelines mandated life in prison.

Today, the context of the relationship would be considered. Ms. Bozon Pappa grew up a religious female in a male dominated culture was a child when she married. She was subject to her husband's will. He was dominant physically, as well as financially. When individuals were arrested, the control continued, Ms. Bozon Pappa went to the police, while he fled to Columbia taking her children with him. Today, the testimony of the expert in domestic violence would explain the subservience of Ms. Bozon Pappa.

(E) Evelyn Has A Family In Columbia That Will Ensure Her Success When Freed

Evelyn's husband, ▆▆▆▆▆▆▆▆▆▆▆ is no longer a threat to Evelyn or anyone else. ▆▆▆▆▆▆▆▆▆▆▆▆▆▆▆ The connections that Evelyn does have left are strong and can't be broken. Which are her mother and 3 daughters and 1 son:

- ▇▇▇▇▇▇▇▇▇▇▇▇ (first born), age 40, married with 3 kids; Graduate of San Martin University with a Degree in Medicine. She know works at ▇▇▇▇▇▇▇▇▇▇▇▇

- ▇▇▇▇▇▇▇▇▇▇▇▇ (second born), age 39, married with 1 kid, Graduate of Autonoma del Caribe University with a Degree in Architecture. He is now an independent contractor doing work as an architect.

- ▇▇▇▇▇▇▇▇▇▇▇▇ (third born), age 37, with 2 kids; a Graduate of Autonoma del Caribe University with a Degree in Fashion Designer and works as independent contractor as a clothing designer.

- ▇▇▇▇▇▇▇▇▇▇▇▇ (fourth) age 34, 1 kid; Studied 6th Semester at Del Norte University with a Degree in International affairs and works at ▇▇▇▇▇▇▇▇▇▇▇▇

There is nothing more that Evelyn's kids would want than to see her free, to be able to hold her again, to be a family again, and they will do everything they can to make sure she is independent and they have the means to do so and they want to more than anything in the world. See Attachment B, Letters From Evelyn's Children To President Trump.

Fortunately, and amazingly, Evelyn's mother Gloria Pappa, who is 95 years old, would truly consider it a miracle to see her daughter free and for the first time in over twenty-four years. See Attachment E, Photographs of Evelyn's Family.

Unfortunately, Evelyn's mother is not in the best of health and nor is her's. Evelyn has suffered a stroke, had tumors on her neck, vaginal tumors, hypothyroidism, and circulatory problems.

(F) <u>Evelyn Is One Of Only A Few Ladies In The United States Serving Life Without Parole For A Nonviolent Drug Offense.and One of The Longest Imprisoned Ladies For A Non-Violent Crime (24 years)</u>

The United States is one of very few countries (many third world) that sentence people to life without parole for nonviolent drug crimes. There are currently over 3,000 federal prisoners serving lwop for a nonviolent crime in the federal system. From what research shows nor more than five of those are women.

In the height of the War On Drugs in the 1990's many believed severe punishments were the solution for battling against drug offenders. But as justice Kennedy noted in Graham v. Florida, where **the Supreme Court held that the Eighth Amendment Cruel and Unusual Punishments Clause does not permit a juvenile** offender to be sentenced to life in prison without parole for a non-homicidal crime:

> "Society changes, knowledge accumulates, we learn, sometimes from our mistakes, punishments that did not seem cruel and unusual at one time, may, in light of reason and experience, be found cruel and unusual at a later."

Even if Evelyn's life sentence was considered appropriate at the time, experience, wisdom and most important the person Evelyn has shown who she truly is in prison clearly illustrates it is not appropriate now. The commutation of Evelyn's sentence would make a statement to this country and others that life without parole should not be the only available option for a woman that commits a nonviolent offense.

CONCLUSION

Evelyn has suffered the last 23 years she has been in prison. But the reality is she has suffered her entire life. But not all is lost, or can be lost. Her mother who is 97 is still alive. She has three daughters and 1 son, who have defied the odds and have become individuals who are successful, independent, and who still greatly love their mother. The reality is that if the President does not use his executive power to commute the sentence of Evelyn she will more than likely die in prison.

Evelyn has spent 23 years in prison. Indeed, Evelyn's freedom would be a huge lose to the women at the prison she is at for they rely on her knowledge, care and love for them when they are in need, when they are in times of crisis. But it is time now for Evelyn to start doing so for her own children.

Please President Trump, release Evelyn who no doubt will make this world a better place to live.

Respectfully Submitted this _____ day of _____, 2018

x._____
Evelyn Cecilia Bozon Pappa

Federal Number #48576-004

FCI Tallahassee

501 Capital Circle NE

Tallahassee, Florida 32301

APPENDIX M: LETTER TO PRESIDENT BY EVA PALMA'S DAUGHTER

July 10, 2018

Mr. President Donald Trump
The White House
1600 Pennsylvania Avenue NW
Washington, DC 20500

It is my pleasure to attempt to write this letter to let you know about 2 people that are very important in my life, my mother Eva Atencio Palma and Edward Atencio. Both have been in prison the past 15 years. They were arrested for a non-violent drug crime and sentenced to life in prison without the possibility of parole.

We were separated from our parents at a very young age. Life for my brothers and sisters and for me has not been easy because we have had to live apart from our parents and we have missed them very much. Since I was a little girl, I have dreamed of them being by our side and able to spend a day at the park, a birthday next to them. It is beautiful when your mother and father go together to a school conference to see their child succeed. I only remember how my friends' parents would go to those conferences and in our case, our grandparents were the ones who were in charge of us. Even though they demonstrated their love and support, it was not the same. This destroyed me.

The only memory I have of my parents is the way they were arrested, it was very traumatic and difficult for me to forget how a police officer held my mother down on the floor and how hard he hit her. Those are memories that stay with you for life. In that instant, our life changed forever, to have everything one second and then in an instant, lose it all. I now know that money does not buy everything in this world, it does not buy a family, having your siblings, your parents together it is something I was not able to have as a child. I ask God for a miracle to demonstrate to them how much I have missed them, hug them and never let them go and tell them I love you mom, I love you dad.

And now that I am a mother, I know how much we can love our children. I have a three year old daughter named Sofia who I adore with all of my soul. I give her all of the love that I could never get and I know that it is never too late to enjoy my parents. But my father has a heart illness and my mother's hair is falling out and she is being treated for anemia. I am very worried about her well-being and not being able to take care of my parents. I worry about them dying in prison, I think there are no words to describe that.

However, I continue living with the hope that my parents are set free. I would be immensely happy to see them enter through the door of my house, and I know my family would feel the same as I do.

With all due respect thank you for reading this letter and may God bless you.

Sincerely,

APPENDIX N: LETTER TO PRESIDENT BY DAVID BARREN'S SON

President Barack Obama
The White House
1600 Pennsylvania Avenue
Washington, D.C. 20500

REF. FEDERAL INMATE DAVID MORRIS BARREN # 09803-068

April 29, 2016

Dear Mr. President:

I am Seaman Andre Barren of the United States Navy. I am very respectfully requesting that you use your power of executive clemency to pardon my father, David Barren. I am currently in the second year of a six year contract for the United States Navy. I am attending the Defense Language Institute in Monterey, California and am currently in my final week of the 47 week Hebrew course here. In this course I have become a fluent Hebrew speaker, listener and reader, with the intentions of serving my country. As you may know of the program here, it is very demanding and takes a special person to attend this school. My father is the person that instilled the intelligence and drive into me so that I may be able to serve my country in this way. I believe in second chances, and I also believe that as a service member it is our duty to look out for our own.

As a child growing up my Father was my hero, and still is. He gave me the wisdom and self-respect that is necessary to be a man in this world. Every day I strive to be as strong as my father. When I was 14 years old as a freshman in high school my father was incarcerated and it flipped my world upside down. I went from living in a home in Houston, Texas to a 2 Bedroom shotgun home in the remnants of Hurricane Katrina in the 8th Ward of New Orleans, without my father to leans on. I all of a sudden had to take all of the strength and wisdom that my Father had instilled in me and apply it to my life at that moment as a 14 year old young man. I did that and although I may have had some downfalls, my father always encouraged me and told me to continue to strive and be the best man that I could be despite his situation.

And so, I am here standing to graduate from my language school in the next two weeks with High Honors in the Hebrew language respectfully requesting from the highest ranking man in my chain of command to make the biggest change in my life of the last 8 years, and that is to return my father home. He deserves a second chance as well as me and my siblings. He has not spent these last 8 years of prison alone, he has done it with his family as well. When he received his sentence of life plus 20 years for a non-violent crime, we did also. Now I am respectfully requesting from you, Mr. President, that you use your power of executive clemency to pardon my father, David Barren, and return him home.

Very Respectfully,

SN Andre Barren

APPENDIX O: LETTER TO PRESIDENT BY DAVID BARREN'S MOTHER

Dorothy Barren

My name is Dorothy Barren I am the mother of David Morris Barren. David is the third child out of five children between my husband and me. My son has always been a very respectful and valued son. As a child growing into a man, I have never had any trouble with him. He went to school regularly, having perfect attendance, and utilizing his time wisely. After graduating from high school, David chose to take on a trade as a draftsman, and eventually found employment with GNC. Wanting to strive for more opportunity, David moved on to an Architectural Firm in Maryland. While in Maryland, David married and within that union gave me four beautiful grandchildren. Though David divorced, he decided to take on the ongoing responsibility of raising his children. Because David was always and is still to this day, thoughtful, hardworking, and selfless, I felt obligated to take on any necessary duties to assist him with raising my grandchildren. Often times, David had to work late, going on summer vacations, and going to school functions with him, helped David shape who my grandchildren are today. In fact, because of David's morals, values and beliefs that I have instilled within all of my children, they are living very productive lives. Two are in college, one is in the Navy, and the one is currently working, taking an absence from school with the intentions of returning.

My other children, who are David's 4 other siblings have been affected by David's incarceration though, they still maintain productive lives as well. Ironically, my youngest son is a lawyer who currently works for the department of education, my youngest daughter has her own consulting business, my second daughter holds two degrees in Business, and has been employed by PPG for 35 years, and my oldest daughter, is a retiree from Verizon, and has taken on a second career opening several Spa Salons with her husband. Though David has missed many celebrations and milestones, my children continue to be very active in David's life, assuring the closeness and bonds they have maintained since they have come into this world.

As a part of instilling morals, values, and beliefs, religion was also a staple of my family. David attended church regularly, and still maintains a strong religious faith. I firmly believe because of his strong faith system, he remains hopeful and prayerful to this very day. Often times when my husband and I go and visit David, he speaks about his faith and how it has carried him these past 8 years. As, you know David is serving a Life sentence, which I never knew could happen to someone who has never murdered anyone, been to prison before, and holds no threat to society. I marvel of his strength and courage, and the fact that he maintains immaculate conduct while incarcerated. This truly demonstrates that no one is perfect, and hopefully my son will be able to show society the morals, values, and beliefs that shaped him prior to his setback as he often speaks of his regret for selling drugs and putting his family through the anguish.

If David is released, I would love for him to be released to my home, or his sister's home, who also resides in Pittsburgh. My husband and I have two vehicles that David could certainly drive upon receiving his driving credentials. As a supportive family, David has no worries as far as coming home to a home where he can make a good transition after being away for so long.

I am 79 years old and my husband is 81 years old, we visit our son every Sunday unless the weather permits us to do otherwise, fortunately, my husband and I can still live on our own, but my biggest wish is for President Obama to commute our son's sentence so that I can spend my last golden years or days with him. Please have mercy on my son as he can still give back to society in the most productive way.

God Bless You,

Dorothy Barren

Dorothy Barren

APPENDIX P: LETTER TO PRESIDENT BY CHURCH OFFICIAL FOR DAVID BARREN

This is the
Church of the Living God
The Pillar and Ground of the Truth
(1Tim 3:15)

President Barack Obama
The White House
1600 Pennsylvania Avenue
Washington, D.C. 20500

RE: FEDERAL INMATE DAVID MORRIS BARREN # 09803-068

April 29, 2016

Dear Mr. President:

I am writing on behalf of David Morris Barren. I am humbly requesting that you exercise your power of executive clemency to commute David Morris Barren's sentence to time-served. I honestly believe a commutation of David's sentence would be in the best interest of our society, justice, and last but not least, the family members, friends, and loved ones who also continue to suffer each day that David continues to be incarcerated. David Barren is currently serving his 8th year of a life sentence plus 20 years for a non-violent drug offense that he regrets based on the teachings of his faith, mind, and soul.

I have known David since we were 10 years old and during the time I have always known David to be respectful, nice, caring, honest, and a very hard worker. In fact, I was rather shocked to learn of his incarceration due to the way David and I were raised. Being in the Hebrew faith, we were taught to be respectful, caring, morally bound, and to obey the laws of the land to the best of our ability. As a Minister of our faith, and knowing David, he lost track of some of the teachings to place him in his current state. Through these trials, because these are simply trials, in which he may reflect back to his teachings to endure these trials that I am as humbled as the Minister asking to find him worthy of a second chance to share this experience to assist others in the community. Our community is deteriorating in many areas, and one being faith. David can greatly impact our community. Our youth today, needs to see a person who has made a tremendous mistake, speak and walk the faith to keep the next generation from making the same mistake.

I would really like to see David home from this abhorrent sentence to assist in our ministry and help better our community. The people of color in the City of Pittsburgh is suffering from wounds of oppression and a person such as David, can help stop the bleeding.

Mr. President, I truly hope you find David a worthy candidate to commute his sentence, at 51 years of age, possesses no threat to society, please find compassion, to release David, who is serving the rest of life in prison for a non-violent drug offense.

God Bless You,

Apostle David White

Shalom, Apostle David White

325 S. Second Street, Duquesne, PA 15110

APPENDIX Q: LETTER TO PRESIDENT BY COMMUNITY MEMBER FOR DAVID BARREN

Pittsburgh Faison K-5

7430 Tioga Street | Pittsburgh, PA 15208
Phone: 412-247-0305 | Fax: 412-247-0105
www.pps.k12.pa.us/faison

Dr. Russell Paterson, Principal
Kira Henderson, Assistant Principal

President Barack Obama
The White House
1600 Pennsylvania Avenue
Washington, D.C. 20500

RE: FEDERAL INMATE DAVID MORRIS BARREN # 09803-068

Dear Mr. President:

I am writing in support of David Morris Barren's clemency petition. I humbly request that you grant David's request for commutation. David is currently serving his 8th year of a life sentence plus 20 years for a non-violent drug offense that he humbly regrets.

I learned of David's sentence through his family. As a Principal in the very community David grew up in and also being a product of a community Washington D.C. very similar to the community, I clearly understand how one can be succumbed to selling drugs to merely stay above water, though I am also aware how lucky and fortunate I am to steer the children of the Homewood Community to choose a different path not so destructive as selling drugs. Because of the Homewood Community being very small, I have learned a lot about the Barren Family; being hard workers, morally bound, and having a strong religious faith. In fact, David has an aunt who was once my Secretary that took pride in her work and ran the school office like a fine tuned clock! I have also heard repetitive sentiments about David as well, i.e. hard worker, humble, helpful, considerate, which leaves me to believe, he made a huge mistake and deserves a second chance at life.

I believe David would be a valuable asset to our community due to his experience of being incarcerated, finishing a paralegal program while there, and being able share with our youth the cons of selling drugs deterring the next generation of making such a mistake. I would welcome David to speak to our youth if he is given commutation which I am hoping he receives Mr. President. As I often tell my students, "It's okay to make a mistake, but make sure you have learned something from the mistake!" I honestly believe David has definitely learned a lot from this experience.

In conclusion, I hope you give strong consideration to David's clemency petition and find him worthy of compassion, and have mercy on David. He is still young enough to set a great impact on our community, as we need him to do so.

Sincerely,

Dr. Russell Patterson, Ph.D.

Our Kids. Our Neighborhood. Our Faison.

We are an equal rights and opportunity school district. | Parent Hotline: 412-622-7920 | www.pps.k12.pa.us

APPENDIX R: LETTER TO GOVERNOR BY HOMEBOY IND. FOR DAVID DIAZ

Board of Directors

John Brady, Chair
Taylor Adams
Javier Angulo
Sean Arian
Joe Argilagos
Gregory Boyle
James Burk
Rosa Campos-Ibarra
Alex Chaves, Sr.
Rick Creed
Fr. Allan Deck., SJ
Renee Delphin-Rodriguez
Oscar Gonzalez
J. Michael Hennigan
Bruce Karatz
Pernille Lopez
Christine Lynch
Mercedes Martinez
O'Malley Miller
J. Mario Molina, MD
Ashley Palmer
Viktor Rzeteljski
Alan Smolinisky
Rob Smith III
Elizabeth Stephenson
Carlos Vasquez
Chris Weitz

January 18, 2017

To Whom It May Concern:

I write to you on behalf of David Diaz #P61959, who is scheduled to appear before you soon. I have known David through, my capacity as Executive Director of Homeboy Industries, a non-profit organization that provides hope, job training and support for previously incarcerated and formerly gang-involved men and women, allowing them to redirect their lives and become contributing members of the community.

Upon David's release I am committed to assist by providing him with mentoring and counseling services, in addition to assisting him with locating employment. Our free post release services will aid David in his transition to life on the outside. They include: tattoo removal, employment services, twelve step meetings (AA/NA/CGA), GED tutoring, case management, mental health counseling, legal services solar panel installation training and more.

David can also receive services such as: 1) obtaining his Social Security card, Driver's License or California ID; 2) creating a resume, learning interview techniques, building job skills; 3) obtaining his GED through prep classes and one on one tutoring; 4) learning life skills, anger management, parenting, Building Healthy Relationships, interpersonal communication, leadership, Alternative To Violence, etc.

It is my sincerest hope that you will consider the above as you review David's suitability for release. I greatly appreciate your attention to this letter.

Sincerely,

Fr. Gregory J. Boyle, S.J.
Fr. Gregory J. Boyle, S.J.
Founder/Executive Director

Hope has an address
130 West Bruno Street, Los Angeles, California 90012 • 323.526.1254 • homeboyindustries.org

APPENDIX S: LETTER TO SENTENCING JUDGE BY JASON

7008 0150 0001 6760 0575

UNITED STATES DISTRICT COURT
ATTN: UNITED STATES DISTRICT JUDGE PAUL E. BROWN (RETIRED)
101 E. Pecan St., Suite 112
Sherman, Texas 75090

RE: IN THE MATTER OF U.S. V. JASON HERNANDEZ, Case No.498cr14(2)

TO THE HONORABLE SENIOR UNITED STATES DISTRICT JUDGE PAUL BROWN:

My name is Jason Hernandez. I'm not sure if you exactly remember who I am, but in 1998 I was a Defendant in your court whom you tried and sentenced to LIFE imprisonment.

The main factor that resulted in me receiving LIFE imprisonment was the fact that my conspiracy involved crack cocaine. At my sentencing you stated that the penalty for crack as opposed to cocaine was "too great a disparity" and that you had personally asked Congress to do something about it. You further stated, by referencing to statements you made at another co-defendant's sentencing (who also received LIFE) that you took "no pleasure" in sentencing me to LIFE imprisonment. But that under the Sentencing Guidelines you were bound to impose such a sentence. See Attachment C.

Recently, the Sentencing Commission amended the puishment range as it relates to crack cocaine. However, the Commission and the Supreme Court have both acknowledged that this amendment is "only...a partial remedy" and have instructed Congress to do more. Based on this minor adjustment by the Commission the amendment had no impact on my sentence.

After eleven years I have exhausted all my appeals and habeas proceedings--to no avail. Now that I have no available remedy to obtain a sentence reduction I am going to ask the President of the United States to commute my sentence to twenty years. It is a long shot, and indeed my only shot, but I have everything to gain and nothing to lose by trying.

Which dictates the purpose behind this letter. The reason I have written you is because I am in need of knowing would you be willing to write a letter to the President, which would be attached to my commutation request, stating that the LIFE sentence I received does not promote respect for the law and it is greater than necessary to accomplish the goals for sentencing in this case. See Attachment F.

I'm not sure if you still feel the same way today as you did the day you sentenced me. Since then you may have encountered situations which may have led you to believe that someone as myself deserves to be in prison for the rest of my life.

I realize I deserve to be in prison for all the wrong and harm I caused on people and the community of McKinney. How long do I deserve to be incarcerated? I am in no position to say. I can say this Mr. Brown; I am truly a changed man from the boy that stood before you eleven years ago. And if I was given another chance at life I would not let you down, my parents, child, or society. I would do everything in my power to right all the wrong I have done and try to assure no one else made the same mistakes I did. Attachment D

Please do not come under the impression that only after serving a substantial amount of time, with no end in sight, that I am finally accepting responsiblity and remorse for my unlawful actions. I was willing to plead guilty immediately after my arrest. However, the Government would not allow me to unless I cooperated.

I have enclosed several documents which I hope demonstrate that I was not a bad kid, but just a kid who made bad decisions. I will not waste anymore of your time Mr. Brown, for I am sure you retired so you wouldn't have to deal with situations like this. Attachment A, B, and E

If you do wish to contact me to obtain any information pertaining to my incarceration or anything else you wish to know please contact my parents at the address below.

I thank you for your time in this matter.

Sincerly,

Jason Hernandez

Parent's Address and Phone No.

APPENDIX T: LETTER TO INVESTIGATING NARCOTICS OFFICER BY JASON

July 3th, 2010

Dear Mr. █████████

....writing this letter ███ nothing but memories of my past flash through my head. Still trying to figure out how can a person...a kid at that.... cause so much pain and destruction; and in the same breath trying to figure out how can I make right all that I have wronged.

....time after time i am asked the question "If you could go back would you have cooperated?" And I respond, "Well not cooperating wasn't my mistake. My mistake was selling drugs."

I don't know ███, maybe because I was stupid, young or just didn't want to acknowledge it but i thought when I was selling drugs I was actually doing something honorable, something to be proud of. I thought because of me the East Side streets of McKinney were better, my friends were better off. To me selling drugs wasn't a crime like murder, rape, or child abuse. Now I realize i was worse than all of them. Here I am selling drugs in the community I was born and raised i selling drugs to people I grew up with, most of whom were either friends or family. Everybody I came in contact with I was destroying in one way or another.

And not just those who used them, but also to their families who had to suffer through the pain of having a loved one as an addict. A pain I knew first hand. And also to the people who I encouraged to sell drugs that ended up losing years and decades of their lives in prison, which resulted in someone having to live without a husband, son, brother, and/or father.

Stevie tells me you feel bad about what happened to me/us, and that you feel you may have contributed to it. As for the grief, that is a personal feeling that is uncontrollable. As for feeling you may have contributed to the events that came to pass after my arrest, that is nothing you should feel came at your hand. If anyone feels grief about that it is me, and believe there is not a day that goes by that i don't acknowledge that had I not have been so arrogant and dumb my friends wouldn't have gone to prison, and my brother would still be alive.

I could never understand why you were so gung ho about getting drugs off the street, but i guess that being from ████████ you knew first hand the impact drugs could have on a community if not prevented. You were doing what was necessary. Having become a father and being what I have been through I now see exactly where you were coming from.

You might not believe me when I say this but I wish there were hundreds of ████████████, cause if that were the case I know my boy would be in a safer environment, McKinney would be a safer environment.

I don't harbor any ill feelings towards you ▓▓▓. In fact, I think because of you I still have a chance to make something of myself. Had you not stopped me I am more than sure I would have dug myself into a hole were most assurelly I wouldn't have been able to get out of.

Stevie has informed me that you are more than willing to assist me in obtaining a sentence reduction. I'm grateful. I know you are not on street time, and nor am I, but I give you my word that your assistance in this matter will not be in vain. I have dreams ▓▓▓ big dreams. And not just dreams of being free but dreams of being someone who's going to make a difference in this world. You might think I am crazy when I say this but to speak of my goals as dreams doesn't do them justice, because I can see everything it is that I want to accomplish and how I am going to accomplish it as clear as day. As if its a car that I assembled out there just waiting to be set in motion.

I hope that if you have had any doubt of assisting me or concerns of my state of mind after being imprisoned for over over twelve years, after reading this letter and the attachments your doubts or concerns are no more.

I thank you for allowing me the time to set forth my position.

Sincerly,

Jason Hernandez #07031-078
F.C.I. El Reno
Post Office Box 1500
El Reno, OK. 73036

---

* If you choose to help me the following is what I will need:

(1) Well as Stevie told you I will be seeking a sentence commutation from the President of the United States. It is a long shot, but I have everything to gain and nothing to lose by trying. As well there is a buzz that the President will exercise his power to commute sentences more freely than past Presidents, especially in cases involving crack cocaine. A letter to the President should contain.

    (a) your job title and the period you worked for the McKinney Police Department;

    (b) any current community programs you are currently invovled in;

    (c) the role you played in my investigation;

APPENDIX U: LETTER TO PRESIDENT BY JASON

September 23, 2011

President of the United States
1600 Pennsylvania Ave. NW
Washington, DC. 20500

> RE: LETTER BY FEDERAL INMATE JASON HERNANDEZ #07031-078 IN SUPPORT OF HIS PETITION FOR COMMUTATION OF SENTENCE

Dear Mr. President:

Greetings. My name is Jason Hernandez. I am sure you have no idea who I am, and probably wondering why on God's earth am I writing to you. Well, to summarize it as best as I can I am a 34 year old federal inmate who has served over 14 years on a sentence of life without parole, which I was given for conspiracy to distribute crack cocaine and other controlled substances. As a result therof, I have filed a Petition for Commutation of Sentence with the Pardon Attorney in hopes you determine there is sufficient cause to grant my request.

As you are aware there has been major support to completely eliminate the disparity between powder cocaine and crack cocaine. But that is not what the substance of this letter is about. I'm not going to sit here and try to downplay the effects crack cocaine or any other drugs have on our nation. I know first hand the distruction drugs cause on people, families, and communities.

Nor will I attest that because I didn't kill anyone, commit rape, or a crime against a child, that I shouldn't be in prison for an excessive amount of time. Because the simple truth Mr. President is that I was a drug dealer. And what I didn't know then that I've learned over the years is that it would not be an overstatement to view my crime as equivalent, if not more detrimental, than those just stated. I realize this because I was selling drugs in the community I was born and raised in. I was selling drugs to people I grew up with, most of whom were either friends or family. Everybody I came into contact with I was destroying in one way or another. From the addicts and the families of those addicts, and the individuals I encouraged to sell drugs that ended up losing years of their lives in prison; resulting in parents being without a son, wives without a husband or kids without a father. Now I can see the cycle of destruction that drugs have caused on my neighborhood and those across the United States.

I acknowledge that I deserve to be in prison. For how long? I am in no position to say. I'm sure there are people who could argue either for or against my current sentence of life without parole. What I can say for certain Mr. President is that I am a changed man from that boy who ran those streets over 15-20 years ago. And if I were given a second at life I would not let you, my family, or society down. I would do everything I could to right what I have wronged and try to prevent kids from making the same mistakes I did when I was young.

    If you review my Petition for Commutation you will see I have dreams Mr. President, big dreams. And not just dreams of being free, but dreams of becoming someone who is going to make a difference in this world. But to speak of my goals as dreams doesn't do them justice, for I can see everything I want to accomplish and how I am going to accomplish it as clear as day. All I need now is for you to give me a chance to turn those dreams into reality.

    I thank you for your time Mr. President, and I hope that after you read my Petition for Commutation you come to the conclusion that I was not a bad person growing up, but a person who made bad decisions.

                                           Sincerly,

                                           Jason Hernandez #07031-078
                                           Federal Correctional Institution
                                           Post Office Box 1500
                                           El Reno, Oklahoma. 73036

APPENDIX V: LETTER TO PRESIDENT BY EVELYN PAPPA

President Trump
The White House
1600 Pennsylvania Ave. NW
Washington, DC, 20500

RE: LETTER FROM EVELYN C. BOZON PAPPA ASKING THE PRESIDENT OF THE UNITED STATES TO COMMUTE HER SENTENCE OF LIFE WITHOUT PAROLE WHICH SHE WAS GIVEN IN 1997 FOR A NONVIOLENT DRUG OFFENSE (Docket 1:95CR000084-004)

Dear President Trump,

I'm sure you are surprised to receive a letter from me. And I am sure you will even be more shocked to hear of my request. However, I hope I may find grace and favor in your sight as I share with a repented heart events that have occured with me since my incarceration and changes that have made me a better person.

Getting involved in this conspiracy was the worst decision I have ever made. Not a day goes by that I do not regret my involvement in the conspiracy and I am profoundly remorseful and sorry for the crimes I have committed and as a result, wronged others, and abandoning my four children who had to grow up without a mother. I have been unable to be there for them as they faced the pains of growing up, unable to embrace them as they went through difficult times in their lives, and unable to share their accomplishments, celebrations, and birthdays marriages

These are incredibly important things that I should have been there for, but instead of me being there, there was only an empty seat. To this day, they express to me the void and emptiness that exists in their lives because I am not present with them. Even as adults, they have told me many times that they will never have complete happiness in their lives until we are all together again. Even my 95 year old mother, who through only God's grace is still alive, has expressed to me the need to see my in person before she dies. She sent me a picture she had someone take holding a sign asking for help.

I understand that these are the consequences of my actions for conspiring with my husband. Because of my stupidity, greed, and selfishness, my children's lives and lives of other families have been and will be adversely affected forever. I hate myself for causing so much pain. The remorse and the guiltiness I have felt have caused extreme stress to the point that I have had a stroke and other several health issues in prison for the past 23 years.

As I began my prison sentence, I made the decision to improve and be a better person in every area of my life. I have accomplished many things since my incarceration but I think my greatest accomplishment, in my life actually, is caring for others in this prison. I have made it a priority to help other women deal with their incarceration in a positive manner. Staff counts on me to help with many daily activities in the Honor Unit, the drug program, and the religious services department. I have applied myself by working hard and not partaking in not committing or partaking in negative behavior. I am a committed Christian and being a student of God's word has allowed living a positive life, even behind bars

I would like to think my conduct in prison for the past 24 years shows I wasn't a bad person, I was a person who made dumb and bad decisions. A person who has learned from them, who has changed her life, and is helping others change their lives based on my mistakes.

President Trump, I am asking for your mercy to please grant me clemency. I am asking for another opportunity. I do not want to die in prison. I am 57 years old, and yes, I will be deported to my native country of Colombia, where my four children are at, including my 95 year old mother, awaits me before she dies.

Please give me mercy and a second chance. I will never take part in such senseless destruction of lives as I once was. My goal is to be a productive citizen of my country and bring awareness of others of the consequences of any kind of involvement in drug activities.

May God continue to bless you and this Country, the World.

_____

Evelyn Bozon Pappa #48576-004
FCI Tallahassee
501 Capital Circle NE
Tallahassee, Florida 32201

APPENDIX W: LETTER TO MICHELLE ALEXANDER BY CRACK OPEN THE DOOR

TRULINCS 07031078 - HERNANDEZ, JASON - Unit: ERE-A-A

FROM:
TO:
SUBJECT: Message to Michelle Alexander

Dear Michelle:

    This message/request comes with the utmost respect sincerity. First, my name is Jason Hernandez (brother of Stevie). I am a federal inmate serving life without parole for crack cocaine. More importantly, however, I am one of the Co-founders of the Organization Crack Open The Door. Which is an offspring of your book The New Jim Crow. Surprised? You shouldn't be. For Martin Luther King was right in believing that although the arc of history is long, it eventually bends towards justice. So lets just say after I read your book, a "greater vision, courage and determination" did come over me as you had hoped for.

    As you are aware Crack Open The Door was initiated with the intent of seeking sentencing reform. However, in addition to this, our vision and goal is to also educate people on the disastrous effects of the drug war on minorities while at the same time bringing to our peoples' attention that we are also contributing to this cycle of destruction.

    Your book has been vital in informing a multitude of prominent individuals and organizations that the greatest contributor to our peoples suppression is or judicial and prison system. Nevertheless, I believe your discoveries and teachings are not reaching a certain category of people: the blacks and Hispanics whom your book is based on. I know this to be true cause I am in an environment surrounded by the statistics that make up the findings in your book. I was from and still associate with people who are from the hoods, barrios, ghettos, your book speaks of and I would estimate nine out of ten never heard of Michelle Alexander or her book the New Jim Crow. What is most distressing, however, is that most of these individuals never even heard of the term "Jim Crow" or even knew what it meant. And it made me think Michelle, and I figured maybe the problem is that our people have been in a cycle of destruction for so long that we seem to think its part of our culture or DNA to drop-out of school, join a gang, use/sell drugs, go to prison, "to make peace with mediocrity [and failure]."

    I don't fault them for thinking like this for I shared the same belief and, even worse, I contributed to this cycle. Based on this I believe before we experience significant progress and upliftment our people as a whole must be made aware of this new method of Jim Crow that has been implemented against us and how, unlike our forefathers, we are voluntarily subject ourselves to such lashings: That we are not a race of "characterless and purposeless people", but that we come from a race of great men and, therefore, can become great again. And i think it is incumbent on whose who are fortunate enough to have become of aware of this knowledge to spread it to those who don't know.

    You have done more for our cause than we could have ever wished for and now we request your assistance again. Steve and me seek to add a section to our site entitled "War On Drugs Or War Against Minorities", which would basically entail the findings of your book. However, we believe that if we were to construct it ourselves it would not be viewed as credible, anti-government, and dismissed as the typical conspiracy against the black man rhetoric. The same Achilles heal many others before you have suffered from who have chose to speak on the subjects set forth in your book. You on the other hand are not viewed as such. People not only listen to you but they believe it as if it is the gospel. Thus the favor we ask is would you be interested in dedicating a couple of pages to our site with passages, pictures, statistics or whatever you felt would capture the attention of our visitors and compel then to go to your site, read your book.....and awaken them.

    I don't know how our people will respond when they learn of what you have discovered, but I can tell you this Michelle; after I read your book......."my [cell] shook and my chains fell off...."

    I thank you.

APPENDIX X: LETTER TO CONGRESSMEMBER BOBBY SCOTT BY CRACK OPEN THE DOOR

Congress Bobby Scott
400 N. 8th Street, Suite 430
Richmond, Virginia 23219

RE: SEEKING PERMISSION TO ADD YOUR NAME TO A PETITION THAT WILL REQUEST THE PRESIDENT OF THE UNITED STATES TO COMMUTE THE SENTENCE OF FIRST TIME AND/OR NON-VIOLENT CRACK COCAINE OFFENDERS' SERVING LIFE WITHOUT PAROLE.

Dear Congressman Bobby Scott,

My name is Jason Hernandez. I am a federal inmate serving life without parole (LWOP) for the distribution of crack cocaine. In addition, I am the initiator of a grass roots sentencing reform group called **Crack Open The Door**. Our mission is to bring awareness to a class of federal inmates that will die in prison for reasons that have been dispelled by research, no longer supported by scientific evidence, and viewed by the public as racially discriminatory: first-time and/or non-violent crack cocaine offenders serving LWOP.

The purpose of this letter is to request your support by signing a petition that we will be submitting to the President of the United States at the beginning of 2014. This petition will request the President to commute the sentences of first-time and/or non-violent crack cocaine offenders serving LWOP who meet a certain criteria.

I have enclosed the petition for your review along with my profile and the profile of two other individuals who are serving life sentences for crack cocaine.

President Barack Obama has only commuted the sentence of one federal inmate during his first term in office. However, we believe based on this administration's prior efforts to completely eliminate the crack cocaine disparity along with support from highly esteemed individuals such as yourself, the President will strongly consider commuting the sentences of non-violent offenders who received a life sentence as a result of the disparity.

If you wish to sign our petition you can do so by simply contacting my brother Steve Hernandez and inform him that he has permission to add your name to the list. If you are interested in learning more about our cause, please feel free to use the contact information listed below.

Thank you for your time and we hope to hear from you soon.

Sincerely,

Jason Hernandez #07031-078
Federal Correction Institution
P.O. Box 1500
El Reno, Oklahoma 73036

Stevie Hernandez

Email: crackopenthedoor@gmail.com
Website: www.crackopenthedoor.com

APPENDIX Y: LETTER TO CONGRESSMEMBER SHEILA JACKSON BY CRACK OPEN THE DOOR

FROM: Crack Open The Door
TO: Representative Sheila Jackson (D. Tx.)
SUBJECT: website dedicated to crack cocaine offenders serving life sentences
DATE: September 14, 2011

Dear Representative Sheila Jackson;

Enclosed you will find a packet pertaining to a website that will be implemented in the coming weeks entitled, "Crack Open the Door." The contents enclosed consist of an overview of the websites purpose, and the goals we seek to accomplish. Also enclosed are profiles of ten inmates incarcerated at El Reno, Oklahoma's Federal Facility; <u>all of whom are serving sentences of life without parole for offenses involving crack cocaine</u> (9 of which are african american and 1 mexican american and make up the individuals in the group picture).

We are currently in the process of locating individuals throughout the federal system that are serving life without parole for offenses involving crack cocaine. We believe when said and done, based on what was unvelied at El Reno F.C.I., all the individuals will be either black or hispanic.

The reason you were sent a packet is because one of the two individuals who is initiating the website (Jason Hernandez, who is also one of the ten inmates at El Reno F.C.I. serving life for crack cocaine) believes you would be interested in the information that will be uncovered. As well Jason, based on your prior/current actions to eliminate sentencing injustices, hopes that you could offer some insight as to how to make the public more aware of the site.

If you are interested in offering advice or in obtaining the information we uncover you may contact either of the two individuals initiating the website at the address's below.

Thank you for your time. We hope to hear from you soon.

Cordially,

Jason Hernandez #07031-078
F.C.I., P.O. Box 1500
El Reno, Oklahoma 73036
(e-mail is available but need
your e-mail address in advance
to get it approved)

Stevie Hernandez (Jason's Brother)

E-mail: crackopenthedoor@gmail.com

APPENDIX Z: LETTERS MAILED OUT TO ORGANIZATIONS BY CRACK OPEN THE DOOR

TRULINCS 07031078 - HERNANDEZ, JASON - Unit: ERE-A-A

FROM: 07031078
TO: Hernandez, Stevie
SUBJECT: letter for the site
DATE: 02/21/2013 01:39:18 PM

As you are aware Crack Open The Door's mission is to put a spotlight on the injustices caused by the crack cocaine/powder cocaine sentencing disparity, especially in those cases were the disparity resulted in life without parole (LWOP) for nonviolent offenders. As well, we also put forth workable alternatives that would eventually result in the release of these individuals back to their families and community, instead of the current status quo of allowing them to perish in prison of old age or disease.

One of these alternatives is President Barack Obama's executive power to grant clemency. Which allows the President to reduce any federal inmates sentence whom he believes is grossly inappropriate, among other reasons. Based on this we are requesting the President to commute the sentences of crack cocaine offenders serving LWOP who meet the following criteria: (1) have never been convicted of a violent crime, (2) would not be subject to LWOP if the crack/powder cocaine ratio was 1:1, (3) conviction became final prior to United States v. Booker, and (4) have been model inmates while incarcerated.

Admittingly, President Obama has only commuted the sentence of one federal inmate during his first term. However, we strongly believe that based on President Obama's prior efforts to completely eliminate the crack cocaine disparity, along with public support, he will issue justice to those individuals who's sentences are extremely harsh.

In an effort to bring awareness to the people we seek to help we have posted on our website profiles of three individuals who meet the criteria stated above. In addition, our facebook is also filled with pictures of others who either meet all or a majority of the criteria listed.

If you would like to voice support for President Obama to commute the sentences of first time and/or nonviolent crack cocaine offenders serving LWOP you can do so by either (1) sending a letter to the President stating your reasons why these individuals sentences should be reduced or (2) you can print a letter we have posted on our site (setting forth our reasons for commutation), sign it, and then mailing it to the White House.

We look forward to you supporting our cause.

TRULINCS 07031078 - HERNANDEZ, JASON - Unit: ERE-A-A

FROM: 07031078
TO:
SUBJECT: Do U need info on 1st time/nonviolent LWOP Inmates
DATE: 05/30/2012 12:18:23 PM

Greetings:

    For those who are not familiar with our cause we are a grass-roots organization who's sole purpose is to bring awareness and propose viable alternatives for a class of federal inmates that will die in prison for reasons that are no longer supported by medical science, have been dispelled by research, and viewed by the public as racially discriminative towards African-Americans: FIRST TIME AND/OR NON-VIOLENT CRACK COCAINE OFFENDERS SERVING LIFE WITHOUT PAROLE.

    Through are research and studies we have learned there is little known as it relates to this type of offender and other first time and/or non-violent inmates serving life without parole. Such as, how many non-violent offenders are serving life without parole: what do they experience in prison: what do there parents, wives and kids go through: what effects does it have on their communities and the economy?

    Recently, however, there have been sentencing advocates, judges, and law professors who have questioned the wisdom of imprisoning non-violent offenders for their entire lives. See subnote. Through our limited resources (we are only staffed by two individuals, one of whom is in prison serving life) we have discovered a number of factors which may be of interest to you or individuals you know. For example,

* of the 38 first time and/or non-violent offenders serving life without parole for crack cocaine 36 of them are African Americans and two are Hispanics:
* some of these individuals sentences are based on conduct they started while in there teens and some were 21 years old or younger when sentenced:
* a number of the judges who sentenced these individuals to life without parole expressed they did not want to impose such sentence but the Guideline's gave them no discretion to impose a lesser sentence:
* a portion of these individuals have been incarcerated twenty years or more:

    If you are interested in learning more about these inmates, speaking to their family members, obtaining there sentencing transcripts/PSI, or anything else you feel that could be of significance in demonstrating the injustice of imprisoning this class of inmate till they die of old age or illness, or if you are interested in assisting us in seeking sentencing reform contact me.

    Sincerly.

---

*/ See Professor David Dow's article "Life Without Parole Is A Terrible Idea" in THE DAILY BEAST (2012): and The University of San Francisco's School of Law Center For Law and Global Justice Report, "Cruel and Unusual", U.S. Sentencing Practices In a Global Context.

TRULINCS 07031078 - HERNANDEZ, JASON - Unit: ERE-A-A

FROM:
TO:
SUBJECT: Introduction and Request
DATE:

Dear Mrs. Ashley Nellis:

Greetings. My name is Jason Hernandez, one of the individuals behind the grass-roots organization Crack Open The Door. Our mission is to bring awareness to the unfairness of sentencing non-violent offenders with minimal to no criminal history to life without parole (LWOP). In furtherance of this cause we are submitting a request to the Sentencing Commission (for the amendment cycle 2012) with the intent it will persuade them to reevaluate how offense level 43 of the Guideline's is applied to non-violent offenders.

The reason I am reaching out to you is because I have discovered you, as well, disagree with how LWOP is used in this country ("No Exit" & "Throwing Away the Key"). As a result i was wanting to send you a copy of the report I am sending to the Commission. We hope after you evaluate it you will support our cause to revise this unfairness created by Guideline level 43 by either: (1) signing a petition we currently have on www.change.org, entitled "abolish life without parole for offenders who commit non-violent crimes": and/or (2) send your own personal reason why the Commission should make our proposal a priority.

I will not occupy any more your time. The information enclosed should be helpful in making your decision to assist us in this cause and maybe even on other ideas we have. In addition, even if you decide not to assist us, we have discoved a lot of information on individuals serving LWOP that you may be interested in, and which we would be more than willing to share with you.

We hope to hear from you soon.

Sincerely

Jason Hernandez, co-founder
Crack Open the Door
P.O. Box 1500
El Reno, Ok. 73036

Stevie Hernandez, co-founder

e-mail: crackopenthedoor@gmail.com
website: crackopenthedoor.com

APPENDIX AA: PROFILE PRISON TEMPLATE

(INSERT NAME)
PROFILE OF PRISONER SEEKING CLEMENCY

NAME AND #:

AGE:

SENTENCE:

YEARS IN PRISON:

RELEASE DATE:

OFFENSE:

NEED/REASON FOR COMMUTATION:

(Insert Picture)

- Picture may have to be cut to fit or reduced on copy machine.
- If you have the benefit of a loved one or advocate on the outside copies in color are preferred
- If copying in color is not possible a copy of photo in black and white is perfectly fine.

CONDUCT WHILE INCARCERATED:

PERSONAL INFORMATION:

CONTACT INFORMATION:

APPENDIX BB: PROFILE OF EVELYN MADE IN PRISON

EVELYN BOZON PAPPA

PROFILE OF PRISONER SEEKING CLEMENCY FROM THE PRESIDENT

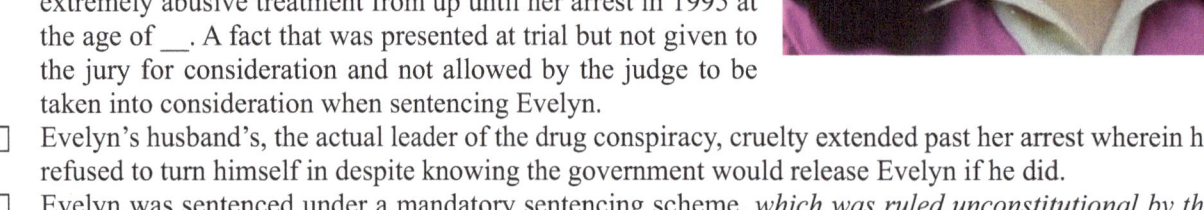

NAME AND #: Evelyn Bozon Pappa #48576-004

AGE: 58

SENTENCE 9 life without parole sentences

YEARS IN PRISON: 24 years in prison

RELEASE DATE: deceased

OFFENSE: cocaine conspiracy

NEED/REASON FOR COMMUTATION:

- Evelyn is a non-violent drug offender who has been incarcerated since 1995.
- Evelyn's connection to the conspiracy was a result of her husband whom she married at the early age of 14 and experienced extremely abusive treatment from up until her arrest in 1995 at the age of __. A fact that was presented at trial but not given to the jury for consideration and not allowed by the judge to be taken into consideration when sentencing Evelyn.
- Evelyn's husband's, the actual leader of the drug conspiracy, cruelty extended past her arrest wherein he refused to turn himself in despite knowing the government would release Evelyn if he did.
- Evelyn was sentenced under a mandatory sentencing scheme, *which was ruled unconstitutional by the Supreme Court in 2005,* requiring the judge to impose a life without parole sentence.

CONDUCT WHILE INCARCERATED: In the past 24 years in prison Evelyn has been an exceptional individual having never received an incident report. She has completed dozens of classes and obtained her High School Diploma. She has served as a role model and mentor for younger and new woman at the prison. She works in the Chapel where she translates sermons from English to Spanish and teaches Religious Service reentry faith based classed that equip prisoners with skill that help them transition back to their community. *Evelyn has eight letters of support from prison staff requesting the President to commute her sentence*

PERSONAL INFORMATION: Decades of imprisonment have only made Evelyn's will and faith stronger. However, the decades of incarceration have taken a toll on her physically. Evelyn has suffered a stroke, vaginal tumors, tumors on her neck, hypothyroidism and circulatory problems. If released, Evelyn will be deported to Columbia. However, a positive in Evelyn's life is in Columbia she has three daughters and one son who are college educated and have their own families and would love nothing more than to care for their mother. Evelyn's mother is still alive at the age of 95 and prays to see her free one day.

CONTACT INFORMATION: Prison: 501 Capital Circle, NE Tallahassee, Fl. 32301 Fb: Clemency For Evelyn;

APPENDIX CC: PROFILE OF JASON MADE IN PRISON

INMATE PROFILE

NAME: Jason Hernandez #07031-078 **AGE:** 36

CHARGE: crack/meth conspiracy

SENTENCE: life+ **YEARS IMPRISONED:** 15

COST OF INCARCERATION: $1,482,000

COMMENTS MADE BY SENTENCING JUDGE: Prior to sentencing Jason to life without parole the district court stated that he disagreed with the disparity between crack cocaine and powder cocaine and he written Congress to do something about it. He also said through reference that it was hard for him to sentence someone as young as Jason (who was 21 at the time) to life but that under the Guidelines he could not give a lesser sentence.

CONDUCT AND ACCOMPLISHMENTS IN PRISON: In addition to having haver received an incident report Jason has done much to better himself and others. After obtaining his GED he completed a number of college courses such as Microsoft Applications, Culinary Arts, and Blackstone's Paralegal/Legal Assistance Program. He has also obtained 1200 hours of vocational training in welding and fabricating metals. Furthermore, Jason serves on El Reno's Suicide Watch Companion Program and was one of six inmates selected from the prison to participate in a program called "A Better Path" which allowed Jason to talk to troubled youth from the local community about the consequences of breaking the law and the hardships that prison poses on a person and their families

NOTABLE FACT: If the Fair Sentencing Act of 2010 had completely eliminated the crack/powder cocaine disparity Jason's sentencing range would have been reduced to 262-327 months. Moreover, the Head Narcotics Officer responsible for Jason's federal imprisonment has stated that although Jason should be punished for his involvement with drugs a sentence of life without parole was to severe.

APPENDIX DD: PROFILE OF TONIE DOUGLAS MADE IN PRISON

INMATE PROFILE

NAME: Altonio Douglas #2398-077   **AGE:** 50

CHARGE: crack cocaine conspiracy

SENTENCE: life   **YEARS IMPRISONED:** 20

COST OF INCARCERATION: $1,222,000

COMMENTS MADE BY SENTENCING JUDGE: Before imposing a punishment of life without parole the district court stated that Altonio showed he was a "compassionate" person and that he was not "at ease" about sentencing him to life in prison. At the time of Altonio's sentencing the Federal Guidelines were mandatory and not advisory as they are now.

CONDUCT AND ACCOMPLISHMENTS IN PRISON: While incarcerated Altonio has done much to better his life and that of others. For example, after completing the Welding Program offered at El Reno FCI, Altonio was recruited by staff to assist in teaching other inmates the trade of welding and fabricating metals, which he has done for the last five years. As a result, the prison has presented Altonio with the "You Make A Difference Award" the last three years in a row. He was also selected by Prison Staff to be part of a program called "A Better Path" which allowed Altonio to talk to troubled youth from the local community about the consequences of breaking the law and the hardships that prison poses on a person and their families. In addition, Altonio has not received a disciplary report in 12 years.

NOTABLE FACT: If the crack/powder cocaine ratio would have been 1:1 at the time Altonio were sentenced his Guideline Sentencing range would have been 292-365 months instead of life. Assuming the district court would have imposed a sentence at the lowest end Altonio's release date would have been in 2014, less than a year from now.

APPENDIX EE: CRACK OPEN THE DOOR'S FACTS & STATISTIC SHEET ON CRACK COCAINE DISPARITY

Crack Cocaine Disparity Fact Sheet
Created by Crackopenthedoor.com

In 1986, before the enactment of federal mandatory minimum sentencing for crack cocaine offenses, the average federal drug sentence for African Americans was 11% higher than for whites. Four years later, the average federal drug sentence for African Americans was 49% higher.

In 2003, whites constituted 7.8% and African Americans constituted more than 80% of the defendants sentenced under the harsh federal crack cocaine laws, despite the fact that more than 66% of crack cocaine users in the United States are white or Hispanic.

African American women's incarceration rates for all crimes, largely driven by drug convictions, increased by 800% from 1986, compared to an increase of 400% for women of all races for the same period

African Americans now serve virtually as much time in prison for a drug offense at 58.7 months, as whites do for a violent offense at 61.7 months.

There is no rational medical or penological reason for the 100:1 disparity between crack and powder cocaine, and instead it causes an unjustified racial disparity in our penal system.

In 1995, the average federal prison term for a crack cocaine offense surpassed that of murder.

If African Americans and Latinos were sentenced at the same frequency at which whites are sentenced, the American prison population would be cut in half

Overwhelming scientific evidence now demonstrates that the difference between crack and powder, is like the difference between ice and water or beer and wine.

African Americans alone make up almost 40 percent of the federal prison population, although they constitute only 13 percent of our country's population.

APPENDIX FF: JASON'S COMMENTS & RECOMMENDATION TO USSC

FOR AMENDMENT CYCLE ENDING MAY, 2013

REQUEST TO THE SENTENCING COMMISSION TO MAKE A PRIORITY REVISING OFFENSE LEVEL 43'S RECOMMENDATION OF LIFE WITHOUT PAROLE FOR OFFENDERS IN CRIMINAL HISTORY I&II (WHO DO NOT COMMIT CRIMES OF VIOLENCE) TO 360 MONTHS-TO-LIFE WITHOUT PAROLE

Submitted by: Jason Hernandez, #07031-078
Federal Correctional Institution
P.O. Box 1500
El Reno, Oklahoma 73036

&

Stevie Hernandez

Website: crackopenthedoor.com
e-mail: crackopenthedoor@gmail.com

TABLE OF CONTENTS

A. STATEMENT OF THE ISSUE PRESENTED FOR CONSIDERATION..................2

B. WHY THE SENTENCING COMMISSION SHOULD MAKE REVISING OFFENSE LEVEL 43 A PRIORITY...2

C. POSSIBLE SOLUTION..5

D. SUBNOTES...6

E. APPENDIX

---

* This is a request to the Sentencing Commission to make revising offense level 43 a priority for Amendment Cycle Ending May, 2013. It is submitted pursuant to 28 U.S.C. §§ 994(s), 994(o), and U.S.S.C. Rules of Practice and procedure. Section 994(s) is referenced because one of the individuals submitting this request is a federal inmate and effected by offense level 43.

* It should be noted that the two individuals (one of which is incarcerated) who prepared this request did so with limited resources. However, to the extent possible, all statements, resources cited to, and attachments are accurate and verifiable.

A. STATEMENT OF THE ISSUE PRESENTED FOR CONSIDERATION

The Issue presented to the Sentencing Commission for consideration is revising offense level 43's recommendation of life without parole for offenders in Criminal History Category I and II (who do not commit crimes of violence) to 360 months to life without parole, and apply the revision retroactively.

B. WHY THE SENTENCING COMMISSION SHOULD MAKE REVISING OFFENSE LEVEL 43 A PRIORITY

(1) OFFENSE LEVEL 43 MAKES NO DISTINCTION BETWEEN OFFENDERS WITH MINIMAL TO NO CRIMINAL HISTORY FROM THOSE WHO ARE CONSIDERED HABITUAL OFFENDERS

As currently constructed offense level one through forty-two of the Guidelines Sentencing Table share one or two important characteristics. For instance, each of these offense levels gives courts a recommended sentencing range to choose from (e.g., offense level 32, CHC I recommends 121-151 months imprisonment). Second, each offense levels recommended sentencing range increases in years the more criminal history points a defendant has (e.g., offense level 34, CHC I recommends 151-180 months and offense level 34, CHC VI recommends 262-327 months; 111-170 month increase).

However, in formulating the sentence for offense level 43 the Commission abandoned not only one, but both of these approaches. Under level 43 it makes no difference what Criminal History Category is applicable because only one sentence is recommended—life without parole.

The Commission has published three reports on recidivism acknowledging that the criminal history rules were never based on empirical evidence.[1] The same reports also establish that offenders with minimal to no criminal history points "have substantially lower recidivism rates than offenders who are in Criminal History Category IV, V, and VI." The Commission has also found that there is "no correlation between recidivism and the Guidelines offense level. Whether an offender has a low or high guideline offense level, recidivism rates are similar." However, despite these findings offense level 43 continues to hold offenders in all six criminal categories equally culpable.

-2-

(2) **THERE IS A NATIONAL CONCENSUS AGAINST IMPRISONING NON-VIOLENT OFFENDERS WITH MINIMAL TO NO CRIMINAL HISTORY TO LIFE WITHOUT PAROLE**

A review of the criminal punishments enacted within this country seems to produce only one state that mandates a sentence of life without parole for an offender with no criminal history who commits a felony that is not a "crime of violence."[2] Several states have recidivist statutes that allow courts to impose life sentences on non-violent offenders, but none mandate it or recommend it, and only one state allows the life sentence to be without parole.[3]

There are federal statutes which mandate life without parole for non-violent crimes (even if they are a first-time offender) but Congress has limited this punishment to only the most serious of crimes, which are known as "Kingpin Statutes."[4] Under the Guidelines, however, just about any crime can be subject to a recommendation of life without parole. This appears to be the only sentencing scheme in the nation to do so.

Based on our limited resources we were unable to determine the actual practice of district courts who sentenced defendants that had compiled a base offense level of 43.[5] What we did learn though was that prior to U.S. Booker, 543 U.S. 220 (2005), numerous federal judges expressed dissagreement with sentencing defendants to life as required by level 43 or a statute and would have imposed a lesser sentence had they the discretion.[6] See Tab (District Judge's Who Stated They Did Not Want to Impose Life Without Parole). Since the Guidelines were rendered advisory, however, district courts now seem less likely to impose a life sentence or a sentence equivalent to it when it is recommended by offense level 43.[7][8]

(3) **THERE IS A GLOBAL CONCENSUS AGAINST IMPRISONING NON-VIOLENT OFFENDERS TO LIFE WITHOUT PAROLE**

The United States is among the minority of countries (20%) known to researchers as having life without parole sentences.[9] The vast majority of countries that do allow such punishment have high restrictions on when they can be issued, such as only for murder or two or more convictions of life sentence-eligible crimes.[10] Whereas in the United States LWOP can be recommended, under the Guidelines for example, for a non-violent crime such as drug dealing or fraud.[11]

Currently, there are around 7,000 inmates in the Bureau of Prisons serving LWOP for violent and non-violent crimes. In contrast, this population dwarfs other nations that share our Anglo-American heritage, and by the leading members of the Western Community. For instance, there are 59 individuals serving such sentences in Australia,[12] 41 in England,[13] and 37 in the Netherlands.[14]

The United States as party to the International Covenant on Civil and Political Rights has agreed that the essential aim of its correctional system shall be reformation and social rehabilitation.[15] Regional Human Rights experts have agreed that long sentences can undermine the rehabilitative purpose of corrections. As the Special Rapporteur on Prisons and Conditions in Africa has stated, "Punishments which attack the dignity and integrity of the human being, such as long-term and life imprisonment, run contrary to the essence of imprisonment.[16] Thus it would appear that offense level 43's recommendation of LWOP (regardless of what crime is committed) contradicts not only this countries obligation to the International Community, but is also a sentencing practice rejected by a great majority of the civilized world.[17]

(4) LIFE WITHOUT PAROLE IS A CRUEL AND UNUSUAL PUNISHMENT

Life without parole is the second most severe penalty permitted by law. It is true that a death sentence is unique in its severity and irrevocability; yet LWOP sentences share some characteristics with death sentences that are shared by no other sentences.[18] The offender serving LWOP is not executed, but the sentence alters the offenders life by a foreiture. It deprives the convict of the most basic liberties without giving hope of restoration. As one jurist observed, this sentence "means denial of hope; it means that good behavior and character improvement are immaterial; it means that whatever the future might hold in store for the mind and spirit of (the convict), he will remain in prison for the rest of his days".[19] Indeed, some believe it to be more humane to execute an individual than "to keep them in prison until they actually die of old age or disease."[20]

Because LWOP forswears altogether the rehabilitative idea, the penalty rest on a determination that the offender has committed criminal conduct so atrocious that he is irredemable, incapable of rehabilitation, and will be a danger to society for the rest of his life.[21] It is a determination primarily made by a judge or jury if certain set elements are present. The Guidelines, on the other hand, makes this same condemnation of a defendant based solely on a mathematical equation.

Lastly, the Commission's rejection of rehabilitation for all offenders in level 43 goes beyond a mere expressive judgment. Federal inmates serving LWOP are normally required to serve the initial eight-to-twelve years in a United States Penitentiary;[22] prisons which are known to have "a predatory environment...engendered by gangs, racial tension, overcrowding, weapons, violence and sexual assaults.[23]" Because in such prisons safety and security override rehabilitation, programs are limited and without substance. And in prisons where vocational training and other rehabilitative programs are available inmates serving LWOP are not allowed to participate or passed over for prisoners with release dates. This despite offenders in Criminal History Category I and II are in most need of and receptive to rehabilitation.[24]

C. POSSIBLE SOLUTION

Change offense level 43's recommendation of LWOP for offenders in Criminal History Category I and II to 360-months to LWOP. This change would still advise district courts that LWOP should be considered, but it is not the only punishment to be considered. See Tab, Judge Roettgers Solution to Level 43.

Make such change retroactive so that district courts who were required to sentence a defendant to LWOP under level 43 (when the Guidelines were mandatory) will have the discretion to consider imposing a sentence of no less than 360-months; but exclude offenders convicted of homicide, acts of terrorism, rape, and crimes against children.

Although the Guidelines are advisory they are still "the starting point and the initial benchmark" in determining a sentence.[25] And currently, offense level 43, CHC I and II sets a "benchmark" which is viewed by the greater part of the civilized world to be a punishment that is "cruel and unusual."[26]

WHEREFORE it is prayed that the Sentencing Commission make revising offense level 43 a priority for the Amendment Cycle ending May, 2013.
Respectfully submitted.

                                                Jason Hernandez #07031-078
                                               Federal Correctional Institution
                                               Post Office Box 1500
                                               El Reno, Oklahoma. 73036

                                                            &

Stevie Hernández

website: crackopenthedoor.com
e-mail: crackopenthedoor@gmail.com

---

1. U.S. Sentencing Comm'n, Measuring Recidivism: The Criminal History Computation of the Federal Sentencing Guidelines (May 2004): U.S. Sentencing Comm'n, Recidivism and the First Offender (May 2004): U.S. Sentencing Comm'n, A Comparison of the Federal Sentencing Guidelines Criminal History Category and the U.S. Parole Comm'n Salient Factor Score (January 2005),

2. See Alabama Code 13A-12-231(2)(d)(provides LWOP for a first-time offender who possesses 10 kilograms or more of cocaine).

3. See Nevada Rev. Stat. §§ 207.010(1)(b)(1)-(3)(1995)

4. See 21 U.S.C. § 848(b).

5. Again, as stated on page 1 we are operated by two individuals, one of which is incarcerated.

6. See U.S. v. Miller, 2010 U.S. Dist. LEXIS 79763 (Dist. of Minn. 2010) ("The court has no hesitancy in stating that a mandatory life sentence

6. without the possibility of parole is vastly to long for this defendant. []....he accumulated a dreadful criminal record - and at an early age ...but a non-discretionary sentence, assuring he will die of old age in federal prison, is to heavy a burden.").

7. See U.S. v. Faulkenberry, 759 F.Supp.2d 915 (S.D. Ohio 2010)(despite obtaining an offense level of 47 for fraud violations district judge imposes sentence of only 120 months): and U.S. v. Watt, 707 F.Supp.2d 149 (D.Mass. 2010)(despite obtaining an offense level of 43 for fraud violations district court imposes sentence of 24 months).

8. The Supreme Court stated in Roper v. Simmons, 543 U.S. 551, 563-64 (2005) that in determining whether a punishment is "cruel and unusual" a factor to be considered is the "objective indicia of society's standards, as expressed in legislative enactments and state practice.").

9. See University of San Francisco's Report entitled Cruel and Unusual: U.S. Sentencing Practices In A Global Context, at p.8.

10. Cruel and Unusual, supra at p.24.

11. Under 18 USC § 1341 a defendant can not be sentenced to more than thirty years. Nevertheless, a defendant convicted for fraud can still attain an offense level of 43, and under such circumstances the Guidelines instruct courts that if the count carrying the highest statutory maximum is less than the total punishment, then the sentence imposed on one or more of the counts shall run consecutively.." See U.S.S.G. 5G1.2(d); and also U.S. v. Okun, 453 Fed. Appx 364 (4th Cir. 2011)(where defendant obtained an offense level of 43 for Ponzi Scheme district court imposed consecutive sentences equalling 1200 months to equal recommendation of LWOP); U.S. v. Lewis, 594 F.3d 1270 (10th Cir. 2010)(sentenced to 330 years as a result of obtaining offense level 43 for fraud); United States v. Robert Allen Stanford, (fraud, sentenced to 150 years);

12. See Englan Vinter and Others v. United Kingdom, App. Nos. 66069189 and 3986/10 Eur.Ct.H.R., 37 (2012)

13. Vinter, supra note 12, para. 37

14. Dirk Van Zyl Smit, Outlawing Irreducible Life Sentences" Europe on The Brink?" 23 Fed.Sent.R.39, 41 (2010)

15. International Covenant on Civil and Political Rights, Dec. 16, 1996, S.Treaty Doc. No. 95-20 (1992, Art. 10(3) 999 U.N.T.S. 171

16. African Commission on Human and Peoples rights, Reports of the Special Rapporteur on Prison Conditions in Africa.

17. See Thompson v. Oklahoma, 487 U.S. 815, 830 (1998)(in ruling that a 14-year-old convicted of murder could not be executed the Supreme Court stated, "We have previously recognized the relevance of the views of the international community in determining whether a punishment is cruel and unusual" and "by other nations that share our Anglo-American heritage..."

18. Graham v. Florida, 176 L.Ed.2d 825, 842 (2010)(Kennedy, Justice).

19. Naovarath v. State, 105 Nev. 525, 526, 779 P.2d 944 (1989):

20. Holberg v. State, 38 S.W.3d 137, 140 (Tex.Crim.App. 2000); and S v. Nehemia Tjiji, April 9, 1991 (unreported) quoted in Nanibia Supreme Court Feb. 6, 1996, S v. Tcoeib (1) SACR 390 (MnS)(1996)("The concept of life imprisonment destroys human dignity reducing a prisoner to a number behind the walls of jail waiting only for death to set him free").

21. See Harmelin v. Michigan, 115 L.Ed. 836, 887 (1991)(Justice Stevens disent)("Because [LWOP] does not even purport to serve a rehabilitative function, the sentence must rest on a rational determiniation that the punished criminal conduct is so atrocious that society's interest in deterrence and retribution wholly outweighs any consideration of reform or rehabilitation for the perpetrator. Serious as this defendant's crime was, (drug possession) I believe it is irrational to conclude every similar offender is wholly incorrigible.").

22. See Bureau of Prisons Program Statement 5100.08(I)(Inmate Security Designation and Custody Classification)("A male inmate with more than 30 years remaining to serve (including non-parolable LIFE sentences) will be housed in a High Security Level Institution unless the [Public Safety Factor] has been waived.").

23. Quoting U.S. v. Silks, 1995 U.S.App.LEXIS 35355 (9th Cir. 1995); Holt v. Bledsoe, 2011 U.S.Dist.LEXIS 73631 (Mid.Penn. 2011)("Inmate-on-inmate violence is commom and uncontrolled at USP Lewisburg."); Penson v. Pacheco, 2011 U.S.Dist.LEXIS 52856(D.Colo. 2011)("...USP Victorville housed violent prison gangs and was where dozens of assaults and a murder had occured."): Jones v. Willingham, 248 F.Supp. 791 (Kansas 1965)(describing USP's as "powder keg[s]".): and Leah Caldwell's Article in Prison Legal News, Sept. 2005 p.10-13 entitled "USP Beaumont, Texas: Murder and Mayhem in the Thunder Dome.").

24. See Graham v. Florida, 176 L.Ed.2d at 846 ("...the absence of rehabilitative opportunties or treatment makes the disproportionality of the sentence [LWOP for juveniles], all the more evident.").

25. Quoting Gall v. U.S., 552 U.S. 38, 49 (2006).

26. S. v. Dodo 2001 (3) SA 382, 404 (CC) at ¶38 (S.Afr.)("To attempt to justify any period of penal incarceration, let alone imprisonment for life...without inquiring into the proportionality between the offense and the period of imprisonment, is to ignore, if not to deny, that which lies at the very heart of human dignity..."): and U.S. v. Miller, 2010 U.S. Dist. LEXIS 79763 (Dist. Minn. 2010)("The Court is of the view that the Supreme Court will visit within the next decade the issue of whether mandatory life sentences for nonviolent crimes committed by adults offends the prohibition against cruel and unusual punishment. ...However, I am reluctant to predict the outcome of such a review. Were this Court a member of the Supreme Court, this Court would follow the reasoning of Justice Kennedy in Graham v. Florida and conclude that such a sentencing regime that resulted in the defendant's life sentence does violate the Eighth Amendment...").

APPENDIX GG: JASON'S PETITION UNDER 994(S) TO COMMISSION PERTAINING TO LEVEL 43

<u>PETITION PURSUANT TO TITLE 28 U.S.C. § 994(s)</u>

NAME OF PETITIONER/DEFENDANT: _____
CASE NO.: _____ : CHARGE: <u>distribution of_____</u>.
TOTAL OFFENSE LEVEL: ___. CHC: ___. SENTENCE IMPOSED: <u>LIFE_____</u>.
REQUESTING MODIFICATION OF SENTENCING GUIDELINE: <u>Offense level 43.</u>

TO THE HONORABLE MEMBERS OF THE SENTENCING COMMISSION:

This petition to the Commission is filed pursuant to Title 28 U.S.C. § 994(s), which states:

> "The Commission **shall** give due consideration to any petition filed by a defendant requesting modification of the guideline utilized in the sentencing of such defendant, on the basis of changed circumstances unrelated to the defendant, including changes in (1) the community view of the gravity of the offense: (2) the public concern generated by the offense; and (3) the deterrent effect particular sentence may have on the commission of the offense by others."

(A) <u>BASIS FOR PETITION</u>

The Guideline at issue in this Petition, which was also utilized in the sentencing of Petitioner, is offense level 43. As currently constructed offense level 43 recommends a sentence of life without parole (LWOP) without regard to a defendants criminal history or if the offense is a non-violent crime. Recommending only LWOP for non-violent offenders with minimal to no criminal history is contrary to evolving standards of decency of a maturing society and is a sentencing practice rejected by nearly all the fifty states and a great majority of civilized nations of the world. Extensive studies by the Sentencing Commission show that non-violent offenders with minimal to no criminal history are less likely to commit more crimes and are more susceptible to rehabilitation. There simply is no reason for the Guidelines to recommend that only a sentence of LWOP should be considered for this type of offender, **and ask the Commission** to implement some sort of modification of level 43 so that LWOP is not the only sentence recommended and to make such change retroactive.

Respectfully submitted this 16th day of July, 2012.

Fed. No. · _____
Federal Correctional Institution
Post Office Box 1500
El Reno, Oklahoma. 73036

APPENDIX HH: CRACK OPEN THE DOOR FACT SHEET

TRULINCS 07031078 - HERNANDEZ, JASON - Unit: ERE-A-A

FROM: 07031078
TO: Hernandez, Stevie
SUBJECT: E-Mail for filling out Profile
DATE: 02/20/2012 08:04:05 PM

WHAT IS CRACK OPEN THE DOOR? AND WHAT IS THERE MISSION?

Crack Open the Door is an Organization whose purpose is to bring awareness to a class of federal inmates that will die in prison for reasons that are no longer supported by science, have been dispelled by research, and viewed by the public as racially discriminatory toward African-Americans: first time and/or non-violent crack cocaine offenders serving life without parole.

Our mission is to represent this class of inmates by presenting alternatives to permanent incarceration that will one day reunite these individuals with there families, while also advocating that Federal Sentencing Laws should be the product of common sense and not Politicians unwillingness to work together or fear of not being re-elected.

AND JUST HOW DOES CRACK OPEN THE DOOR PLAN ON DOING THIS?

Though the War On Drugs is responsible for creating many absurdities and racial injustices, with no other drug has it been overwhelmingly demonstrated than that of crack cocaine. Unfortunately, the statistics have not been enough to make Congress completely eliminate the disparity between crack/powder cocaine. We believe, however, by putting a face to the statistic and showing how imprisoning minorities for the rest of there lives adversely effects their families and the community the public will demand change. Though are cause is limited to crack cocaine offenders serving life many of the changes we are advocating for would effect more than this class of inmate if achieved.

WHO EXACTLY STARTED CRACK OPEN THE DOOR, AND WHY DO YOU CARE?

Crack Open the Door is the result of two brothers: Stevie and Jason Hernandez. Stevie is a former federal inmate who received a mandatory ten year sentence for crack cocaine. He was released in 2005 and is now a successful hairstylist in South Beach, Florida. Jason is currently in federal prison serving life without parole for crack cocaine. Jason has been in prison since 1998. Both individuals know what your going through, the pain your parents are experiencing, and the struggles and hardships placed on your wives and children. They want nothing more than to change unfair and unwise drug laws.

IF I'M INCARCERATED CAN I HELP FURTHER CRACK OPEN THE DOOR'S CAUSE?

Yes, you can. Currently our Organization is looking to put profiles on our website of first-time and/or non-violent offenders serving life without parole for crack cocaine. If you fit this profile and would like to have your profile posted on our website, simply send an e-mail request to--crackopenthedoor@gmail.com. After your approved we will send you a questionnaire to fill-out. After you complete it send it to the address below along with a family picture (preferably a recent one taken at visit).

It is important that you know, however, that just because you fit the profile we are looking for does not mean you will automatically be posted on our site. Nevertheless, we feel it is important you complete the form and send it immediately for we feel we will be making contact with organizations who will be interested in contacting you and/or posting your profile on their site.

Additionally, to prevent any misrepresentation on our part or yours, you will likely be required to send your P.S.I. and/or sentencing transcript to verify you fit the profile before you are posted on our site. You can mark out any personal information on these documents, but nothing pertaining to the crime, criminal history, or comments by sentencing judge.

HOW DOES CRACK OPEN THE DOOR DEFINE FIRST TIME OFFENDER?

Any individual who was in Criminal History Category One of the Guidelines. Juvenile convictions are not counted as priors unless you were certified as an adult for the crime. In any event, priors will not prevent you from be posted on our site unless they were for crimes of violence.

SO WHAT IS CRACK OPEN THE DOOR'S DEFINITION OF A "VIOLENT OFFENDER"?

Well, this is a slippery slope. And if your familiar with law then you know not even the Supreme court has been able to come to agreement with what "violent offender" or a "crime of violence" means. As for purposes of being posted on our site (and it is subject to change) we define "violent offender" and "crime of violence" an an individual who has any prior convictions, whether state, federal or juvenile crimes which you were certified as an adult, which involved an actual act of violence. As well

TRULINCS 07031078 - HERNANDEZ, JASON - Unit: ERE-A-A

---

if any of the charges you are currently incarcerated for required the jury to determine you committed an act of violence in order to find you guilty of the offense or if you were enhanced under the Guidelines for a actual crime of violence you will be considered "a violent offender". There may be exceptions for offenders who were enhanced under the Guidelines for a crime of violence being that the judge and not the jury found you guilty of this act.

DOES YOUR ORGANIZATION HELP INMATES OBTAIN LAWYERS, FILE BRIEFS, OR ANSWER LEGAL QUESTIONS?

NO. We do not have attorney's, legal researchers, or a team of people assisting us. Again, we are self funded, and ran by two individuals (one of which is incarcerated). So please, do not send any e-mails pertaining to these matters for they will not be answered.

We thank you and hope to hear from you soon.

Stevie Hernandez, President of Crack Open The Door.

e-mail: crackopenthedoor@gmail.com

APPENDIX II: CRACK OPEN THE DOOR SOLUTIONS

TRULINCS 07031078 - HERNANDEZ, JASON - Unit: ERE-A-A

FROM: 07031078
TO: The Door, Crack Open
SUBJECT: IS THERE A SOLUTION? WHATS OUR SOLUTION? ETC.
DATE: 03/01/2012 08:08:34 AM

IS THERE A SOLUTION? WHATS OUR SOLUTION? WHAT DO WE RECOMMEND
(YOU DECIDE WHAT SOUNDS BEST FOR THE TITLE/SECTION T BONE)

The Federal Sentencing Laws responsible for creating racial disparities and sentencing absurdities are to many to name. Admittingly, there is no quick fix or simple solution that would address or correct the causes of these problems. Fortunately, with research now suggesting that the "War On Drugs" is a major cause of poverty, chronic unemployment, broken homes, and crime, a major push for sentencing reform has begun. Unfortunately, many of the new sentencing changes being proposed would not effect the inmates most desperately in need and egregiously harmed by unfair sentencing laws: federal inmates sentenced to life imprisonment (which no matter what their crime is, lack of criminal history, or age at which the crime was committed, is life without parole). See subnote 1.

There is a national consensus that first-time and/or nonviolent drug offenders serving life without parole is "cruel and unusual punishment". Yet, despite this acknowledgment, little to nothing has been proposed by lawmakers to correct or prevent this injustice. We have, therefore, took it upon ourselves to not only spotlight this tragedy of the drug war, but to also propose sensible alternatives to leaving these individuals in prison till they die of old age or illness. Are proposals are, but not limited too,

(1) COMPLETELY ELIMINATE THE SENTENCING DISPARITY BETWEEN POWDER COCAINE AND CRACK COCAINE: Federal Drug Laws punish crack cocaine offenders 18x more severely than powder cocaine offenders, despite extensive studies establishing there is no basis to treat the two drugs differently and that doing so disproportionately affects African-Americans. [click here for more details]

(2) COMMUTE THE SENTENCES OF FIRST-TIME AND/OR NONVIOLENT CRACK COCAINE OFFENDERS SERVING LIFE
WITHOUT PAROLE: President Barack Obama has steadfastly expressed the powder/crack cocaine disparity is unwarranted and should be completely eliminated. However, Congress has failed to do so. President Obama now has the executive authority to correct the sentences of defendants in which unfair crack cocaine drug laws have created the greatest injustices. [click here for more details]

(3) CHANGE THE SENTENCING GUIDELINES RECOMMENDATION THAT A DEFENDANT WHO HAS AN OFFENSE LEVEL
OF 43, REGARDLESS OF THE DEFENDANT'S CRIME OR LACK OF CRIMINAL HISTORY, SHOULD BE SENTENCED
TO LIFE WITHOUT PAROLE: Life without parole is the second most severe penalty permitted by law. The Sentencing Commission should recommend this penalty only for the most heinous crimes or criminals who have shown they are beyond rehabilitation and will forever be a danger to society. Not offenders of non-violent crimes who have minimal to no prior criminal history. The Commission could accomplish this by changing its recommended sentence of life imprisonment for defendants who have a offense level of 43 (CHC 1&2) down to 360 months to LIFE. [click here for more details]

(4) RETROACTIVELY APPLY UNITED STATES SENTENCING GUIDELINE 5H1.1 TO DEFENDANTS WHO HAVE MINIMAL
TO NO CRIMINAL HISTORY (CHC 1&2) THAT WERE SENTENCED TO LIFE IMPRISONMENT UNDER OFFENSE LEVEL 43: In 2010, Guideline 5H1.1 was amended by instructing courts it could consider a defendant's age (youth or old age) in determining whether to depart from a recommended sentencing range. However, this amendment is only applicable to defendants sentenced after November 1, 2010. Thereby, depriving courts the opportunity to consider in previous cases whether the defendant's age at the time of sentencing warranted a departure from the Guideline's recommendation of life: a departure (from what we have discovered) many judges would have given had they not been instructed by the Guidelines not to do so.

As you can see we by no means suggest that all laws resulting in such life without parole should be repelled or that every inmate sentenced to such punishment should be reevaluated and considered for leniency, we propose only that there should at least be a crack in the door to correct the laws and sentences that have been demonstrated to be unwarranted, unwise, and unjust.

1. For example, Senator Patrick Leahy (D-VT) has introduced bill S.1231 (The Second Chance Reauthorization Act) which would increase federal good time credit by an additional 60 days, and Representative Sheila Jackson Lee (D-Tx) has introduced bill H.R. 223 (The Federal Prison Bureau Nonviolent Offender Relief Act) which would authorize the release of non-violent inmates who are over the age of 45 that have completed 50 percent of there sentence with no disciplinary infrations. Though we praise Senator Leahy and Representative Lee for submitting these legislative proposals, they would not apply to first-time and/or non-violent offenders serving life without parole.

APPENDIX JJ: PETITION TO PRESIDENT BY CRACK OPEN THE DOOR

PRESIDENT BARACK H. OBAMA
THE WHITE HOUSE
1600 Pennsylvania Ave.NW
Washington, D.C. 20500

RE: REQUEST FOR THE PRESIDENT OF THE UNITED STATES TO COMMUTE THE SENTENCES OF NON-VIOLENT CRACK COCAINE OFFENDERS SENTENCED TO LIFE WITHOUT PAROLE.

Dear Mr President:

This is a plea requesting you to strongly consider commuting the sentences of non-violent crack cocaine offenders serving life imprisonment who meet the following criteria:

(1) Have never been convicted of a violent crime;
(2) Would not be subject to a sentence of life imprisonment if the crack/powder cocaine disparity were completely eliminated;
(3) Their conviction became final prior to the Supreme Court's decision in <u>United States v. Booker</u>; and
(4) Have been model inmates while incarcerated.

In 2010, Congress passed a bill, which you signed into law, entitled The Fair Sentencing Act that reduced the penalty for crack cocaine from 100-to-1 down to 18-to-1. Though this legislation was lauded as being a significant step in sentencing reform, Congress's failure to completely eliminate the crack/powder cocaine disparity has resulted in thousands of individuals (over 80% of which are African Americans) to languish in federal prison serving extremely harsh sentences that are universally viewed as racially discriminative, unwarranted, and unjust. Leading many jurist and members of Congress to label The Fair Sentencing Act of 2010 as anything but fair.

While many individuals and families suffer as a result of Congress's fear of appearing "soft on crime" no one has been more affected than in those cases where the crack cocaine disparity resulted in life imprisonment: which in the federal prison system is life without parole (LWOP).

Drug distribution is a serious offense and should be punished as so. However, to allow a person to spend the rest of their life in prison until they die of their illness or old age based on the determination of a mechanical mandatory Guideline system-which has been since ruled unconstitutional, and for beliefs about a drug that have been dispelled by research and science is a complete miscarriage of justice. Furthermore, LWOP for non-violent crimes not only contradicts this countries obligation to the Internal Covenant on Civil and Political Rights, but it is also a sentencing practice rejected by other nations that share our Anglo-Saxon heritage and by leading members of the Western Community.

During your first term as President, and even during your days in Congress, you advocated for a complete elimination of the crack cocaine disparity. Because Congress has failed to do so it in now requested of you Mr. President to exercise your executive authority to commute the sentences of those individuals whom have been most severely affected by the disparity, who have demonstrated while incarcerated they can become productive members of society.

Mr. President it is prayed for these individuals and their families that you act upon this plea of mercy.

Sincerely,

APPENDIX KK: CRACK OPEN THE DOOR OP-ED

TRULINCS 07031078 - HERNANDEZ, JASON - Unit: ERE-A-A

FROM: 07031078
TO: Leal, Abel; The Door, Crack Open
SUBJECT: Editorial
DATE: 10/18/2011 10:58:44 AM

DO THE JIM CROW LAWS STILL EXIST IN OUR JUDICIAL SYSTEM?

There are over 6,000 federal inmates serving life without parole. The expected cost to incarcerate these inmates for the rest of their lives will cost the tax payers over 6.5 billion dollars. At a time where are economy is on the brink of collapse this is an extremely high cost, but a necessary one if we are to be successful in our fight against crime. After all, if these individuals were sentenced to life without parole surely they must be this country's most dangerous and violent criminals. Right? Wrong.

What if you were told there were a class of these inmates who were first-time and/or non violent drug offenders who received life sentences simply because their crime involved crack cocaine as opposed to powder cocaine: Two drugs which scientific evidence has now demonstrated the difference between the two, is like the difference between ice and water or beer and wine.

That in nearly everyone of these individuals cases the sentencing judge disagreed with Congress' decision to punish crack cocaine offenders so severely, but stated under the United States Sentencing Guidelines they had no discretion to impose a sentence less than life without parole.

What if i also told you that the Sentencing Guideline system these individuals were sentenced under was subsequently ruled unconstitutional by the Supreme Court of the United States, but that these first time and/or non-violent crack cocaine offenders were not entitled to be resentenced simply because they were sentenced before the Supreme Court's ruling.

That despite the very real likelihood of these individuals dyeing in prison, a great majority of them were model inmates. Many of whom took action do not only better themselves, but others as well by teaching their fellow inmates job skills, assisting inmates in obtaining their G.E.D., counseling inmates who were suicidal, or by speaking to troubled youths from the community about the consequences of breaking the law, being in prison.

There has to be something I'm not mentioning. Right? Something that justifies the basis for leaving these men in prison, some of whom were 21 years old or younger when sentenced, to be kept in prison until they die of old age or illness. A reason no one has come to their rescue. And there is. Though many would argue against it and others, such as the NAACP and LULAC, have just simply failed to recognize or believe it to be true. The race of these inmates.

There is a website called crackopenthedoor.com. An organization which seeks the eventual release of first time and/or non-violent crack cocaine offenders serving life without parole. If you visit this site you will see all that has been stated in this article to be true. But the most extraordinary revelation of this website, or should i say frighting, (depending on your race) is that all the individuals shown are minorities.

This racial make-up is alarming being African-Americans make up only 13 percent of our countries population. Though not shocking if you consider African-Americans make up almost 40 percent of the federal prison population; 1 out of 3 black children will eventually be incarcerated; of the 2,500 juveniles serving life sentences 1,500 of them are black; if blacks and hispanics were sentenced at the same frequency as whites our prison population would be cut in half, etc., etc.,.

If what our country stood for was to be determined by our judicial system, what would our's say about us as a nation?

APPENDIX LL: CLEMENCY CONTACT LIST

<u>**CLEMENCY CONTACT LIST**</u>

NAME AND TITLE OF PERSON CONTACTED: _____

NAME OF ORGANIZATION/BUSINESS/: _____

THEIR MISSION/FOCUS (if known): _____

_____

CONTACT INFORMATION: address:_____

phone no. _____: email._____. social media handle:_____

HOW I LEARNED OF CONTACT AND WHY I CONTACTED THEM:_____

_____

IMPORTANT NOTE(S) ABOUT CONTACT: _____

_____

DOCUMENT SENT & DATE SENT:_____

RESPONSE: (Y/N):_____

DOCUMENT SENT & DATE SENT:_____

RESPONSE: (Y/N):_____

DOCUMENT SENT & DATE SENT_____

RESPONSE: (Y/N):_____

DOCUMENT SENT & DATE SENT:_____

RESPONSE: (Y/N):_____

DOCUMENT SENT & DATE SENT: _____

RESPONSE: (Y/N):_____

APPENDIX MM: CHANGE.ORG PROFILE OF ELISA CASTILLO

Profile of Elisa Castillo on Change.org

Clemency for Elisa Castillo serving Life without parole

My name is Nidia Cano. One of two Daughters of Elisa Castillo who was sentenced to life without parole at the age of 53 for a nonviolent drug offense. She has been in prison since 2008. She is now 64 years old.

Our mother was arrested just six months after our father past away in 2007. It has really affected our entire family mentally and physically. Life hasn't been the same ever since .She is our back bone and all we have left we really need her in our lives.

My kids are growing up knowing there grandma only by visitations on the weekends.
When I take my kids to visit my mother and she ask "How are we doing?" I always tell her "We are doing good." But it is with a fake smile, knots in our throats and holding back tears. It gets harder and harder because each time she is getting older and older and just the thought of the only time she would be leaving will be when her heart stops beating is killing me inside.

Our Grandmother (my mom's mother) passed away recently and we can only now pray that my mother does not pass away while she is in prison.

President Trump believe me when I tell you my mother is not a bad person. Please grant her clemency so she can be with us once again and not die in prison. Please.

https://www.facebook.com/Clemency-For-Elisa-Castillo-299581527637433/

APPENDIX NN: CHANGE.ORG PROFILE OF EVELYN PAPPA

PROFILE OF EVELYN PAPPA ON CHANGE.ORG

Grant Clemency to Evelyn Bozon Pappa serving a Life Sentence for a nonviolent drug offense

My mother, Evelyn Cecilia Bozon Pappa is a 57 year old grandmother serving life without parole for a first time nonviolent drug offense. She has been in prison 23 years without any incidents and will die there unless President Trump grants her clemency.

Evelyn is the mother of 4 children and has 6 grandchildren and 1 great grandchild. She married my father when she was 14 and became a mother at that age. **My father was a very abusive man and was involved in drug trafficking in Colombia. For many years, my mother, Evelyn was subjected to many types of abuse from my father. She is a domestic abusive survivor.** After 20 years of marriage, she decided to leave him and fled to the United States. I will never forget it because I was there too. We always had to run because of my father!

I am now 34 years old and a mother myself. I was 11 years old when my mother was arrested. She was sentenced to life in federal prison. I lost my sense of security and have never felt the same since she was taken away from me. My life changed forever and my heart will never be the same until she is with us. I am aware she is one of thousands of first time, nonviolent offenders who were given a draconian, life in prison.

My mother has accepted full responsibility for her actions and used that experience to better her life and the lives of others. Since being incarcerated she has been a model prisoner who is a mentor for women in that institution. My mother completed many rehab programs. She graduated from High School, gardening, sewing, painting, theology and much more. She is the leader of the church. We need your help! Please help us! Please help us, help- her, help my family. She is in the process of submitting a clemency petition.

It serves no purpose or benefit to society to have her locked up for life. Her large and loving immediate and extended family and friends would welcome her return and she has a stable environment to return to when she is released and will receive all the help she needs for a smooth transition back into society.

Please sign this petition and ask President Trump to grant clemency to a mother, grandmother, sister, aunt, and friend who wants to use her experience to assist others and give back to her community.

To learn more about Evelyn' story, please go to: https://www.candoclemency.com/evelyn-bozon-pappa/

Thank you!

APPENDIX OO: POSTER BOARD OF DAVID DIAZ

GOVERNOR JERRY BROWN
PLEASE COMMUTE DAVID DIAZ CDCR P61959

David Diaz is currently in prison serving a **37 year-to-life sentence** for a shooting that happened in 1998. The victim of this crime has stated that David is innocent and not the person who shot him and the key witness has confessed to **"randomly"** accusing David under police pressure.

David Diaz CDCR P61959

Has already served 20 years in prison for a crime he did not commit.

80 days left help ask Governor Jerry Brown to commute his sentence

David was just 19 years old when he was arrested. He is now 40 years old and has served 20 years.

APPENDIX PP: POSTER BOARD OF ELISA CASTILLO

FREE
ELISA IDALIA CASTILLO

LIFE WITHOUT PAROLE FOR A FIRST TIME NONVIOLENT DRUG OFFENSE

64 YEARS OLD

11 YEARS IN PRISON

IF ELISA DOES NOT RECEIVE CLEMENCY

SHE WILL DIE IN PRISON.

#ClemencyForElisa

www.candoclemency.com justice through clemency

APPENDIX QQ: POSTER BOARD OF EVELYN PAPPA

FREE
EVELYN BOZON PAPPA

LIFE WITHOUT PAROLE FOR A NONVIOLENT DRUG OFFENSE

58 YEARS OLD.

25 YEARS IN PRISON

IF EVELYN DOES NOT RECEIVE CLEMENCY

SHE WILL DIE IN PRISON.

#ClemencyForEvelyn

APPENDIX RR: EVA PALMA'S COVER TO PETITION FOR COMMUTATION

BEFORE THE PRESIDENT OF THE UNITED STATES OF AMERICA
ON BEHALF OF FEDERAL INMATE EVA PALMA ATENCIO #21868-051

EVA PALMA ATENCIO'S PETITION TO COMMUTE HER SENTENCE OF LIFE WITHOUT PAROLE FOR A NONVIOLENT DRUG CRIME TO THIRTY YEARS IN PRISON

Eva Palma Atencio #21868-051
FCI DUBLIN
CAMP PARKS, CALIFORNIA
SUBMITTED: July __, 2018

IMPRISONED SINCE 2003

APPENDIX SS: EVA PALMA'S COVER TO MEMORANDUM IN SUPPORT OF PETITION FOR COMMUTATION

EVA PALMA ATENCIO'S MEMORANDUM IN SUPPORT OF HER PETITION TO COMMUTE HER SENTENCE OF LIFE WITHOUT PAROLE

Eva With Her Three Children

During A Prison Visitation in 2006

EVA PALMA ATENCIO

Fed No. 21868-051

FCI Dublin

5701 8th Street

Dublin, CA 94568

Prepared With The Assistance of

Jason Hernandez, Formerly Incarcerated

And 2013 Clemency Recipient

Sent: December 2, 2019

APPENDIX TT: EVELYN PAPPA'S COVER FOR PETITION AND MEMORANDUM

BEFORE THE PRESIDENT OF THE UNITED STATES OF AMERICA

ON BEHALF OF FEDERAL INMATE EVELYN CECILIA BOZON PAPPA #48576-004

EVELYN CECILIA BOZON PAPPA'S PETITION TO COMMUTE HER SENTENCE OF LIFE WITHOUT

PAROLE FOR A NONVIOLENT DRUG OFFENSE

AND A MEMORANDUM IN SUPPORT THEREOF

Evelyn Cecilia Bozon Pappa

Fed. No. 48576-004

FCI Tallahassee

501 Capital Circle NE

Tallahassee, Florida 32301

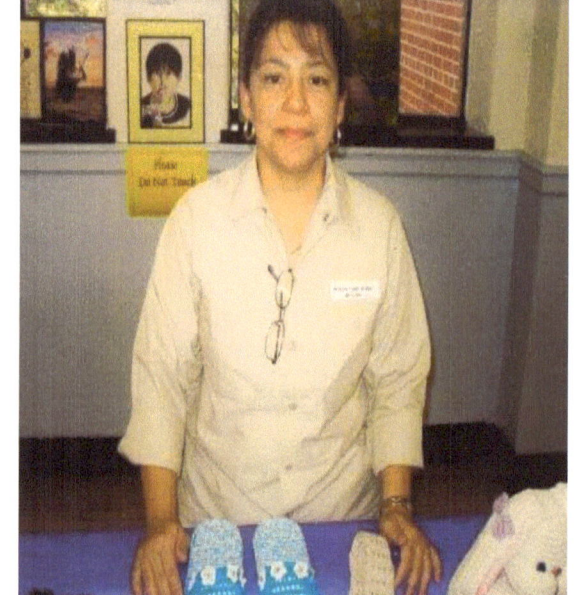

Prepared By Damaris Ramos (Formerly Incarcerated With And Mentored by Petitioner) & Jason Hernandez (2013 President Obama Clemency Recipient)

SUBMITTED:

NOVEMBER 2018

APPENDIX UU: THREE BUSINESS CARDS OF JASON HERNANDEZ (FRONT & BACK)

FED. NO. 21868-051 — Eva Atencio Palma

"Eva was sentenced to life without parole for a nonviolent drug crime in 2003. She has been incarcerated of 13 years, and will more than likely die in prison unless her sentence is commuted."

Jason Hernandez

Founder,
Crack Open the Door

First Latino to receive clemency from Presidente Obama

crackopenthedoor.com
972-480-7516
jhernandez121913@gmail.com

BLACK + CRACK = LIFE

TOP ROW
- Wayne Bledsoe #60866-080 LIFE
- Ellis Russell #06939-424 LIFE
- Bobby Reed #72743-079
- Jason Hernandez = granted clemency
- Timothy Fields #24509-077 LIFE

BOTTOM ROW
- Kenneth Evans #24606077 LIFE
- Samuels Lavert #270120-077 LIFE
- Kirtman Eugene #0802-0062 35 YEARS
- Altonio Douglas = free, reduce by 2

[Scan QR code for more information about their cases and how to help]

NOT PICTURED
- Michael Holmes #07030-078 LIFE
- James Ortega #07056-078 24 YEARS
- Jesus Olivares #20583-077 LIFE
- Corey Blount #83126-079 LIFE
- Douglas Dunkins #22619-077 LIFE
- William Underwood #04849-016 LIFE

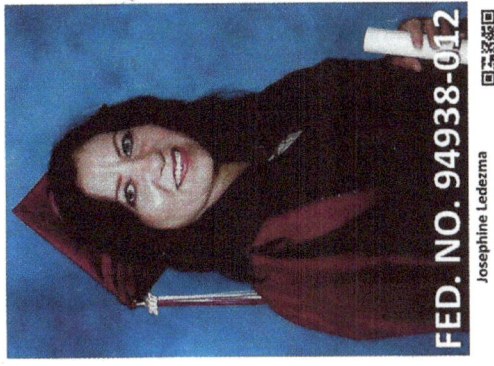

FED. NO. 94938-012 — Josephine Ledezma

[Scan QR code for more information about her case and how to help]

"Josie was sentenced to life for a first time, non-violent drug crime in 1992. She has now been incarcerated over 24 years and will likely die in prison if her sentence is not commuted."

Jason Hernandez

Founder,
Crack Open the Door

First Latino
to receive clemency from
President Obama

crackopenthedoor.com
972-480-7516
jhernandez121913@gmail.com

Endnotes

INTRODUCTION: Why I Created This Guidebook

[1] Terry Frieden, "Bush Pardons 19, Commutes Sentence of Meth Dealer," CNN, Dec. 23, 2008. https://www.cnn.com/2008/POLITICS/12/23/bush.pardons/index.html.

[2] Drug offenders serving life without parole, especially those who were black or brown.

[3] For more information on William Underwood and how to help see: https://www.change.org/p/president-trump-30-years-is-too-long-free-our-father-william-underwood; Ebony Underwood, "30 Years is TOO Long: Free Bill Underwood," petition on Change.org, 2014, https://www.change.org/p/president-trump-30-years-is-too-long-free-our-father-william-underwood.

[4] The petition for Josephine Ledesma (who received clemency) was created by me and a school teacher named Tracey King who knew absolutely nothing about clemency or the law.

[5] Michelle Alexander, The New Jim Crow: Mass Incarceration in the Age of Colorblindness (New York: The New Press, 2012).

PART ONE: The Federal Commutation Process

[6] "Standards For Consideration Of Clemency," The United States Department of Justice, April 2018, Accessed Jan 1, 2020, https://www.justice.gov/pardon/about-office-0.

[7] In the event you feel something stated in this Guidebook conflicts or is at odds with what is stated in one of these four documents, always side with what is stated in these four documents.

[8] Mark Osler, "Fewer Hands, More Mercy: A Plea For A Better Federal Clemency System," Vermont Law Review 41 (2017): 465, 477-489, accessed Jan 1, 2020 http://lawreview.vermontlaw.edu/wp-content/uploads/2017/05/03-Osler.pdf.

[9] Joe Patrice, "Can Trump Issue A Pardon Via Tweet? Apparently Yes," Above The Law, Aug. 24, 2017, https://abovethelaw.com/2017/08/can-trump-issue-a-pardon-via-tweet-apparently-yes/.

[10] The DOJ does state that a clemency petition should be filed through the prison you are incarcerated at but does not state the process for supplementing a clemency petition at a later date. I always recommend sending documents you obtain later directly yourself to the OPA certified mail return receipt. You can request your Case Manager to send it for you, but there is no policy statement saying they are required to send for filing anything after you initially send your clemency petition.

[11] PSR's are always sealed by the district court. You can try getting it unsealed from the court, but it is a tedious and difficult process and you could lose valuable time trying to do so. Better to try other alternatives.

[12] Normally the Bureau of Prisons will start the day of your confinement or when you were sentenced. However, sometimes you can spend months in jail if not years waiting to be sentenced. More than likely the OPA will know exactly how long you have been in prison, but if you were not released on bond I would put down the day you were arrested.

[13] If you feel your sentenced was enhanced improperly based on a prior conviction then you can assert that as a basis for commutation but I would not recommend you do so under Question Six.

[14] Melissa Jeltsen, "Cyntoia Brown Will Go Free. What About the Countless Others Just Like Her?" Huffpost, Jan. 8, 2019, https://www.huffpost.com/entry/cyntoia-brown-released-prison_n_5d4ab5f7e4b0066eb70aac07

[15] This article speculated that the woman's cancer may have contributed in addition to other factors, leading to President Obama granting her clemency. Kim Bell and staff, "Commuted: Obama Commutes Sentence of Alton Woman In Cocaine Case," St. Louis Post Dispatch, Nov. 11, 2011https://www.stltoday.com/news/local/crime-and-courts/obama-commutes-sentence-of-alton-woman-in-cocaine-case/article_c30d817e-1523-11e1-8e09-0019bb30f31a.html.

[16] Associated Press, "Illinois Governor's Blanket Pardon Spares Lives of 167 Condemned Inmates," Fox News, Jan. 11, 2003, https://www.foxnews.com/story/illinois-governors-blanket-pardon-spares-lives-of-167-condemned-inmates. See also Herrera v. Collins, 506 U.S. 390 (1989), stating that a proper remedy for claim of actual innocence based on new evidence, which is discovered too late to file a new trial motion, would be not federal habeas relief, but rather executive clemency.

[17] When I use the word "memorandum" or "addendum," I am specifically referring to the document attached to your actual Petition For Commutation. When I use the word "supplement," I am referring to any additional document or attachments you send at a later date in support of your Petition For Commutation.

[18] During a period of incarceration, dozens of programs and courses can be completed. It is my belief that specifically listing every certificate you received (which could range up to 30 or more) and including a copy of the actual certificates does not strengthen your case for clemency and could possibly distract from other important parts of the petition. I would recommend only stating how many courses you have completed and then highlighting and attaching the certificate of those you feel are of significant importance.

[19] An analysis by ProPublica showed a clemency applicant with congressional support were three times more likely to receive a pardon. Dafna Linzer, "Details Emerge on Government Study of Presidential Pardons," ProPublica, Aug. 8, 2012, https://www.propublica.org/article/details-emerge-on-government-study-of-presidential-pardons.

[20] No actual letters by prison guards or prison staff are included in the Appendix, but there are several individuals who I have filed petitions for who were able to get support letters from guards/staff. Nevertheless, it is not easy to get these types of letters.

[21] Sentencing judge and prosecutor support prisoner Clarence Aaron's request to have his sentence commuted by the president. Dafna Linzer, "Pardon Attorney Torpedoes Plea For Presidential Mercy," ProPublica, March 13, 2012, https://www.propublica.org/article/pardon-attorney-torpedoes-plea-for-presidential-mercy.

[22] If you only include your Petition For Commutation then that is all that should go on the cover page, if you elect to include a cover page: it's not required. However, if you send your Petition For Commutation and Memorandum in Support of the Petition simultaneously you should mention that on the cover page. See Appendix RR, Eva Palma's Cover To Petition For Commutation; Appendix SS, Eva Palma's Cover To Memorandum In Support of Petition For Commutation; Appendix TT, Evelyn Pappa's Cover For Petition and Memorandum

PART TWO: *How to Advocate for Clemency*

[23] Part Two, Fighting For Your Freedom From A Prison Cell is geared for a person who is in prison but many of the tactics and principals equally apply to someone who is advocating on the outside. As well, if you are collaborating with a person who is incarcerated, you both will want to strategize on many of the tactics set out and the best way to execute them.

[24] In regards to my own request in the box below, it should be noted that I personally felt our sentences should have been commuted to twenty years or less and the guideline range should have been changed to twenty years to life. However, I believed the former and not the latter was easier to get the most support around and actually achieve, and that is why I chose to pursue a goal I totally was not on board with.

[25] Michigan Women's Justice and Clemency Project Facebook Page, accessed Jan 1, 2020, https://www.facebook.com/Michigan-Womens-Justice-and-Clemency-Project-136575696544868/;
CAN_DO Foundation – Justice Through Clemency Facebook Page, accessed Jan 1, 2020, https://www.facebook.com/candoclemency/;
Buried Alive Project Facebook Page, accessed Jan 1, 2020, https://www.facebook.com/buriedaliveproject/;
Mercy Me 924c Facebook Page, accessed Jan 1, 2020, https://www.facebook.com/ianordevon924c/.

[26] Free David Diaz Facebook Page, accessed Jan 1, 2020, https://www.facebook.com/freedaviddiaz;
Clemency for Elisa Castillo Facebook Page, accessed Jan 1, 2020, https://www.facebook.com/Clemency-For-Elisa-Castillo-299581527637433/;
Free Eva Palma Facebook Page, accessed Jan 1, 2020, https://www.facebook.com/FreeEvaPalma/;
Clemency for Evelyn Pappa Facebook Page, accessed Jan 1, 2020, https://www.facebook.com/Clemency-For-Evelyn-1511441555652738/.

[27] Michigan Women's Justice and Clemency Project Facebook Page, https://www.facebook.com/Michigan-Womens-Justice-and-Clemency-Project-136575696544868/;
Buried Alive Project Facebook Page, https://www.facebook.com/buriedaliveproject/.

[28] In my home state of Texas, for example, you have Lone Star Justice Alliance, https://www.lonestarjusticealliance.org/; Texas Advocates for Justice, https://grassrootsleadership.org/programs/texas-advocates-justice; The Buried Alive Project, https://www.buriedaliveproject.org/; Epicenter, https://secondlooktexas.org/; Texas Inmate Families Association, https://tifa.org/. See also Michigan's Women's Justice and Clemency Project, http://umich.edu/~clemency/women_summaries.html; Daughters Beyond Incarceration, https://www.dbinola.org/

[29] Endnote pertains to the story of David Diaz, described in the text box below. The Inner Voice, https://theinnervoices.com/page/482467614/; Mommie Activist and Sons, http://www.mommieactivistandsons.com/?fbclid=IwAR2f59TNIvpHWly8QN3c07JzOiUxhQTMoyjf3Alwd4VBb844o0Cx0njxNZ8; Decarcerated Podcast, https://www.marlonpeterson.com/decarceratedpodcast

[30] Section 994(s), which gives prisoners an extraordinary platform to speak out about Guidelines they have been sentenced under, is one that is rarely used and many are not even aware it exists. In making the must of this outlet, I simply drafted fill-in-the-blank documents that I passed out to other prisoners serving life without parole and asked them to fill in the blanks and send them to the United States Sentencing Commission.

[31] I wrote several op-eds while incarcerated and would send them out to my list of contacts when I would finish with one. I would also pass them out to those who were in incarcerated with me so they could understand the nature of the War On Drugs. Two of those articles, that were written back in 2011-2012, would be published online, including: https://www.latinorebels.com/2015/07/16/latinos-unidos-pushing-for-criminal-justice-reform-together/. One titled "Brown and Out" was published in 2015 when I was released and read by other social justice advocates and would open the door for me to be involved with criminal justice reform on a national level and offer more opportunities to write about criminal justice reform and clemency for The New York Times, Huffington Post, ACLU, The Guardian and other media outlets. Just another example of "you never know how long something you do will take to have an impact but when it does it could be life changing."

PART THREE: *Advocating From the Outside for Someone on the Inside*

[32] Part Three, Advocating on The Outside For Someone On The Inside is geared for a person not in prison but you should definitely read it and apply what is doable to your advocacy. As well, if you have an advocate on the outside who is assisting you, you will want to talk about and strategize on many of the tactics that are set out and the best way to execute them.

[33] For other information on how to use social media to advocate see Facebook, Twitter & Dot What? Social Media Primer by Campaign for Youth Justice.

[34] The Buried Alive Project Instagram Page, accessed Jan 1, 2020, https://www.instagram.com/buriedaliveproject/.

[35] Endnote applies to data in text box: Courtney Seiter, "How to Gain a Massive Following on Instagram," Buffer (blog), Aug. 6, 2019, https://buffer.com/resources/instagram-growth.

[36] The Crazy Egg found that users spend no longer than 15 seconds when viewing a website. "The 15 Second Rule: 3 Reasons Why Users Leave A Website," The Crazy Egg (blog), Feb. 26, 2019, https://www.crazyegg.com/blog/why-users-leave-a-website/.

[37] Websites you can look at that can help in giving you a visual of what one should look like: http://www.iamsharandajones.org/; https://www.freerodneyreed.com/

[38] It is very important to remember a Change.org petition or any type of petition you create that you are requesting signatures for is not an actual clemency petition. You must file an actual clemency petition with the Pardon Attorney in order to start the commutation process. I have unfortunately seen this happen a couple of times.

[39] See the following for Change.org petitions pertaining to clemency: https://www.change.org/p/donald-j-trump-clemency-for-elisa-castillo-serving-life-without-parole; https://www.change.org/p/president-trump-30-years-is-too-long-free-our-father-william-underwood; https://www.change.org/p/grant-clemency-to-evelyn-bozon-pappa-serving-a-life-sentence-for-a-nonviolent-drug-offense.

[40] For more information on vigils and rallies see Campaign For Youth Justice's 30 Minute Vigil Toolkit.

[41] Endnote applies to statistics in text box: Nichole Elizabeth DeMere, "How to Design Business Cards People Will Remember You By," Canva, https://www.canva.com/learn/how-to-design-business-cards-people-will-remember-you-by/.

ABOUT THE AUTHOR

Jason Hernandez was sentenced to life without parole plus 320 years for a nonviolent drug offense in 1998 at the age of 21. While incarcerated, Jason became a "jailhouse attorney" and began litigating on his behalf along with others incarcerated with him. In 2011, he started his own grass-roots organization in prison called Crack Open the Door, which advocated for crack cocaine offenders serving life without parole. In 2011, Jason prepared his own Petition for Commutation and sent it to President Obama, along with a letter, asking for his sentence to be reduced.

On December 19, 2013, Jason became one of the first to receive clemency from President Obama: known as the "Obama 8." Since his release in 2015, Jason has assisted over half a dozen individuals receive clemency through the Obama and Trump Administration: six of whom were serving life without parole. He has become a leading voice and advocate for criminal justice reform. Jason has written for and appeared in media outlets such as The Guardian, The New York Times, MSNBC, and CNN.

Jason has been a recipient of a Latino Justice Fellowship, Soros Justice Fellowship, JLUSA Fellowship and was awarded the Volunteer of the Year in his city for the work he does with students. He is currently working on his memoir.

If you are interested in having Jason speak at your school, university, conference, or prison, you can email him at getclemencynow@gmail.com or go to getclemencynow.org

www.ingramcontent.com/pod-product-compliance
Lightning Source LLC
Chambersburg PA
CBHW040902020526
44114CB00037B/37